THE PHANTOM CARAVAN

AUTHOR. LISBON. 1946

[*Frontis.*

THE PHANTOM CARAVAN

SIR OWEN O'MALLEY, K.C.M.G.

A Moment's Halt—a momentary taste
Of Being from the Well amid the Waste,
And lo! the phantom Caravan has reacht
The Nothing it set out from. Oh make haste . . .

Rubáiyát of Omar Khayyám
(trans. E. FitzGerald), 4th ed., XLVIII.

LONDON
JOHN MURRAY, ALBEMARLE STREET

There are no fields of amaranth on this side
of the grave : there are no voices, O
Rhodope ! that are not soon mute, however
tuneful : there is no name, with whatever
emphasis of passionate love repeated, of
which the echo is not faint at last.

WALTER SAVAGE LANDOR

First Edition . . . *1954*

Printed in Great Britain by Butler & Tanner Ltd., Frome and London
and Published by John Murray (Publishers) Ltd.

CONTENTS

LIST OF ILLUSTRATIONS

* Photo. Leinster Studios, Dublin.

FOREWORD

THERE are three reasons why this narrative is a good deal duller than my life has been. The first is that, for obvious reasons, I cannot write about the most—to me— exciting and interesting parts of it which had their source in intimate personal relations. The second is the Official Secrets Act. The third is described on page 157 in the following words : " The efficient conduct of business in the Foreign Office depends almost more than anything else on complete frankness between the Secretary of State at the top and the latest joined member of the Service at the bottom. This would be shattered if any member of the brotherhood, high or low, had reason to fear that words spoken within this citadel of mutual trust and confidence might afterwards be made public."

O. ScC. O'M.

ROCKFLEET.
  August 1953.

CHAPTER 1

DENTON

MY father spent nearly all his life abroad as Attorney-General or Chief Justice of various colonies and as Judge of the former extra-territorial court in Egypt and the Ottoman Empire. During the early years of his married life he took wife and children with him, but when my two elder brothers reached school age and my two sisters were aged, respectively, two and six years, it became impracticable to do this any longer, and he began to look round for a permanent home for his growing family in England ; meantime leasing successive temporary residences. Of these, the one in which the family was settled in the year 1887 was " Ellerslie ", a modest little house in Burlington Place, Eastbourne. It was here, during one of his periods of leave in England, that I was born at about half-past two o'clock in the afternoon of May 4th in that year. He does not seem to have been much stirred by the event. The entry in his diary for that day says only " May 4, 1887, Wednesday. Political work. Baby born about 2.30 p.m. Thank God for all his mercies, may the child be one of his faithful ones." In the autumn of that year my father got possession of Denton in Oxfordshire. He was never altogether satisfied with it and hankered after a house in Mayo, but for one reason or another the family lived there till his death in 1932. It was Denton, therefore, which became the dearly loved background of all my youth.

Denton is a hamlet of the village of Cuddesdon which lies about seven miles to the south-east of Oxford and is separated from the city by the ridge running between Shotover and Garsington. Anyone coming to our village from Oxford had to traverse the dreary Cowley Flats where Morris's motor factory now stands, but when he had crossed the old Roman road from Dorchester to Bicester (close to the railway line and at the south-east limit of the factory) and breasted the

Garsington Hill, the prospect which would have met his eyes in the 80's and 90's of the nineteenth century was of great beauty and dignity. This section of South Oxfordshire is alternately drained and flooded by the sluggish river Thame which joins the Thames at Dorchester. Cuddesdon is built on an outcrop of oolite about five miles upstream from Dorchester, and Denton lies below it in the deep hollow between Cuddesdon and Garsington. Until the turn of the century all the low country to the south-east of Garsington in the direction of Chiselhampton and Little Milton seemed to be covered with forest rather than grass farms. Wire had not replaced hedges, and most hedges were thickets of thorn and bramble in which full-grown elms stood shoulder to shoulder. These elms were not much good as timber, but their beauty is engraved on the memories of us who grew up among them. In winter the tracery of their branches rocked against the watery sky ; in summer they sheltered the stamping tail-swinging short-horns, and in autumn evenings when the golden sheaves were cocked and the partridges were calling in the stubble, they stood in towering black lines contemplating the immemorial labour of the husbandman and receiving into their leafy dormitories an unending stream of rooks heavy with wireworm and dungbeetles and leatherjackets. But, for all their beauty, these trees were not to the liking of farmers, for the elm is a greedy tree and, as the agricultural depression pressed more hardly upon them, they represented to the landlords—Magdalen, The Queen's College and Lord Macclesfield—that they could not grow trees as well as grass on the one land. So there came about between 1890 and 1900 what my mother called " the slaughter of the innocents ", and all the winters of those years the fellers' axes and saws were busy. During our schoolroom walks we invented games to play on the flat sawn-off stumps along the hedges and prised off the dead bark from the trunks, looking for spiders and woodlice and earwigs. Some of the trunks were sawn into boards by farm labourers just outside our garden wall : the top-sawyer standing at ground level and the bottom-sawyer in a pit which is now fallen in and full of nettles. The rest of the timber went to

2

Wycombe to make coffin boards and cheap furniture ; and now the visitor from Oxford sees from Garsington Hill only water meadows and undulating pasture.

Denton House was a rectangular stone block with accretions at the back containing about twenty rooms besides offices. When Domesday Book was compiled the site was occupied by a cell depending from the Abbey of Abingdon, and a large stone structure later converted into a coachman's cottage had at one time been used for the collection in kind and storage of tithes. The entrance hall was paved in black and white squares ; on the right was a room furnished with ash panelling of the Queen Anne period, and on the left a room panelled in oak of an earlier date. A massive twisting oak staircase bore the date 1614. At the back of the house was a small courtyard with a heavy gate onto the road, pierced by a barred and shuttered peephole suggesting that the lonelier valleys in South Oxfordshire were at a comparatively recent date not secure from violence. At the time when we went to live at Denton what estate agents call " conveniences " were defective. Water was pumped by hand from a well under the stables, and there was not much of it. Sewage found its way through unglazed drain-tiles under the house to a cess-pit in the orchard. The kitchen range, which consumed a vast amount of coal, was the only source of supply to one hot-water tap upstairs and one downstairs. There were only two old-fashioned w.c.'s. Everyone bathed every day in their bedrooms in tin tubs to which many heavy cans of hot water were carried by the maids. The staff included three men in the garden, two in the stables, and in the house, four maids, two washerwomen, and a nurse or a governess or both ; but money went a long way in those days, and I doubt whether my mother's total expenditure when my father was abroad came to more than £1,200 a year. Until we left the place in 1932 the only kind of artificial light used was paraffin lamps and candles, with the result that on winter evenings occasional pools of soft golden lamplight left many corners and passages in obscurity. In winter then, to us children the house was full of mysteries and alarms ; and for me the daily

3

journey at half-past six in the evening from the cosy society of the library or drawing-room was a spine-tingling and hair-raising adventure : up a dark staircase, past curtains concealing goodness knows what, past doors of lumber rooms which might well be full of burglars or skeletons and down shadowy passages hung with portraits whose eyes pursued me all the way to the nursery door.

This house was certainly a magical place ; and like any house that is worth bothering about, it had a strong personality of its own. There it stood at the bottom of a green pool over-topped by the great trees in the garden, clothed in magnolia and wistaria and roses and jasmine. Perhaps it was from the monastic occupants of the site that it had collected into itself a store of sweet fortitude and quiet. I think that it was not so much warmly or intimately concerned with the doings of the O'Malley family which lived in it for a bare half-century, as preoccupied with the secular life of the land and of the crops and herds which the land nourished. Though the comparison may seem unduly fanciful, the house used to remind me of a portrait which hangs at Knole of Lady Catherine Fitzgerald, Countess of Desmond, who was born in 1484 and died in 1604. If I had had the good fortune to be her guest at Inchiquin in the year 1584 or thereabouts, she would, I feel sure, have received me with the courtesy and benevolence appropriate to so distinguished a hostess ; but having conversed for a little while about this and that, it would have been borne in upon me that she would welcome it were I, while making free of her house and its amenities, to leave her alone to reflect upon things important to one who had outlived all the passions and preoccupations of a normal life but hidden as yet from a man at the top of his strength and activity. That at least is an impression I derive from her portrait, and that is the sort of kindly detachment with which Denton always seemed to regard us. It was a house which no disappointments, no suspicions, no ambitions, no quarrels could disturb. I can remember well the sound of restless or angry feet padding from room to room, but I can remember too that the house itself absorbed and dissipated the message of those steps as soon as they had passed, offering instead a reassurance of wisdom and patience to the attentive heart.

The garden was a proper setting for the house. Lawns green as only a rich soil can make them surrounded it on three sides ; and on these, when on dew-soaked summer mornings I knelt at the dining-room window for family prayers, I could watch the blackbirds and thrushes and starlings and green woodpeckers and the red squirrels too, digging for their breakfasts. Beyond the lawns stood forest trees of great size and beauty—oak, lime, chestnut, poplar, acacia, sequoia, pine, walnut, holly, thorn and yew. These overshadowed shrubberies of laurel, box and syringa, and among the flowers stood medlar, quince and mulberry trees. All the common warblers, tits and finches frequented the garden, where I have also found the nests of such less common birds as stockdove, tree sparrow, nuthatch, wryneck and lesser spotted woodpecker. On still sunbathed summer evenings when the Red Admirals and Tortoiseshells had already left the heliotrope and the stocks, wood-pigeons cooed from the big trees, belying the look in their wild and wary red eyes ; and in autumn nights the brown owls would snore and squawk and hoot—a miraculous noise, piercing the October mists, teaching little boys in warm nursery beds how rich and adventurous their lives were going to be.

My father remained in England till the end of the year 1887. He would have liked to enter the House of Commons. " I feel more than I have often done any public thing " he wrote in his diary " the brutality and injustice with which the Irish Party in the House of Commons are being treated. Oh how I long to help them ! " But he had a living to make, and so he went back to Hong Kong (where as Attorney-General he could earn £100 a day in private practice) at the end of 1887, and was subsequently appointed Chief Justice first in the Straits Settlement and later in British Guiana. Consequently until I was eight or nine years old I was entirely dependent for parental love and support on my mother who had not, I think, welcomed my arrival into the world.

Her life had been permanently blighted by the death a year earlier at the age of eleven of her second son, Peter,

5

who, full of beauty, talent and spirit, had been adored by both parents. When a few months afterwards another pregnancy was declared, I feel sure that friends and relatives must unwisely have assumed that one child could take the place of another, and that my birth would fill in her half-broken heart the place which my brother's death had left empty ; and I can well imagine the distress which their ill-judged congratulations must have caused. Debilitated by her affliction and illness, my mother hung at the point of death for weeks after my birth while I was given over to a wet-nurse ; and when she at last recovered, she found herself without that abundant supply of spontaneous affection on which a baby, if it is to be normal and healthy, needs to feed. Parents did not, of course, in those spacious days bother about their children as much as they do now. They generally had more of them and always more nurses and governesses to look after them. This was a good thing because nannies, however devoted to their charges, do not make the same sort of emotional demands on children as do parents. However, in properly balanced family life a mother's passionate physical love for her baby has its use, even if she is not fussing around in the nursery all the time ; and although I am sure she always did her very best to do her duty, I think my mother after my birth no longer had it in her to irradiate my infancy. As a consequence my recollections during very early years are mostly of nurses and maidservants.

These were a mixed lot. The presiding figure in the nursery was an old woman called Smith who had been nannie in the family for many years. I think I learned later that she was dying of cancer when I and my sister Eva, three years older than myself, were in her charge. I remember her slashing at me with a little brown cane and my saying " I should like to put you on the fire and burn you ! " All the hard work in the nursery was done by a younger woman, Agnes Edwards. She came from Writtle in Essex and brought some of the nipping East winds of Essex with her. However, I know she did her best and I bear her memory nothing but goodwill. Then there was Fanny Sellar from Garsington, the housemaid,

who was nearly always feeling ill and nearly always cross. I
remember her best as cleaning and trimming innumerable
paraffin lamps in the pantry. Perhaps it was because there
were so many lamps that she was so often cross, but of course
I didn't think about that at the time. Exceptionally, the
parlourmaid, Waring (parlourmaids were always called by
their surnames), who came from Littlemore, was an angel.
She was never cross. I think she was one of the nicest people
I have ever known. These characters stand out against a
background of boiled chicken which I detested, rice pudding
which I liked ; first pram-rides and later walks along muddy
lanes ; visits to cottages where I was received with great
intimacy and respect ; terrors at night of the skeleton arm
which Smith told me would come in through the window and
haul me off to limbo ; tearful attempts to repeat the Lord's
Prayer which mysteriously ended with the words " ever en-
deavour our men " ; being read to by my mother, and, more
particularly, being scolded or disapproved of by my mother.

The happiest memories I have are of the evenings when
the lamp was lit, and my sister and I would sit up to the
nursery table covered with brown American cloth in front of
a roaring fire while Aggie and Fanny and Waring sewed. I
would catch flies and tie them up in a contraption made of
pins and sewing-cotton while Aggie and Fanny and Waring
sang " Sweet Belle-Mahone " ; or " Shall we Gather at the
River ? " Another happy memory is of the base of the big
chestnut tree where, in the hollows between the exposed
beginnings of the roots, I used to construct a little lean-to
shed about eight inches high with a roof woven of twigs and
moss. I had a tin dolls' teapot two inches high and having
pursued with a switch and killed one of the large black bumblebees with a scarlet tip to his abdomen, it gave me great pleasure
to cram him into the teapot and house him thus in my mossy
tabernacle. How quaint a thing is memory, which brings
back to me now the sweet smell of that moss and the sight
of those dead bumblebees, but has allowed me to forget not
only the declension of the verbs in μ and the dates of the
Kings of England, but whose were the lips that first I kissed.

CHAPTER 2

EASTBOURNE

LIFE at Denton was interrupted once or twice a year by visits to Eastbourne which the family had enjoyed as a holiday resort since 1848 when my father at the age of six was first taken there by my grandfather and grandmother. A short account of my grandfather's life will put Eastbourne and my own feelings about it in perspective.

Peter Frederick O'Malley was born in 1804, and brought up at Lodge near Castlebar. He was educated at Trinity College, Dublin, and joined with enthusiasm in the life of a small country house along with three high-spirited brothers, all devoted to horses and dogs and guns. On leaving Trinity College, he was threatened with consumption—always very prevalent in Mayo—and did actually contract smallpox and rheumatic fever. Whether as a consequence of this or not I do not know, but about this time he underwent a process known in those days as " conversion ". Ever afterwards, but without impairment of his brilliant combative and zestful nature, he remained a deeply religious man, beloved by all. His eldest brother Charles (Lever's Irish Dragoon) was already at the Irish Bar, and partly to avoid competing with him, partly perhaps because he saw a larger future abroad, my grandfather was called to the London Bar in May 1834 and before long made a name for himself on the Norfolk Circuit ; acquired an immense number of friends all over Suffolk and Norfolk and in 1839 married Emily Rodwell, the exceedingly handsome daughter of a family which divided with the Cobbolds the best brewing, banking and law business in Ipswich. He took silk in 1850, and in 1857 refused the Chief Justiceship of Bengal as he was confident of being raised to the Bench. But Lord Chancellor Cairns was no friend of his, so he never became a Judge and accepted instead the Recordership of

8

Norwich. A numerous family were brought up at No. 7 Lowndes Street, and it was during this period that my grandparents, when they were not staying with the Rodwells at Holbrook near Ipswich or in other country houses, used to take the children to the sea at Eastbourne. My grandfather died in 1874, and it was very natural that my grandmother and my aunt Elsey should buy a small house in Eastbourne where so many happy family gatherings had taken place, there to live out the remainder of their days. The house selected was No. 8 Burlington Place and they called it Belclare after the place near Westport, Co. Mayo, which had been, so to speak, the capital of our kingdom in the sixteenth century and before the autonomous Irish Lordships were brought under English jurisdiction.

In 1848, according to my father's diary, Eastbourne was not at all like what it is now. What is now called " the Old Town " stood where it stands but was quite isolated. About a mile away and on the sea was a fishing village called Southbourne, connected with the Old Town by a country road lined with low flint-faced cottages. Southbourne was concentrated about the Anchor Inn and Splash Point and besides flint or brick cottages contained small houses with bow fronts and balconies. There was on the " Front " no plate-glass, no big hotels, no pier, no esplanade ; nothing but tar-smelling fishing boats, fishing-nets hung up to dry, the shingly beach, the sandy shallows and beyond, the unchanging restless chalk-blue sea. Only one terrace with any pretensions was being laid out in this land of chalk and poppies and cornflowers. It was between Eastbourne and Southbourne and appropriately called Cornfield Terrace. I stayed there with my nurse in 1892. It did not seem at all pretentious then, being already completely overshadowed by many streets of Victorian mansions.

The journey from Denton to Eastbourne was the principal excitement of the year. It began with a drive of two and a half miles in the brougham or the wagonette from Denton to the station at Wheatley where Mr. Wilmshurst, the station-master, generally secured for us a carriage to ourselves. The line from Princes Risborough to London had not yet been built ; and so, stopping at every station, we proceeded to Paddington via Bledlow and Loudwater. London was crossed from Paddington to Victoria in a four-wheeled cab, called a " growler ", with straw on the floor, and we arrived at our destination late in the evening. By 1892 Eastbourne, as the whole conurbation had now become known, had suffered many changes, but the small Victorian house in Burlington Place preserved its own peculiar reticence and charm. For me it was crammed from basement to garret with romantic significance. The basement kitchen was small and dark : one side was filled by a huge wasteful iron stove. The cook, Mrs. Peak, was very fat and of uncertain temper ; nevertheless, she cooked well and whenever I went down the narrow precipitous stairs to the kitchen, I got something delicious to eat. Can it be that the hygienic kitchenettes in Dolphin Square are storehouses of similar memories ? I hope so ; but it seems improbable. In the hall, cases of tropical butterflies hung on the walls, and two stuffed grouse labelled " Leenane [1] 1835 ". In large glass boxes were a stuffed eagle owl and the front half of a mountain lion which had attacked my uncle St. Clair near his ranch in Buffalo, Wyoming. On the left was a lavatory where sea anemones and crabs and shrimps suffered a lingering death, and from which a delicious smell of seaweed always emanated. A steep flight of stairs led from the ground floor to the bedrooms occupied by my grandmother and aunt and sumptuously furnished, as it seemed to me, with four-poster beds and massive Victorian mahogany wardrobes. A further ascent led to the bedrooms where we children found the usual roaring coal fires if the weather was chilly ; and here on arrival we would dash at once to the window to smell the sea and listen to the receding waves sucking the pebbles after them. Warmth, intimacy and security were encompassed within the mustard-coloured wallpaper and among the flaring gas-jets, each with a purple heart.

Life at Belclare was regulated by the religious outlook of my relatives, but the theory and practice of their religion was

[1] Leenane is on the border between counties Mayo and Galway.

different from what could be found today in most comparable households. The day invariably started and generally ended with family prayers, attendance at which was obligatory. All went to church without fail at eleven o'clock on Sunday, and all activities on Sunday were endued with a religious character : the reading aloud which took place after lunch was from a book of Bible stories rather than from the novels of Sir Walter Scott or Charlotte M. Yonge ; and while they were being read to, the children were expected, instead of knitting a woollen kettleholder or drawing a picture of Ivanhoe's meeting with Rebecca as on weekdays, to illuminate texts later to be hung on the nursery walls. Preparations for bazaars in aid of the Church Missionary Society were always in progress and every child was encouraged to collect money for this and similar bodies. To this end each of us was provided with a card marked in squares which by different colours indicated quantitatively the various religions of the world. Each little square represented a million souls : black for what were collectively known as " the heathen ", green for Mohammedans, yellow for Jews and red for Roman Catholics. In the middle of the card were a very few white squares representing the Protestant community. All the rest were understood to be in urgent need of conversion to Protestantism, and we were led to hope that another tiny white square might one day be added to the rest if enough children with enough cards collected enough pennies to launch enough missionaries against the forces of nakedness and Roman idolatry. My grandmother and aunt also gave in person much faithful service to such societies as the Y.W.C.A. and the Bible Society, and to an institution called " The Welcome ", the object of which was at the time veiled from us, but which we afterwards learned was a home for unmarried mothers. A gloomy view was held about the prospects for these both in this world and the next, even if they gave every sign of regretting their indiscretion.

The idiom in which my grandmother and aunt expressed the religion impelling them to this unselfish devotion is much less often used in corresponding circles today. They thought and spoke of God—or *Guard*, as they pronounced it with downcast eyes—as an individual in the same sense that we regard the King or the Archbishop of Canterbury as individuals. They had, I think, no doubt that after death they would wake up with a start in a new environment indeed, but carrying with them each her own little bundle of memories and tastes and capabilities and ideas—an unbroken continuum which had indeed a definite beginning in the cradle but which had no end anywhere ever. They thought of Christianity as " true " and other religions as " false ". They believed in the validity of a code of ethics which in most respects was as definite as the law of the land or the rules of a club. They held that a whole series of definable actions were " sins ", irrespective of the circumstances in which they were performed.

To these simple and potent habits of thought and action was added compliance so regular as to seem spontaneous, with the commandment to " honour thy father and thy mother ". Consequently, and in spite of discrepant tastes and temperaments, my grandparents and their children formed a very solid four-square family edifice in which it was wholesome for me and my brothers and sisters to grow up. I like to imagine that my grandfather brought the plans for it with him from Mayo along with the stuffed grouse ; for, in spite of our many failings, none can deny that family solidarity is an outstanding characteristic of Irish rural society.

It was at Belclare in, I think, the year 1893 that I first remember actually seeing my father. He was about five foot eight inches in height, strong and active, with a noble brow, closely-trimmed dark beard and china-blue eyes. As I grew up I discovered progressively how rich he was in intellectual, artistic and social gifts, but all I can recall of him when he was fifty-one years and I six years of age, is his benevolence, humour and dignity. It was he who in 1893 first took my sister Eva and myself and the nurses to that wonderful place " Abroad " where he had spent and where I was to spend a large part of my working life. The place chosen was Dieppe. My father had first visited this in 1856, and his reminiscences of the things he best remembered report that " . . . on market days we spent hours amidst the profusion and animation and

SIR EDWARD O'MALLEY (1900)
Judge of H.B.M. Supreme Court in Egypt and the Ottoman Empire

DENTON (see p. 3)

picturesque life of the market in the Place St. Jacques, never
tired of coveting all the pretty things in the beautiful ivory
shops, especially the pink-coloured ivory knives and figures and
crucifixes . . . and watching a review of the garrison—red-
trousered, white-gaitered, blue-coated, shakoed little soldiers ".
My recollections of 1893 are precisely the same ; additionally
I recall the old women in the market continuously chanting
" *Un sou là piè-è-èce* " to the tune of a yellow-hammer's spring
song ; and the little soldiers, when told to stand easy, running
as fast as their legs would carry them to the tin *pissoir* at the
edge of the *plage*. If what psychologists write is true, I suppose
there is some deduction to be made from this similarity of
recollection. However that may be, what I feel sure of is
that it was my father, with his insatiable appetite for travel,
who made me also to seek and to find great riches in all my
departures and journeys and arrivals by sea and land ; in the
fatigues and homesickness and surprises and delights of living
in foreign countries and—not least—in my returns from distant
and famous places to the white cliffs of Dover and to Victoria
Station and to Denton and Bridgend and, at long last, to
Rockfleet.

CHAPTER 3

SOUTH OXFORDSHIRE

I DID not go to school till I was eleven years old. Between
the nursery days which I have been writing about and the
year 1898 when I was sent to Mr. Hussey's preparatory
school at Folkestone, my horizon was expanding because, as
my legs grew longer and stronger, I and my sister Eva were
allowed to go alone for walks together within a few miles of
Denton. I think also that it was towards the end of this
period of my life that that superb invention, the bicycle,
became available to us. And so, on bicycles or on foot, along
the white dusty roads and green lanes, across pasture and
field and along the sluggish river Thame we explored the
countryside and the neighbouring villages : Garsington,
Wheatley, Chiselhampton, Stadhampton, Great and Little
Milton, Great and Little Hasely, Marsh and Toot Baldon,
Dorchester, Clifton Hampden and Waterperry. It was from
the people who lived in them and the way that they behaved
to each other that we got our ideas—soon to be outdated—of
what normal human society was.

Though the parson and the squire and some of the gentle-
men's servants might be " foreigners ", most of the people who
lived in these villages were midland English to the backbone.
Here are some of the names of Cuddesdon men : Buswell,
Ryman, Gale, Sellar, Turner, Dover, Godfrey, Jennings, Bur-
gess, Hicks, Wilkinson, Hinton, Kinch. Besides these there
were a few offshoots of noble families who had come down
in the world, such as Howard, Mortimer and Quarterman.
This society was divided into ill-defined social strata : farmers
at the top ; in the middle, tradesmen—carpenter, smith,
mason, and so on ; and, at the bottom, agricultural labourers.
All but the farmers were collectively known as " the poor
people ". All were tightly bound together by propinquity

and interdependence, and nobody bothered about what is nowadays called " a parity of social esteem ". The farm labourers were " poor " in the sense that they only got four-teen shillings a week and small allowances, but nevertheless they reared five or six healthy children on this. Our head-gardener only got eighteen shillings a week with house and allowances, but I knew his household intimately from the in-side, not from outside, and could see that he did pretty well. The sons of such families could always get work in the towns if there was no demand for them locally. The daughters, as they grew up, were glad to go into service. This was a good thing for them, for in all the vicarages and large houses near Denton they were well-trained and disciplined and con-sequently became good wives and mothers. It was a good thing for people like us too, because our form of life depended on a supply of reasonably cheap and obedient maidservants ; and it was a good thing for everybody because our class was the custodian of most of the qualities which were most valuable in the life of the nation. Of all such—farmers, tradesmen and labourers—I have happy memories : of old Mr. Buswell, who farmed Denton, in his tailcoat and pothat, with an apple in each pocket for the children ; of very old Mrs. Kinch down Plat Lane in the smallest of thatched cottages with her canary and Madonna lilies ; of Mrs. Godfrey, leaving in the mud the imprint of her alder-wood pattens as she trudged up Ryman's Field to church ; of Fred Turner, the sound of whose hammer ringing on the anvil came into the nursery windows before we were up in the morning. It was with such that I and my sister, when we could throw off our governesses, were most at ease and best entertained, and with a succession of our own menservants ; Burton and Goodfellow and Smith and Rowe ; Harry and Albert and Fred.

My mother fitted very well into this little world. She was devoted to the poor people and they were devoted to her and the house and garden were her delight. My father, on retire-ment, did not fit in as well. He never had any warm under-standing of the poor people, enjoyed London and hankered continually for foreign countries. He could have been perfectly happy wandering indefinitely from one end of Europe to the other. They were a highly coloured pair, but piety restrains me from description of the singularities of our family life. I can see them now : my mother in a preposterous hat and expensive low-heeled shoes moving restlessly and purposefully about the house and garden or driving the pony-cart along the country lanes and my father, deep in meditation or a book, walking for hour after hour up and down the terrace or the herbaceous borders ; and I am happy to think that Denton and South Oxfordshire extended to them a detached but benignant protection during the years of their decline.

According to accepted ideas, I ought to have been at school between my eighth and eleventh years. I do not know why I was not, unless it be that my father being abroad, my mother put off the day when she would have to pay my school fees. But, whatever the reason, instead of playing cricket and football and getting broken into the barbarous society of other little boys, I spent those years—when I was not doing lessons —in messing about in Cuddesdon and the other villages mentioned ; poking among the willows by the Thame and watching the rushes bowing in the current and the roach nosing about in the shallows ; watching stoats on dew-drenched October mornings in Coombe Wood ; hunting for pussmoth caterpillars in a jungle of willows at Waterperry ; and on whole holidays marching beyond the furthest limit of our known world till, as from a peak in Darien, I and my sister gazed upon the forest of Menmarsh and the fields and hills of Buckinghamshire leading the eye on illimitably to fresh discoveries. To have spent those years between the ages of eight and eleven at home instead of at a boarding school was likely to make me in some ways peculiar ; and one result of it was that when I did eventually go to school I was never quite at ease with the other boys or they with me. I expect it is from these circumstances that flowed in a long and incalculable series the reasons why, all my life, I was never able to behave quite as I was expected to, nor as other people desired.

16

CHAPTER 4

SCHOOL AND UNIVERSITY

LIFE at home before I went to school is, in retrospect, by no means all happy memories. There was plenty of boredom in it and of being naughty and of being in a general way overshadowed by a watchfulness to disapprove on the part of my elder sisters and governesses and above all of my mother. But these things related to what might be called my public life, and I have largely succeeded in forgetting all about them, because I was secure in my private life in which I include relations with servants ; relations with the animals in or about the house—horses, cows, pigs, dogs, cats, parrots, minnows or caterpillars ; relations with things—straw and oats in the stables, leather in the harness-room, tools of every description in the potting-shed and all the varied and interesting objects which accumulate in the garrets and cellars and cupboards of every country house ; relations above all with the sights and sounds and smells of garden and meadow and pond and spinney. School was a great change. At school it was all public and no private life at all except in bed at night when a small boy could take refuge in secret recollection.

On April 28th, 1898, I arrived at The Grange, Folkestone, a private school of good repute kept by the Reverend H. Hussey. My own children and the children of my contemporaries on going to school for the first time have nearly always been accompanied by one or both parents, but such consideration was much less usual two generations ago. In my own case my mother was at Eastbourne when I set out, and could easily have come with me to Folkestone ; but for reasons which I shall never know I was put alone into the train with a story book by G. A. Henty and told to join the crowd of other little boys which I should meet at Folkestone station. Discipline had been often enforced by my various

17

governesses with the words : " If you won't be a good boy, we shall have to send you to school," and in this and other ways I had been given to understand that school was not at all a pleasant place. It was therefore with a sinking heart that I said goodbye to everything that was familiar and set out to face by myself a life for which nothing in my previous experience had prepared me. After being received by Mr. Hussey with a few kind words and being presented to the matron, I was turned adrift in a large barrack-like room where three classes were normally taught, and left to fend for myself. Supper consisted of thick coarse cocoa, cheese and Osborne biscuits, and when this had been tearfully consumed we went up to bed. I shared a small room under the roof with three other boys. It was furnished with four little hard beds and four chests of drawers, and under the window stood four washing-basins. They were filled with water overnight and the following term I was to find that the water was covered with ice on many mornings.

As I now realize, the climate of Folkestone did not suit me ; and I suffered from a variety of mysterious ailments. Being a somewhat precocious and peculiar child the other boys read in my behaviour a fear and dislike of their way of living which naturally made them suspicious and contemptuous of me. Home was Paradise compared with the sudden deprivation of all privacy, all peace, all beauty, all comfort, all accustomed interests or pleasures. Consequently my first two terms at The Grange were overshadowed by the agonies of homesickness, and the things which I can remember most vividly are the smell of the boot-room, retching before breakfast into the basins in the changing-room, and sobbing fits in the semi-privacy which a range of w.c.'s, smelling of drains and dis-infectant, alone provided. There is no dignity, not even pathos, in the miseries of homesickness : to all but the sufferer his sufferings are trivial, unreasonable and cowardly ; but I sometimes wonder whether the convict starting upon his long journey to Siberia suffers a sharper pang, or the shipwrecked mariner, solitary and adrift upon the ocean. However that may be, I know that at the beginning of the Lent term of 1899

I got to the point of writing to my father, who was paying one of his periodical visits to England, to say that unless he took me home I should run away from school. With my eyes streaming with tears I wrote the letter in pencil against the wall of the w.c. where alone I could not be overlooked. He came straight to Folkestone and took me away with him the same night. I spent the Spring of 1899 with my sister and her governess in Brighton and in the following May, much stronger in health, went to Mr. Eden's Preparatory School at Hillbrow, Rugby. Here I followed a normal and not unhappy course and made several friends of whom Rupert Brooke was one. Rupert was head of the school, a good full back and a promising cricketer. He was as beautiful at that age as he was when he died : a cheerful, talented and perfectly normal boy. He never wrote any serious poetry whilst at Hillbrow.

My brother had been to Harrow as had most of my cousins, which was why I was sent there myself in May, 1901 to Mr. Howson's House, just failing to secure a scholarship. The summer term passed not too unpleasantly, and though I think I must, as previously, have been the object of a certain amount of contempt on the part of my contemporaries, I cannot remember being at all elaborately bullied. But my health there was not good and the doctor advised that I should spend a year at home ; so my mother sent me to inefficient tutors in Oxford for the winter of the year 1901, in the course of which I lost what little scholarship had been acquired earlier. I learned a lot of other things, however, which were most valuable to me but inured fatally to my disadvantage when later I went to Radley.

This year at home was a wonderful year : back again to the horses and cows and dogs ; back again to the stoats in Coombe Wood and to voyages of discovery—but all now upon an ampler scale and with leisure to enjoy a continuity of experience through all the changing months of the year. " Nature Study ", regarded at school as less noble an occupation than cricket and football, became a passion. Nothing in this line came amiss to my sister and myself : flowers, toadstools, birds, moths, rats and newts. We read all the books we could get hold of and made collections of everything, alive if possible, and if not, dead. From these activities I learned to respond to the perfection and innocence of each animal and leaf and flower from which, if we are lucky, we can get an intimation of the true character of our origin and destiny. Additionally I was allowed to drive Tiny in the pony-cart and the carriage horses, Jubilee and Margravin, in the dogcart; and even to ride Margravin by myself to a Meet of the South Oxfordshire hounds or before breakfast in the pasture. This gave us increased mobility and to our other preoccupations we added a study of every church within reach enabling me, with the help of simple text-books, to get a knowledge of architecture and the treatment of interiors which was of great value when I came, later in life, to rebuild two houses, Bridgend in Ockham and Rockfleet. It was in this year too that the apocalyptic experience of the high Alps first came my way and that at Rosenlaui as well as at Denton my acquaintanceships and friendships swept me along into new worlds.

My uncle, the second Lord Monkswell, and his father before him, together with the Elphinstone Grant Duffs, used to take a party of twenty or thirty people to the hotel at Rosenlaui (between Meiringen and Grindelwald) year after year; and here in 1901 I joined them. Monkswell's boys—Robert and Gerard and Eric—had as climbers made the Wellhorn and the Engelhörner to be very much their own, and it was dear Gerard who dragged me up the Dossenhorn and walked with me through the fragrant pinewoods, teaching me the elements of how to walk and climb up mountains, and, though ten years my senior, discoursing to me about the whole duty of man. Here too, at Rosenlaui, as acquaintances if not as friends, I met Reginald Farrer and Gertrude Bell and other distinguished people and fell in love for the first time at the age of fourteen with Iseult, the youngest Grant Duff girl then aged twenty-one. Such contacts and more like them, were to me an incalculable enrichment and more than compensated for having completely unfitted me to make myself acceptable to the rowdy remorseless boys at Radley with whom I was about to be herded.

On May 2nd, 1902, two days before my fifteenth birthday, I drove up to the front door of St. Peter's College, Radley, in the dogcart with Margravin between the shafts. My parents had selected Radley as a more suitable school for me than Harrow because it was near Denton and enjoyed a very good climate. I had attended a preliminary interview with Dr. Tom Field, the Warden, and although I had stumbled over some lines of Euripides, I think he accepted this unusual candidate for a place in the school because he found that—unlike any of my contemporaries—I could read French fluently and German with a hardly perceptible accent. I was placed in the Reverend G. Wharton's " Social " and at once there began for me a dreadful intimacy with the crudities and beastliness of Lower School society.

The outline of the next four years can be drawn in a few sentences. I was academically undistinguished—always just below the level of scholarship boys. I ended up by getting the school prize for an essay on Greek and Roman education, but I never could learn easily to construe the Latin and Greek classics nor to write elegiacs. By specializing in " Gym " of the classical Aldershot kind at which I was good, I got out of regular football and cricket and rowing. All that is dull. The interesting part of my Radley life came out of the dislike felt for me, with a few exceptions, alike by boys and masters. It was not in general a mutual dislike. I should have been very glad to make myself popular with both, but in this I was conspicuously unsuccessful. Nor was what happened inevitable. There were numerous boys more gifted and as sensitive and intelligent as myself, who were popular with everybody or at any rate passed through school without compromising their integrity or irritating their contemporaries. But I was not alone in my misfortunes. There were—and I suppose always are—at schools a small number of boys who attract to themselves all the cruelty and intolerance of the others without having particularly nasty characters. Sometimes it is because they care a lot about books and not at all about games ; sometimes because they squint or stammer ; nearly always it is—among other things—because they are by temperament nonconformists. I was precocious, timid, pious, intolerant, not very good at anything and reeking of a sophisticated background. But more fatal to my happiness I think than all this, was the fact that in spite of despairing efforts to conceal it, I thought I was in a general way superior to other people ! I was therefore fully qualified for inclusion among the persecuted.

Persecution meant being casually knocked about and elaborately humiliated. The second form of torture was worse than the first. Some of the big boys would catch me along with others and haul us off to a lonely corner on a Saturday evening and make us get onto a table, dance, sing and strike ludicrous attitudes. This part of the entertainment concluded, we were beaten and kicked or dragged along the floor by the heels, and only released in time to tidy ourselves up for Evensong. I think, as I still think, that a state of things where such goings-on were possible was atrocious; and when, in my last year, I enjoyed the authority and physical immunity of a prefect I did what I could to stop it. The consequence was the expulsion of several big boys, and a series of school rows of the first magnitude, causing much embarrassment to the Warden and masters and entertainment and excitement to all boys not directly involved. Another consequence was that in my last year I did very little work for the scholarship at Oxford for which I was destined to compete. At the end of my last term the school was examined by a Mr. Peile, a Fellow of New College. My papers showed that I had done practically no work during the preceding thirteen weeks, and while admitting to the Warden and Mr. Peile that this was the case, I explained that I had had other preoccupations. " Well," said Mr. Peile, " you odd people, you sometimes turn out all right and sometimes you don't ; but it is a good thing there aren't too many of you."

And so at the end of July I drove away from Radley for the last time in the same dogcart behind the same little mare, over the ferry at Sandford, back to the heavenly peace and beauty of Denton ; and that evening when I and two other prefects, Noël Smith and Tim Burra, sat and smoked out of doors and

talked about what we were going to do at Oxford and afterwards, the garden seemed more magical than ever. Such as
it was the fight was over. It had seemed like a real fight
about real and important things, although the issue was
befogged at every turn by the eccentricity and intolerance of
my own nature. I asked the Warden, Tom Field, long afterwards, when he was a Canon of Southwell and I had just
returned from Hankow with much credit and publicity, what
he thought about it. " I think you were partly right and
partly wrong," he said, and there I am content to leave it. I
incline to think the school rows of which I was the centre
cleared the air after my departure. In any case, I hear from
many sides that Radley is now a much more civilized community and that the torturing of children is a thing of the past.

After the harsh experience at Radley the amenities of
Magdalen were welcome. I went into residence in October
1906. My rooms were on the ground floor of No. 3 Staircase
in New Buildings. Being no scholar and not wishing to spend
more than three years at Oxford, I decided to take Pass Mods:
and the Honour School in History. If the school of Modern
Greats had existed in 1906, I think I should have been tempted
to take it, for I had an exaggerated respect for philosophy and
metaphysics, supposing that if I learned to use in the right
way the difficult words proper to such branches of learning, I
should get at the truth about myself and the universe. It was
only when I was about thirty-three years old that I discovered
that this truth was a function not of continuous thought or of
language, but of life itself—of the sum of activities of which we
are capable. Having just recovered from a severe operation
for appendicitis, I did not join any of the athletic clubs, preferring to play golf, run with the beagles and take such other
exercise as left me free to follow my own fancy. My allowance
was only £220 a year—enough to hire a punt or buy a bottle
of port, but not sufficient to keep a horse or one of the new-
fangled motor-cars.

As in all universities, groups of undergraduates got together
who amused each other with lively discussion day and night
of every topic under the sun, training themselves for excellence

in one department or another of the metropolitan life they were soon to enter. Having depicted myself in preceding chapters as vividly affected by many different kinds of people and things, it might be supposed that I should soon have attached myself, perhaps even become a valued member of a circle of interesting and congenial friends. But this did not happen. I was too intelligent not to be bored by the bores and not nearly mature or witty or spirited enough to find a secure place in the esteem of my many gifted contemporaries. Consequently, I was as undistinguished socially as I was in the world of books and games. I was not, as at school, an object of active dislike or contempt ; nobody wanted to " rag " my rooms or " debag " me ; it was just that nobody very much cared whether I was there or not. This failure to make myself valued or admired did not cause me to fret. After the storms and stresses of school life I was only too thankful for the independence and physical and aesthetic comfort which life in the shadow of Magdalen tower provided. I was well content watching the Fallow deer in the park out of my window, walking round Addison's Walk every day before breakfast, toasting my muffins over the fire at tea-time and being able at last to make up my own mind how and for what purpose I was going to spend time which now and for the future seemed wholly my own. Indeed, being more or less disregarded may have been good for me, for a lot of people at Oxford and Cambridge got wrong ideas into their heads about the importance of being held high in public esteem.

Besides, I was in love. I had not forgotten Iseult. Far from it ; we had corresponded and occasionally met, and from 1901 to 1907 I had kept safe the recollection of her sweetness and radiant beauty. But what had happened to me now in my twentieth year was something which physical maturity made more formidable. My new young woman lived at some distance from Oxford, and my memories of the years 1906–09 have much less to do with the preoccupations of university life than with cross-country journeys, and letters posted every single night in the box outside my rooms in New Buildings. Of this April of my life, of this uncovering for the first time of a full heart which comes but once, I cannot write but to say that nothing that occurred later, not the separate unfolding of the emotional patterns of what turned out to be divided lives could impair the quality of so well-founded a tenderness and confidence. This accompanied me through all the events related later in this book ; and, of course, it made everything else that happened to me at the university seem relatively unimportant.

In the final History Schools I was placed, to my disappointment, in the Second Class ; and the reasons for this were sympathetically explained to me afterwards by the President, Sir Herbert Warren, and my tutors Grant Robertson and Clement Webb. When my examiners had asked " Was Henry VIII justified in proceeding against Cardinal Wolsey under the Statute of Praemunire ? " they had wanted to elicit from me evidence of knowledge of facts and authorities and intelligent well-expressed comment. What they had not wanted, and what I was fatally inclined to do, was to spend half the statutory three hours analysing the various meanings of the word " justified ". Private schools, they told me, were full of unsuccessful schoolmasters who had got " Seconds " or " Thirds " instead of " Firsts " because of such misplaced activity by an inquiring mind. I took this lesson to heart and when I started to work for the Foreign Office examination I abandoned the pursuit of knowledge in its more recondite forms and devoted myself to learning how to score high marks. This enabled me ultimately to secure the first place over the heads of two Eton collegers who had both been elected to scholarships at Cambridge.

I thought much about how I was going to make a living when I went down, and discussed it with my friends. They did not worry about their future as much as I did, perhaps because for them it was to be so short. Grierson, for instance, was killed by a riding accident ; Gerald Gould died in middle life with but a small volume of poetry to his credit ; Mackworth shot himself ; Davies got a direct hit from a sixty-pound shell in 1914 and Leslie Johnson was shot in the stomach when rescuing a casualty in No-Man's-Land. But I worried a lot. Nobody in my family had ever been " in business " or, as it was formerly expressed "connected with trade", and I accepted this restriction as valid for myself. It never occurred to me to become a doctor ; perhaps because at the beginning of the century medical students were but one remove from dentists and veterinary surgeons who belonged in a world half-way between the butler's pantry and the dining-room. I was not clever enough to get a fellowship and schoolmastering was well known to be the refuge of the destitute. Furthermore, being short-sighted, the Army and the Navy were excluded and I had no vocation for the Church. I might have gone to the Bar like my father and grandfather, but this would have meant postponing the day when I should earn a living—a disagreeable prospect for a young man who wanted above everything to get married and bring up children in the country. Being then without influential connections or natural gifts which could be professionally exploited, my mind turned enviously to the career which annually recruited many of the most brilliant undergraduates : the Indian Civil and Home Civil Services. As a child, visitors had often asked me " And what are you going to be when you grow up to be a man ? " and I had been used to answer that I was going into the Foreign Office. Of course I had not at that time got the faintest idea of what the Foreign Office was ; but my father's job at Constantinople was under the Foreign Office and my cousin Robert Collier, who seemed very grand to me, was in the Diplomatic Service ; and so, as the years passed, I went on repeating, and almost came to believe in the fact that I was going into the Foreign Office. Being fairly good at French and German it seemed by 1907 just conceivable that I might be successful in an examination which was almost, but not quite, as stiff as the examination for the I.C.S. ; and my tutors strongly encouraged me to have a try which, as it proved, was successful. But I have often thought since then how odd it is that I should have been directed onto the long road where my life has been spent by signposts which initially meant nothing to me.

CHAPTER 5

SKIPNESS

I HAD five married uncles and aunts, and thirty first cousins.
Until the latter grew up and got married a constant inter-
change of visits took place.   The cousins I liked best were
the Grahams who lived at Skipness in Argyllshire, and during
the years I was at school and at Magdalen I visited them
constantly and Skipness became for me the most important
place in the world ; more important than Denton or Eastbourne or indeed, the houses which later became my own,
Bridgend and Rockfleet.   Skipness came, it seemed, to be
part of me and I part of it, and I have carried with me my
feelings about it, like a shirt worn next the skin, always and
everywhere.

Skipness lies on the east side of the northern end of the
peninsula of Kintyre, where the county of Argyll stretches out
a long finger towards the hills of Antrim.   When I first went
there it belonged to Robert Graham, who had married my
mother's youngest sister, Emily Hardcastle, and had brought
up there five children of whom the eldest was ten years older
and the youngest four years younger than myself.   A large
house in the Scottish baronial style had been built in 1881.
The estate stretched for about eight miles along a typical piece
of Argyllshire coastal scenery.   At its best it yielded about a
thousand brace of grouse.   The burns were small but quite
good enough to learn to fish in.   I paid my first visit to the
place in the summer holidays of 1902, and thereafter, year by
year, till my aunt died in 1934 I enjoyed her hospitality and
kindness and the society of my cousins, and indulged my
passions for shooting and fishing.   I have written out of a full
heart about Denton and its elms and willows and rich meadows
and slow-flowing streams but Skipness stole my heart away
and it became my home.   I sometimes gave offence to my

cousins by setting up a sort of tacit claim to be as intimate as themselves with their lovely heritage : and I now regret, as they, I am sure, will have forgiven my too ingenuous enthusiasms ; but though I might have been more tactful, there was nothing I could have done to alter the fact that this place was then and for ever my home.

My cousins and I had lots of fun together, but the days that live longest for me are the days I spent alone ; and if we could ever retrace our steps, if some good fairy could give me back a few remembered hours, I should choose to spend them alone at Lochan Fraoich, or on the high beat, or on the upper pools of Glenskibble. Here, if anywhere, would I look for fields of amaranth, and listen for the tuneful voices' still unmuted call.

Waking up early in one of the tower bedrooms, I look out of the window. The weather, I say to myself, is overcast and gentle. You never can tell what it will do till ten o'clock, but it looks good to me. I have breakfast. This coffee and these oatcakes and honey are very good. But this is a very old bicycle and the three miles to Clonaig seem interminable. Never mind, I'll soon be there. I've started : nothing can stop me getting there ; nothing but a little time and effort separates me from the high lochs. Here I am at Clonaig where I leave the bicycle and start to walk, heavy with lunch and gear. The walk is very hard and sweaty. First through a field of oats and then a field of rape. Why are my steps so short? Why do the horizons move so slowly ? Here I am on a hill path where the going is easy though there are many flies. Here is Strone ; and here is Garvelin—a ruined croft where in earlier days I was sure of a glass of milk. Now my way gets steeper. The heather and moss claw and suck at my feet. Never mind, an hour is a very little time. If I go on putting one foot before another for an hour I shall see a white thread near the skyline and that will be my first sight of the loch. Half a mile more ; a quarter of a mile more ; a hundred yards now. Here at last is the loch. Here I am at last on the firm gravelly edge. How nice to walk on firm gravel instead of on the yielding, clawing heather. Now I put up my rod carefully and hastily and soak my cast ; and now I sit down to eat a piece of chocolate and smoke a cigarette and think that here am I at Lochan Fraoich and that this is where I have wanted to be through so many months. There is no longer anything between me and it. Of course it is all slipping away and going to join the past, but for the moment I need not worry about time, for this moment is a kind of eternity ; for this moment I am raised up on the tops of the hills, and all the kingdoms of the earth are mine, and I am a part of them, and even when this evening I have gone down to Skipness again, and indeed when I am dead and have been buried and forgotten, I shall still be here.

Now I push out this leaky old boat and narrow down my thoughts to the business of fishing. It is extremely important to catch fish, but at the same time it is not important at all. I catch some fish, and they are not as big or as many as I should like. But I do catch some fish and they are fierce and cold and very beautiful. And then at last I repack my gear and leave that lovely water and the complaining gulls and walk very fast and easily down off the hill past Garvelin and Strone and down the hill path, through the field of rape and the field of oats on to the hard road, re-entering again the world of rabbits and bicycles and dinner bells, my pockets heavy with the gold of experience which I can never lend nor lose nor give away.

One of the attractive features of shooting and fishing is that no two days are ever alike. Each good day on the hill leaves upon us the imprint of its own individual indestructible beauties and excitements. In winter hill days are shorter and rougher than in summer. On a day in early December I leave the house by the Ploughman's Glen, cross the pier road, and start up across Monibachach to the top of the scars where the burn has since the last ice age been at work cutting a vast trench through the hill and rolling the red soil down into the sea. I reach the scars and look over the edge very carefully where the wind, sucked through this funnel in the mountain, is driven almost vertically upwards ; for below in the hollow, on the face of the scars or like great fruits hanging in the branches of the twisted trees, will be six blackcocks who know me even

better than I know them. They are not in the trees ; I must
scramble through the hollows. I am very much exposed. I
slip and slide down the wet crumbling red earth. Now the
blackcock are suddenly aloft beating the stormy grey air with
their wings and heading for the upper waters of the burn. I
have missed that one. That is because I was not standing
square to him. How can I stand square to him when I can
barely stand at all ? My shot has woken a woodcock out of
his midday sleep and he rises like a butterfly and flops ten yards
further on in the bracken. He can't get away from me now.
He rises again and like a piece of paper swept by the wind
flickers down through the scrub. When he is far enough away
I shoot him in the back of the neck and he falls feather light
among the marsh grasses far below me. Poor woodcock!
your great eyes did not avail you that are now for ever dim. I
am not ashamed of having killed you, of that little bead of
blood oozing from your tawny gentle head. On the contrary
I should have been very disappointed if I had not killed you.
I am not even ashamed of not being ashamed. I have fulfilled
my function and you yours. I go on up the burn onto the
bracken slopes on the high beat, hunting my blackcock all over
again and stalking the cock grouse with his head up in the gale.
There is a little snow here piled against the east side of each
tuft of grass. It is too cold to eat, but I sweat in spite of the
cold and kneel down to drink from the burn. The burn here
runs through small gorges into little pools, feeding in summer
the glen flowers small and sweet. It drains the high mosses
which seem very far away from the sea and the house and the
sheltering plantations. There are always ravens here and
golden plover and few to see them but the shepherd and his
dogs. It is a long way home and I am tired of this strong
sweeping wind. At last I get down to the trees again and here
it is quiet and dark and my feet are light upon the path.
Everyone is at tea in the hall. I feel cut off from them, as if
I had since breakfast been walking on the tundras of Lapland.
Now I am nearly in the same mood with my cousins again, but
not quite ; not quite in the same mood as my aunt Emily, who
sits looking very small and fierce, but not really fierce, with

her silver head and beautiful small hands sewing by the drawing-room fire, her feet in black buckled shoes stretched out on
a footstool to the fire. But when I climb the tower stairs to my
bedroom and say goodnight to Frances, I am glad to see that
she knows, and does not mind, that I have been so far and
been alone, and have added one more link to that chain of
golden incommunicable memories which I shall carry with me
always.

And so the precious days followed each other through all
those years when Skipness was for me the fountain of all ardour
and content. Now Skipness is sold, and all that has gone for
ever ; but I can still comfort myself, when I need comfort, by
reciting like a rosary the lovely names of its hills and farms :
Lagganroaig, Airidh Fhuair, Altagalvish, Culintrach, Monibachach, Caolfin, Achameanach, Gortaneorna, Cnoc a Bhaile
Shios, Oragaig, Eascairt. In those days when I was on the
hill it was always in my mind that some invisible and benevolent spirits accompanied me ; and when some day some other
boy shall travel those hills with rod or gun, perhaps he will
notice that his dog stands from time to time with attentive eyes
and nose fixed on what seems nothing. Wiser than his master,
the dog will I think have seen in the swirling mist or in the
changing shadows of rocks and scrub, the shadow of me who
once walked that way with watchful step and tireless eyes,
gathering into myself such understanding of the wisdom and
kindness of those hills and glens as would nourish me later in
very different circumstances.

CHAPTER 6

ENTRY INTO THE FOREIGN OFFICE

ON going down from Oxford, I spent the summer at Issy-sur-Seine in the family of a manufacturer of "sacred hearts" and other articles of religion. Here in an unlovely, pinchbeck, French suburban villa I passed eight lonely bored and rather profitless weeks of a stifling summer. When I was not doing my lessons or sitting under the pleached limes in the back-garden I explored Paris by myself, but loneliness desolated me. What I liked best was having tea in W. H. Smith's and writing to my young woman on one of their marble tables. "My dear," I wrote, "you are my love, my true love. You are about my path and in my heart. You watch by my bed at my lying down and at my uprising. You are my hope, my citadel, and everything will be all right when I, your true love, come back to you again." I made friends with the daughter of the house, Mademoiselle Rodain, and I talked to her about all this. "Ah," she said, "you have much talent ; you are superior to the other young people we have had working for the English Diplomatic Service. You will be successful, and moreover, you have your happiness, your well-beloved, and all will be well." She was to be wrong on both points, but fortunately I could not see into the future.

In October I returned to England and joined "Scoones", the Foreign Office crammers in Garrick Street. My aunt Mary Monkswell invited me to live with her at Monkswell House, No. 7 Chelsea Embankment, which I did on and off for the ensuing two years. The site of No. 7 had been bought and the house built by the Colliers, when the Embankment was first constructed, at a cost of £16,000. It was very large and comfortable and covered inside with oil paintings of Swiss mountains by the first Lord Monkswell which were more remarkable than the output of his brother John Collier the well-known artist. They were all later destroyed in a furniture depository fire. Chelsea Embankment was a very agreeable place when there was nothing to be heard but the clop-clopping of horses' feet on the wooden pavements. We generally had coffee after lunch on the verandah watching the barges and tugs in the river. All the residents on this part of the Embankment called on each other as people do in the country ; and Chelsea was referred to by the local people as " the village ". At that time I knew nothing of London and had no links with London society except what Monkswell House provided. However, interesting and agreeable people came to the house and I received a number of invitations to dinner-parties which were in general larger, more magnificent and more formal than after the war. Dinner was at eight or a quarter to eight o'clock. No one was ever late. Though we got six different kinds of wine during and after the meal, cocktails and sherry were not handed round while we waited for it, standing talking under the chandeliers. All the men, unless they came straight from the House of Commons, wore starched white shirts and white ties with black waistcoats. We must have looked rather like Du Maurier's illustrations in *Punch*. Walking back to the Embankment on a summer night by Queen's Gate or Prince's Gardens or the Cadogans, I would pass house after house with open lighted windows from which came dance music and the chatter of conversation. Poor people stood by the front doors and thoroughly enjoyed seeing the ladies going in and out in their finery, and lines of carriages stood or walked up and down with the horses stamping and jingling their harness and tossing little balls of white foam from their bits onto their lacquered shoulders. It was all very agreeable but not enough to make me feel anything but a small fish half out of water when I eventually entered the Foreign Office.

I soon abandoned " Scoones " and instead worked with private tutors or by myself in London or at Denton, going to Skipness twice a year and for madly exciting skiing holidays to Switzerland at Christmas. I failed—by very little—in the

Foreign Office examination in August 1910 and decided to try again, partly out of obstinacy and partly because I could not think of an alternative. In the 1911 examination I secured the first place. This was good news ; indeed I cannot think of any bit of news I was ever so glad to get in all my life. The loathly tyranny of examinations which had regulated my life for thirteen years was ended, and the future seemed as secure as any worldly future well could be. I returned to London in good spirits, destroyed the little books in which I had written and from which I had learned by heart fourteen thousand German words and phrases, and took furnished rooms at 71 Eaton Terrace. In the course of a few days I received from the Private Secretary a letter printed in beautiful italics on hand-made paper directing me to " come into attendance forthwith ".

On the morning of October 13th, 1911, I presented myself rather tremulously to the Private Secretary to the Permanent Under-Secretary of State, Lord Cranley, or—as he afterwards became—Lord Onslow, generally known as the Round O. I was pleased to think not only that I had at last finished with academic studies and got a real job of work, but that this was work of a kind which would make me an object of envy and esteem to contemporaries who had had much more distinguished careers than I at school and college. The Private Secretary took me along the passage to the Western Department to which I had been allocated, and introduced me to the head of it, Sir Eyre Crowe, the assistant Mr. Drummond (later Lord Perth), and the members of the " Third Room " ; Gerald Villiers, Lord Drogheda and Lord Colum Crichton Stuart. It was characteristic of the staff of the Foreign Office in those days that four out of six men in my department should have been the offspring of noble families. The three or four members of the " Third Room " sat at commodious desks in Room No. 12 on the ground floor looking out over St. James's Park ; a large coal fire burned in the grate and there was one telephone inconveniently attached to the wall. The clerical staff who kept all our papers were housed nearby, and intercommunicating doors led to the rooms where Mr. Drummond sat and where Sir E. Crowe supervised our labours and received foreign representatives and other visitors. Through these offices passed nearly every document, whatever its importance, treating of the foreign relations of the British Empire with countries in Western and Central Europe.

The economy and despatch with which the Foreign Office transacted business was largely due to a system different from that in use in foreign countries. Our system provided that every paper, with very few exceptions, should pass into the machine at the bottom, and only reach the Secretary of State when each member of the appropriate hierarchy, starting from the bottom, had recorded his opinion of it. In most foreign ministries the presiding politician, less confident in the loyalty of officials or more apprehensive that his own doings should be known outside his own personal entourage, often employed in confidential or shady transactions a small group of adherents whose indiscretions would be as dangerous to themselves as to him. This system automatically impairs confidence between a Cabinet Minister and his department as a whole, leads to delay, confusion and duplication of labour, and renders less valuable the advice tendered by all those who are not in the inner ring. In our Foreign Office, on the other hand, no change of Secretaries of State, no changes of party in power ever caused the Foreign Secretary to withhold his full confidence from even the most junior members of his administrative staff. This being so, there were naturally many papers of the highest interest which it was my initial duty to read, understand and catalogue. It soon became my duty also to write opinions on the papers which reached us and to draft letters carrying out the instructions minuted upon them by the Secretary or Under-Secretaries of State ; and it was in this manner that the education of everyone who joined the Foreign Office was conducted.

Two things struck me at once about the way in which my new associates did their work. The first thing I noticed was that every member of the Western Department, faced with a specific question arising out of a paper on his table, realized that the decision taken on that actual piece of paper would

35

affect the lives and fortunes of human beings, possibly large numbers of them, possibly for a long time to come. Besides this sense of the actuality of their work, my colleagues showed readiness to take just as much responsibility as the Secretary of State or Under-Secretaries of State would concede to them ; and they undertook responsibility without making heavy weather of it and as if it were part of their normal lives. In these two respects our clerks seemed to me, when I had had opportunity to make comparisons, to enjoy an advantage over the ordinary run of civil servant ; and I guess that this was attributable to the aristocratic tradition in the Foreign Office : to the fact that its traditional attitude towards its work had been built up during the nineteenth century by cadets of the governing families of England, habituated to giving orders and regulating the lives of servants and dependants. At any rate I should like to think that this was so, for so general is the tendency nowadays to decry privilege and declare that every-one is as good as everyone else, that these same governing families seem to get less credit than they deserved.

There was very much less work for the Foreign Office to do in 1911 than there is now that governments have got themselves tangled up in such a lot of complicated international machinery. But if an almost cloistral peace reigned in the Western Department, if we got home from work in time to change for dinner and if one of us was generally away in the country from Friday to Tuesday, this did not mean that we did not, on the average, do a good day's work for very little pay ; to be precise, for £3 a week. The Marmadukes and Archibalds of fiction must have long been extinct ; at least I never met them. So far from being lackadaisical we prided ourselves—and I think rightly—upon answering letters from the public and from other government departments quickly, precisely and politely. Sir Eyre Crowe saw to that. Two reasons why work in the Foreign Office or in an Embassy was less of a hurly-burly than it later became were, first, that we had only one master with whom everything began and ended, the Secretary of State ; and secondly, that Sir Edward Grey was very much master in his own house. Nowadays clerks, or " officers " as they are called, in the Foreign Office are obliged to read Cabinet minutes and pay a lot of attention to what other Departments and Ministers than their own think, while Ambassadors are liable to get instructions, often inconsistent, from three or four different Government Departments in London at the same time on the same matter. Further, the Secretary of State's job has been more or less placed in commission ; there is hardly anything the poor man can decide for himself without Cabinet consultations. When Sir Edward Grey, on the other hand, had to make an important decision, he did not as a rule have to discuss it with a score of Cabinet colleagues or indeed defend it in detail in the House of Commons. He very often had no more than a little private unrecorded talk with Mr. Asquith or Lord Haldane and later was able to persuade the House of Commons not to press him on matters better left to " Secret Diplomacy ". The result generally reached us in the form of a telegram precisely drafted on our papers in red ink in Sir Edward's own hand, in respect to which no action was needed except to put it into cypher and send it off. All this, of course, was comfortable for everybody.

In the year 1911, the Foreign Office and the Diplomatic Service were surrounded by a nimbus of prestige and romance, and the reasons for this were not far to seek. In the first place their activities were carried on against a background of Court life in this country and abroad ; and although newly-joined members of the service would not for some years be on terms of intimacy with Kings and Emperors, they were all Ambassadors in embryo, and enjoyed at an early age some reflection of the bright light which beat upon their seniors. In the second place the work upon which we were employed was surrounded by a delicious atmosphere of secrecy, excitement and importance. We dealt with foreign and not domestic matters. States stood in relation to each other in what Hobbes would have called " a state of nature " with every man's hand potentially against his neighbour, and no authority set above the contending interests. Consequently the conduct of foreign affairs compared with internal affairs as big-game hunting compares with deerstalking or a covert shoot ; and an Ambassador or a Minister seemed in a sense to share the responsibilities and catch some reflection of the glamour which surrounds naval and military commanders in time of war. In the third place, the Foreign Service derived prestige from the fact that its personnel was in general drawn from families whose claims to belong to the best society were not open to question. This was due to a variety of causes. A candidate required a nomination from the Secretary of State to compete in the annual examination ; an attaché posted abroad had to have a guaranteed private income of at least £400 a year ; of the sons of middle-class parents some did not realize that the door into the Service was more than half-open to them, and others hesitated to pass through it into a profession where they feared to find themselves out of their element. Accordingly, the majority of the Office was drawn in 1911 from families " in society ", as it was quaintly called. " Society " and politics were the two big driving wheels which had carried London like a powerful locomotive flashing and puffing along the rails of Victorian and Edwardian England. The Foreign Office was the place where political importance and social distinction were most obviously and closely linked, and it was this combination which gave it its legendary prestige.

I was pleased when I entered it to find that some of the prestige of the Service was reflected upon myself, and it was a pity that I did not take more advantage of it. I might, for instance, have enlarged my circle by accepting the invitations which were sent to me—simply because I was in the Foreign Office—by numerous hostesses to whom I had never been introduced. Being old-fashioned, I put all these in the fire ; and of those with whom I did make fresh contacts some did not please me and to many I was not pleasing, being neither rich nor good looking nor talented nor amusing. However, I was constantly picking up people in trains or ships or odd corners here and there with whom acquaintance had all the magic and golden fruits of intimacy ; and with these, and my solid background of family connections, my leisure was fully occupied. Accordingly, I continued in London, as I had lived

in Oxford, in well-deserved obscurity, finding in snow above
the tree-line and on the high lochs as in the depths of my
affections and the interest of my work satisfaction for the
passions and imaginations of an undistinguished life.

CHAPTER 7

PEACE AND WAR

BETWEEN October 1911 when I entered the Foreign
Office and August 1914 when war broke out, three
important events occurred in my life which I will now
proceed to relate : I set foot in Asia for the first time, broke
my back, and got married.

When the pressure of work in the Foreign Office was less
severe than now, it was often possible for a junior clerk to get
permission to substitute one of the regular King's Messengers
who carried official correspondence in what are called " bags "
from London to various Missions, and, on the return journey,
from Missions back to the Foreign Office. The most attractive
route, on which a fortnightly service was maintained, took
the messenger to Berlin, Munich (where a quasi-diplomatic
Mission existed), Vienna, Budapest, Belgrade, Sofia and Constantinople ; and I lost no time in offering myself as a substitute courier for this journey to the Chief Clerk, Sir Chauncey
Cartwright and, under his instructions, setting off some time
in March 1912. I remember as if it were yesterday the delight
of settling down in my mahogany and blue plush sleeping-
berth for a much longer journey than I had yet undertaken,
and the growing excitement as my little moving house rushed
by day and night across the great plain of Hungary, over
the Danube at Belgrade, through the great gorge beyond Nish,
through country stations in Bulgaria where real people still
wore fancy dress, and over the Rhodope mountains and the
downs at Chatalja, coming at last to rest in the Stambul
which my father had so often described to me.

After engaging a room in the Hotel Tokatlian I took my
bag at once to the Embassy, where Sir Gerard Lowther,
having given me lunch, handed me over to his junior attaché,
Harold Nicolson, who was to look after me. In the course

of my three days we visited together all the usual sights of the town, and I came in for a good deal of chaff both from Lady Lowther and others because I insisted on stopping in inconvenient places to watch birds and pick flowers which meant nothing to them but were full of interest for me. One afternoon Harold took me across to Scutari. When, uncertain of our direction, we had stumbled some distance along a road unevenly paved with huge square blocks of stone, he asked an old man what road it was that we had struck. The man answered in Turkish, which Harold translated for me : " This, Effendi, is the road to Bagdad ". I had always had the ordinary boy's ambition to travel, and for me, as for most people, the foreign countries I wished to visit were arranged in my mind in an order of preference. Australia, New Zealand, Canada and the United States came last. Higher up came the windy beaches of Tierra del Fuego and the South Sea Islands ; but Asia—a generalized conception of Anatolia, Persia, Mesopotamia, Khiva, Bokhara and Ferghana with its peach gardens and apricot groves—this was what I really wanted to see ; and so, as I heard the old man's words, I felt that now indeed my feet were set upon the road of my desire. Once again a good while afterwards I was to hear words of equal weight fall from the lips of a Chinese donkey-boy. We were leaning against the balustrade of the Marco Polo bridge outside Peking and wondering whither the road led which it carries across the *Hun-Ho*. The donkey-boy, to whom we turned for information, answered : " Big grand-father, this is the great road to Lhassa." At that time—in 1926 it was—I had not yet given up all hope that these eyes of mine would one day look upon the Po-ta-la.

When I reached Vienna on the return journey from Constantinople I was in so much pain that I could hardly stand or walk. What had happened was this : some weeks before starting for Turkey I had taken my usual winter skiing holiday in Switzerland and in the course of an expedition had had an awkward fall, resulting as it afterwards proved in a fracture of the pelvis and a displacement of the bones in and around it. I paid as little attention to this at the time as I could and did not let it prevent me carrying out the previously arranged journey to Constantinople. This journey, however, had naturally aggravated the injury; by the time I got to Vienna it had almost immobilized me, and it was only with much distress that I managed to carry on to London. I will here finish the story of my back and never refer to it again, although my accident in fact did more to condition my life than any other single thing that ever happened to me. My back ached day and night for about seven years. I spent hundreds of pounds on useless treatment, and it was not till 1919 that Sir Robert Jones diagnosed the real nature of the mischief. But it was too late to cure it, and for the rest of my days I have had to put up with the pain and fatigue of a disability which has interfered with all my favourite occupations. Life would have been very different if I had managed always to keep my knees together when running on ski in deep wet snow.

By 1910 I and my young woman of Oxford and Paris days had decided that we could never get married. By 1913 therefore, the door was wide open for some other rash person to pass through and join their life with mine. On March 13th of that year I and my cousin Bertie Graham arrived back in London from a skiing holiday in high fettle. From Victoria Station we drove to a flat where two of my Skipness cousins were living, and on ringing the bell the door was opened to us by a friend of theirs, a girl of about twenty-three years who turned out to be a Miss Sanders, well known in those days not as Ann Bridge the novelist but as one of the leading English woman mountaineers. Not without reflection on the possible consequences, I started at once to cajole my cousins into asking Miss Sanders to Skipness where I was also hoping to spend the Easter holiday. May in London was for courtship and on June 1st we became engaged to be married. Our wedding took place on October 25th in St. Mark's, North Audley Street.

We spent our five-day honeymoon in Beaminster with which my relations had long been connected. My grandfather, Joseph Alfred Hardcastle, had lived there when he retired

from the House of Commons ; and after him his widow, a
daughter of Lord Chancellor Campbell ; and after her my
Vaughan Johnson cousins and my aunt Mary Monkswell. It
was my aunt Mary's house—the Stone House—which was now
put at our disposal. On that leaf-strewn October evening of
1913, as the hired car showed its headlights coming over the
hill from Crewkerne Station, we were greeted by a full peal
of the minster bells ; some of the finest in the west of England :
eight of them in the key of D, the tenor weighing 25 cwt. I
sent across some money for the ringers to drink our health,
but ever since then have had to live with a secret niggling
shame, for all I sent was a golden half-sovereign. In those
days that would, of course, have bought a good many pints
of beer ; but still, it was mean. I ought to have sent £5,
or anyhow £2. But the fact was that I had very little money
left after all the expenses of getting married, and I can only
hope that those who still survive of that team of ringers will
accept this very belated explanation and apology. At the
Stone House we were greeted by servants who had been in
the family for many years. Grimes the gardener had picked,
and McCoy the parlourmaid had laid on the table for us
two bunches of white geraniums. Why have I seen white
geraniums so seldom since ?

The spring and summer of 1914 rolled along majestically like
many earlier Victorian and Edwardian springs and summers,
with nothing more serious in the air than mutiny in the British
Army and threat of civil war in Ireland. None of my friends
or colleagues measured accurately the stupendous disequil-
ibrium shortly to appear in our seemingly well-ordered lives.
One of nature's curiosities is that *Misgurnus fossilis.* This small
fish spends a lethargic life on the mud at the bottom of sluggish
streams, but from time to time springs suddenly to life and
darts about in all directions in great agitation. This is a
sure sign that an earthquake is imminent, and some of these
creatures are consequently kept in captivity and under constant observation by seismologists in India. Providence had
not provided us with a political equivalent of the infallible
loach, and thus in the spring of 1914 most people, including

my wife and myself, went on with their plans for the summer in much the same way as usual. We had few thoughts to spare for anything but the organization of our private lives on a bare £650 a year in a maisonette at 72A Lexham Gardens. Towards the end of June, when the carpets and curtains had been arranged to our satisfaction and the top rooms had been got ready for the child shortly to be born, my wife went to stay with friends in Sussex and I to Skipness. The daily papers were delivered here at about five o'clock in the afternoon, and returning for tea on Monday June 29th from a day's sailing, I walked up from the boathouse to find Bertie Graham reading *The Times* on the bench outside the billiard-room windows. He told me that the Austrian Archduke Francis had been murdered at Sarajevo and that the news had made a stir in London which then to me seemed almost as far away as Serbia. If I had still been in the Western Department I might possibly have foreseen more fully the events which were shortly to follow, but I had by this time been transferred to the African Department of the Foreign Office, and for this reason among others I, like my cousins, went in to tea without realizing that the death sentence of innumerable Shipnesses and of all they stood for had already been pronounced. In a few days, however, I was recalled from leave and from then on my personal life was carried away on a flood of portentous events.

An account is given in Nicolson's " Life of Lord Carnock " of the circumstances in which a note was delivered to the German Ambassador in London, beginning " The German Government having declared war upon His Majesty's Government . . ." ; of how, when it was ascertained that this was based on wrong information, a revised note had to be substituted affirming " that a state of war would exist as from 11 p.m." ; and of how, in consequence, the text of a whole series of documents had to be corrected and reprinted in order to bring them into conformity with a British rather than a German declaration of war. It was in making the necessary alterations in ink on innumerable copies of some Order in Council or Proclamation that I spent most of that night. I think most of my contemporaries as well as myself were in a state of pleasurable excitement. It was not as silly and wicked as it may seem that pleasure was mixed with our excitement because we had spent the preceding days in nightmarish fear that England would funk going to war to help her friends. Besides that, all members of the Office were glowing with goodwill and warmheartedness towards each other. I remember this well, because I disliked several of them, and a good many of them disliked me. All such unworthy feelings were utterly swept away by shared dangers and anxieties. It is a pity that we do not all of us realize all the time that our immortal souls, if not our physical existence, are in great danger and proper objects for acute anxiety. If we did, perhaps we should all always live in love and charity with each other.

Elaborate preparations had in previous years been made in the Foreign Office for meeting the emergency which was now upon us ; but one side of it had been overlooked, namely, that it would require an unprecedented number of telegrams to be encyphered and decyphered with the utmost possible speed. To meet this need the majority of the staff of the Office was at once divided into three shifts working all round the clock with a very inadequate number of cyphering tables. Anyone available was recruited for the work, and I can remember seeing our Ambassador in the U.S.A., Sir Cecil Spring Rice, peering short-sightedly at the manuscript of a telegram and copying it laboriously on a typewriter with one finger of each hand. I was assigned to the 12-8 a.m. shift of cypherers but had a certain amount of work to do during the day also. I had barely reached home on August 9th when at 6.40 p.m. my daughter Jane was born.

For me the central figure of these August days was not Sir Edward Grey whom I had never met ; nor, though I knew him, his private secretary and *eminence grise* Sir William Tyrrell —a little man as quick as a lizard with scintillating eyes and wit and a great aversion to any work not transacted orally— with whom Crowe was at this time at bitter odds. The central figure for me was Crowe who had by now been promoted from the Western Department to be an Assistant Under-Secretary of State. I went into his room on that agonizing July 31st when the course England would take was still in doubt. He was writing on a piece of blue quarto paper, and over his shoulder I read, in his beautifully clear script :

" The theory that England cannot engage in a big war means her abdication as an independent State. She can be brought to her knees and made to obey the behests of any Power or group of Powers who can go to war . . . If the theory were true, the general principle on which our whole foreign policy has hitherto been declared to rest would stand proclaimed as an empty futility . . ."

A few days later I went into his room again on hearing of the fall of Namur. " It is a bad beat—a bad defeat, I mean," he said. Having had a German mother and having spent his earliest years in Frankfurt-on-Main, his command of English used to break down in moments of stress. Crowe's face was white and drawn and he told me that he felt that his advice was falling upon the reluctant ears of a man—Sir Edward Grey—not qualified by upbringing or study to understand what was going on in the sinister depths of the German mind. I can find no one who knows why he was transferred soon after the outbreak of war from the political and military to the commercial department of the Foreign Office, but we believed at the time that it was because Sir A. Nicolson, Permanent Under-Secretary of State, had become impatient of the vigour with which he pressed his views. Whether this was so or not the transfer was of great benefit to the State, for the Commercial Department rapidly developed into the instrument of blockade, and the decisive nature of this weapon owed as much to the fertility of Crowe's brain as it did to the Tenth Cruiser Squadron.

It is high time somebody wrote a biography of Crowe, for we who knew him will soon all be dead and no one could do it well who had not known him well. It is, in a way, fortuitous that he is famous, for his public reputation is mostly due to his Memorandum of 1907 on " German Relations ", and if there had been no war this would have been buried for generations in the State archives. He had been passed over twice for promotion before I entered the Service ; partly because he never condescended to any of the arts of self-advancement, and partly because he took a rather puckish pleasure in flouting convention. He told me, for instance, that old " Lamps " (Lord Sanderson) had remonstrated with him one day for wearing a bowler during the Season, when of course top hats were the rule or at any rate the fashion. " You say I am not to wear a bowler," Crowe had replied. " Very well, your instructions shall be carried out " ; and for the rest of the summer he came to the Office in a straw hat. It is disquieting that old " Lamps " should have cared more about the straw hat than the 1907 Memorandum.

I can never be sufficiently grateful to Crowe for having given me always his intimate friendship and having encouraged absolutely frank discussion on both sides of all matters personal as well as official. We were quite different. He liked art and literature, I liked pigs and hens; but we both disliked humbug and had a natural sympathy for *frondeurs*. He laughed at me for knitting in the Underground, but I surmise that he saluted in those green woollen socks with purled ribs and basket-stitched heels something which he respected. Anyhow, we always got on very well, and I loved him dearly. What I remember best is not his sensibility and good nature though these were enough to make him a good friend ; not his intelligence and flawless integrity though this would have made him a valued member of any society. There was besides these things such a heat in his spirit that knowledge of history and contemporary politics, acute judgment and power of exposition ran together with a kind of incandescence which lit up everything on which his mind and feeling and words were directed.

On that night of August 4th–5th, 1914, and for the four following years, we never seemed to have time to say a proper goodbye to the world that was spinning away from us ; besides which, of course, we did not know what we were in for. Harking back now to the pre-war years, what I dwell on in my mind is Denton on a summer afternoon ; the smell of newly-mown lawn grass mixed with the scent of very early heliotrope in the front beds ; the clatter of the hay-mower drifting through the windows with the chintz curtains lifting in the draught ; Red Admiral and Peacock butterflies on the creeper ; the stable cat folding herself together on the torrid cobbles of the back yard and the outline of the windows creeping from west to east across the portraits on the landing walls. I suppose these things still go on in some places, but the form and quality of the life which makes this image in my mind is very nearly stone dead. The odd thing is that it died with hardly a squeak of pain or protest. This is like the dissolution of the British Empire, the English being apparently prouder of abdication than of responsibility.

Members of the Foreign Office were forbidden to join the Armed Forces. We were told we should be put in prison if we tried to do so. About halfway through the war we were medically examined and " attested " but we were never called up. Most of my contemporaries were full of martial ardour but I was glad I did not have to be a soldier, knowing very well that with my bad back I should not have outlasted my training and, since a broken sacro-iliac joint is not readily diagnosed, that everybody would have thought I was shamming. So instead of being killed or being very brave or just very frightened, my war consisted in working hard in the Contraband Department from half-past eight in the morning till half-past seven in the evening for about 320 days a year ; learning to write the highly-stylized language of a Government Department and acquiring a mass of curious knowledge about such things as the interlocking directorships of Swiss armament factories : the headings under which silk and cotton can be classified and the difference between the gross nett and dead-weight tonnage of ships. Not having been shot at by the Germans left me with a permanent feeling of inferiority to all the young soldiers who entered the Foreign Service when the war was over.

The end of it all came at last. I asked Sir Sidney Clive, Lord Haig's Chief-of-Staff, some years later at what point he knew that we had won the war. Although Haig says nothing like this in his diary, Clive answered at once that it was on March 26th, 1918, for by the afternoon of that day the momentum of the final German attack had been measured and its ultimate failure foreseen ; but I was not to know that in the spring or even the summer of 1918. When at last the eleventh hour of the eleventh day of the eleventh month came I went to stand at a window of Room 63 in the Foreign Office. The whole of Downing Street was packed to suffocation. Mr. Lloyd George came out of the door of No. 10 and stood with his elbow on the iron railings flicking his eyeglasses up and down in his left hand. " In two minutes," he said, " the war will be over . . ." If he said more than this I could not hear it because of the noise the crowd made.

While all this was going on affairs in Ireland were going from bad to worse. I can never be sufficiently thankful that we had no residence in Mayo at that time, and that I had nothing to do with them. The Chief Clerk, Sir Hubert Montgomery, who was responsible for personnel in the Office, was a Covenanter. I told him he could count me as a Sinn Feiner ; but that was as far as it went. Like many other Irishmen I was ready in the last resort to be killed in the service of England, but I think I comprehended then almost as clearly as I do today how fatuous it was of the English to deny self-government to Ireland, how unwise to kill participants in the Easter Rising and later, how wicked to let loose the Black and Tans and Auxiliaries on the country.

CHAPTER 8

BRIDGEND

I MUST now give some account of how we settled into Bridgend, for this was the little fortress of tranquil family life where my wife and I established ourselves after all the upsetting events of the war; from which we sallied out to go to the ends of the earth in 1925, and to which, with grateful hearts we returned in 1928. Bridgend it was which offered me exactly the kind of life which I had set before myself at Oxford as being most desirable : to be married and have children and live in the country and keep pigs and hens.

In February 1919 my wife and I were spending a week-end at Clandon when we heard of a house to let in the neighbouring parish of Ockham. We bicycled over to look at it at eight o'clock on a snowy morning and at once decided that it was the place for us whatever shape it was in ; and in a few weeks we had got a lease of it from the proprietress, the Dowager Lady Lovelace. The house to which we so precipitately attached ourselves had formerly been a farm. Parts of it dated from the late fifteenth or early sixteenth century, and the latest addition had been made in 1780. A large cottage and five acres went with it. Ockham had belonged to the King family ever since Lord Chancellor King had used in the 1720's to drive up thence in his coach to Westminster Hall ; and with uncommon right feeling and determination our landlady for many years after her husband's death kept the agricultural character of this parish uncontaminated by the extension of London suburbs. In the usual sense of the word there was no village of Ockham, the parish being divided into several congeries of houses known as Bridgend, Church End, Southend, Hatchford End, May's Green, Martyr's Green, Elm Corner and the Wilderness. That part of the parish clothed with heather and self-regenerating pine which the

passing motorist sees on his left hand between Cobham and
Ripley was called the Moor. The woods at the Horsley end
of the parish were called the Forest. Like Bridgend itself,
they were thus denominated when Domesday Book was compiled and since that record was made have never been under
the plough. The bricks for the houses of Ockham came from
one end of the village and most of the timber from the other.
In some, however, were embodied ribs and knee-pieces from
ships broken up at Portsmouth ; for our village formerly sup-
plied oak for building the King's ships and the hauliers had
used to bring back from the coast old ships' timbers rather than
travel empty. The partition walls of Bridgend were made of
wattle and daub, that is to say of hazel hurdles packed with
clay, but had certainly been well-rendered with plaster as far
back as the sixteenth century, for by chipping away more
recent colour-washes we found stencilled designs of that period
on them.

I was the first member of the Foreign Office to live in the
suburbs and go up and down to London every day. Other
members of the Office looked down their noses at this arrangement and it was a good thing for me, in this context, that I
had been immunized by my school experiences against much
minding about what other people thought in a matter of this
kind. My wife and I decided to make the experiment, first,
because we could not conceive of any house or flat in London
being " home ", and secondly, because we thought the children
would miss something, never afterwards to be recovered, unless
they went out day after day along the same dusty or muddy
lanes between the same hedgerows bordered with celandines
and cow parsley, over the same tillage where larks sang and
the same meadows where the cattle stared gloomily at small
intruders before turning, as cattle do, despondently away.
This thing which we wanted for the children is the feeling
only to be acquired in early life, that " home " has been as
it is since the beginning of the world and will go on being
as it is till the end of the world. Long after time has taught
us that such ideas are illusory they can go on being a source
of comfort and strength. Owing to changes of residence my

wife had not had the full advantage of continuity of upbringing in the country. She had been born at Porters in Hertfordshire when her father was making £89,000 a year. In her second year he had moved to Englefield Green on about £30,000 a year. In her sixteenth year he had declined to a beggarly £6,000 a year in Elm Park Gardens. Her parents' ultimate descent was in her twenty-first year to a residential hotel in Stanhope Gardens and £600 a year, after which she and all the six other children had to shift for themselves. We were both determined that our children should, so far as possible, enjoy the advantages which I had enjoyed at Denton in the apparently changeless, timeless world of familiar gardens, woods and meadows.

There were only two children so far, but Grania, or Kate as she came later to be called, was born at Bridgend on May 7th, 1921, at about twenty minutes past five in the afternoon. We were all having tea in the drawing-room when my wife said to the doctor : " I think I shall now go upstairs and I think you shall come with me." Kate entered this world an hour later so fast that Dr. Kitching told me afterwards he had barely time to give a whiff of chloroform with one hand and catch the baby with the other.

Our net income when we went to Bridgend was about £1,200 a year gross, to which my salary contributed £594 12s. 8d. gross. It rose gradually to about £3,000 in 1937, when I was sent to Mexico and we were obliged to give up the house. Of this £1,045 represented my net salary and £1,300 my wife's net literary earnings. As most of our money—in Ireland as in England—is now taken away by the Government and spent in the manner most likely to induce the lower orders of society to vote for them at the next General Election, it may be of interest to record the kind of life it was possible for people in our financial position to lead between the years 1919–37 ; bearing in mind that school fees and expenses, amounting to about £600 a year by 1929 and nearly £1,000 a year by 1933, were for the most part paid out of rapidly dwindling capital, and that to set against this we received much hospitality from friends and relations richer than ourselves.

Bridgend, before we improved and added to it, was hardly more than a cottage, but being conducted with knowledge and industry it provided us with something differing not so much in atmosphere as in degree from the sort of life we had enjoyed at Denton. Our staff consisted, besides casual labour, of a gardener, a nurse or nursery-governess and two or three maids. My wife took a proper pride in the delightful business of housekeeping and the storeroom was always full of pickled eggs, hams, jam, honey and bottled fruits produced on the place and often prepared with her own hands. The silver, linen, glass and china cupboards as well as the book-shelves were similarly well furnished by inheritance, gift and careful purchase. A house with cottage, stables, garage, sheds, cars, electric-light engine, garden, walls, and fences needs for good maintenance many trades and much labour, and it was to this that I devoted all my spare time. Among other things I built for myself in brick a workshop twenty-four feet by ten by thirteen, and I think I had more peace here than anywhere else in my life ; spending long days with the smell of glue and shavings in my nostrils and the exquisite texture of oak or pine in my hands. At the height of Bridgend's productivity I had a boar and two sows in full profit, about 150 chicken, a number of geese and ten stocks of bees. I sold most of the pigs at eight weeks, but to get dung, fed some up to twelve stone. We used to cut these up in the garage and I would deliver pork by car to London customers at retail prices on my way up to the Foreign Office. We made a few hams but the work was heavy for my wife. Our egg trade was similarly run on a retail basis, and we never used less than seven to ten dozen eggs a week in the house. The rearing was heavy work before I could afford incubators and brooders. I once had as many as twenty-nine sitting hens to lift every day before breakfast.

Fresh-laid eggs have the same serene beauty as old silver or fine linen, and pigs are affectionate and intelligent companions, but more than these and indeed above all other things at Bridgend it was bees that I loved and reverenced. There is something divine about the hive and the honeycomb and the meticulously ordered existence of a community which carries social obligation and technical skill to almost un-exampled heights. Most of a man's trouble he owes to his women or his children or both. What are we to think of a society where three sexes live in unquestioned harmony? Where males never do any work at all? Where the mother of the hive can produce three thousand offspring in twenty-four hours having recourse to her male but once in her life? Where females incapable of mating can produce at will males fit to fertilize a queen? But if anyone who has never handled bees wishes to learn why we, who know the hive, can draw from it a kind of grace and consolation, he would do well, instead of reflecting on these fantastic arrangements, to sit some calm day in June for an hour or two in the morning and again in the evening close to the entrance of the hive and watch the procession of the foragers. As soon as the sun is high enough the older workers come out like arrows from the bow, soaring unhesitatingly towards the lime trees. Only the young bees newly released from nursery duty swing to and fro to mark well the hive's location. Later in the day bees pour out helter-skelter and all the long hot hours there is the appearance of confusion but no confusion on the alighting board among those coming and those going and the fanners and the sentries. When the sun gets low no bees any longer leave the hive but all the air about it and the long grasses will be full of tired, heavy-laden workers dropping out of the scented sky, and from the doorway will come a sweet smell, a steady ecstatic hum. To see the summer day close thus is in itself a benediction.

Everyone gets tired of their own place from time to time, and so of course the labours here described, beginning for me about half-past six in the morning winter and summer, and bringing at the best about £160 profit per annum were inter-rupted by holidays abroad and visits to Skipness or elsewhere. At Bridgend itself we had the best of society, that is to say the society of our own chosen associates who would come down and dine and sleep or spend Sunday with us. For the rest we enjoyed the friendship of the villagers who lived round us and of four or five families resident in Ockham in much the same circumstances as ourselves. I spent my days in London and generally went to bed dog tired at about half-past nine o'clock. Multifarious engagements seemed to take my wife also to London three or four times a week. It was a good life. It was just the sort of life I had meant to live. I should have enjoyed great wealth or a great position if I had been born to the one or called to the other, but without these I yet felt that I had achieved a kind of equilibrium between the Foreign Office on the one hand and the land on the other. A just balance between the two sides of my life ought, it seemed to me, to make me at once a better clerk and a better workman.

This general account of life at Bridgend covers the whole eighteen years during which it was ours, and particularly the years 1919–1925 during which I was employed in the Northern Department of the Foreign Office.

CHAPTER 9

NORTHERN DEPARTMENT

THERE will be very little in this book about official and political personalities because most of those I worked with are still alive. However, during and after the war three eminent men had been Foreign Secretaries who are now dead, and to the record of these I will make my minute contribution. It is minute because my own position was too humble to bring me close to them. Such interest as it has, lies only in this : that in every case where I did come into direct touch with them, what they said or did seemed full of significance. Snapshots are often more revealing than studio portraits. It looks as if we were all of us being intensely typical of ourselves every moment of our lives and in everything we did and said. If that is so, all the trouble we take to appear more attractive or talented than we by nature are is trouble in vain.

One summer evening, about the year 1930, I was standing on the platform at Waterloo station waiting for a train to take me back to Ockham, when I noticed a big man, obviously a gentleman, in a deerstalker's hat, old grey flannel trousers and heavy black spectacles making his way through the crowd towards the platform entrance. He was carrying a rucksack and a fishing-rod, and what I—though not the ticket-collector —well knew to be defective eyesight caused him to blunder into the line of city clerks pressing through the barrier. In 1930 the lower orders had already learned to speak disrespectfully to their betters and the inspector on duty at the gate pushed him a little roughly aside with the words : " Now then, my man, stand back. Don't push, there's plenty of time." Sir Edward Grey, or Lord Grey as he then was, waited obediently till the whole crowd passed in onto the platform with a humility characteristic alike of the blind and

56

the great and doubly moving in one who was both. Both men would, I am sure, have been very much put out if I had told the inspector to whom he was speaking. The next time I saw Grey was when about a year before his death I found myself sitting next to him at a luncheon party. With diffidence I did my best to entertain him with information about the Office as it was at that time, and was touched to find that so small a thing, coming from anyone as unimportant as myself, could apparently give real pleasure to a man who had in his time commanded the attention of the whole world. He asked me to stop at Fallodon when next I should be driving up to Barmoor, and it is my great loss that he died before I could do so. Even if I could not have maintained his interest in my small talk about the Foreign Office, he would have felt that I shared the love of his birds and his Northumberland.

Grey was followed at the Foreign Office in the last days of 1916 by Mr. Balfour, and by this time I had reached a position where I was very occasionally summoned to the Secretary of State's room to explain some point arising out of our departmental papers. When this happened he seemed so little interested in what I had to say that I was covered with embarrassment. I was left in no doubt that he would —very reasonably—forget my name and face and everything about me as soon as I had left his room. Balfour took temporary charge of the Foreign Office again a few years later, and on one occasion I accompanied him to the House of Lords where he opened a debate on Russian affairs. Grey countered from the opposite side, and as we left the Chamber Balfour made a comment which threw a new light for me on the technique of parliamentary debate. " That was an excellent reply," he said, " of Edward Grey's ; an excellent reply. In my speech, you know, I made what I thought were six very strong points. He ignored them *all* without exception : ignored them *all*. It was an excellent reply."

In 1919 Lord Curzon succeeded Mr. Balfour. The first time I had anything to do with him was when Mr. Gregory, the head of the Northern Department, and I were summoned

to be present at the reception of Mr. Krassin, representing
the Soviet Union. Curzon posed us as if we had been on
the stage : " Mr. O'Malley, you come and stand here behind
my chair—so. Mr. Gregory, you will be standing over there
by the corner of my table, turned towards me—so. That is
right. Now then, when Mr. Krassin comes in we'll put him
in the chair there. No, push the chair a little further away
and turn it half towards the light. Mr. O'Malley, be good
enough to draw up the blind." This little scene—this insight
into Curzon's sense of dramatic form, enabled me to understand, when I later accompanied him to a debate in the House
of Lords, the secret of his virtuosity as an orator. This
depended in part on his noble appearance, beautifully modu-
lated voice, and staggering command of a complicated subject.
Speaking without looking at his notes he would say : " We
now come to the second subsection of clause (b) in Article XI.
With Your Lordships' permission I shall venture to compare
these words with the words employed in the second paragraph
of the Schedule attached to last year's Agreement with . . .
in reference to . . ." and so on and so on without, as I have
said, a glance at his brief. But what struck me most of all
was his exquisite consideration for the dignity of the Upper
House, and the judicious mixture of deference—or the appearance of deference—with authority. Here clearly was someone
who on a familiar stage could play his rôle to perfection.

Curzon was the only political head of the Office I have
known who used to ask for more papers and not less to be
sent to him. A document received in the Office is normally
enclosed in a folder on which everyone concerned writes his
opinion. This folder is sent up to the higher from the lower
authorities with numerous relevant papers put below it in
chronological order, the whole bundle being tied together with
red tape. Most Secretaries of State are content to read the
current paper on the top of the file, but not so Curzon. When
these files returned to the Department with his directions
endorsed upon them, it was evident that during the night
watches, sitting up in his harness with a severe backache, he
had read right through the whole file. If this had not satisfied

his curiosity, he would call the next morning for more and
more back papers. His own minutes written in pencil in a
flowing hand would infallibly draw not too kindly attention
to any weak point in a case presented to him, and if a department had offered him a really good piece of work, he would
but seldom express appreciation or thanks. In some ways,
then, he was a hard master, but I am glad to say that I personally did not have to suffer his reproaches. What I did most
strongly feel was that in any dealings with Curzon I had to
do with an outsize intelligence and character, and that if I
was going to differ from him I should need to have on my
side extremely strong arguments very clearly marshalled.

In contrast to what I have said of Balfour, I got the impression when speaking to Curzon that his restless and brilliant
eye had taken in every detail of my appearance and manner
and stored what he had observed of a very unimpressive
member of his staff in some pigeonhole of his memory.
Whether or not this was so, I recall with gratitude that on
the only occasion when I bothered him about a personal
matter he devoted to it a surprising degree of attention. In
1925 when, as I shall presently relate, I saw a prospect of
visiting Persia, I wanted to prepare my mind for the journey
as well as I could in the intervening days ; and, since Curzon
was the standard authority on the country, I ventured, greatly
daring, to ask him through his private secretary, Vansittart,
for advice on the bibliography of the subject. The next day
I received in reply several sheets of folio paper covered on both
sides with meticulous directions of how I might best employ
the short time at my disposal. Admittedly, an enquiry about
Persia was just the thing to touch off Curzon's enthusiasm, but
I never met anyone else who in comparable circumstances
would have done what he did. In the interests of truth I
must, I suppose, add that this extraordinary man not seldom
showed a strange callousness towards the feelings of other
people. He disliked Crowe, and used deliberately to ask for
the latter on the telephone at the Foreign Office from Carlton
House Terrace or Kedleston at times when Crowe could not
reasonably have been expected still to be there. The following

day he would be plaintive and peevish about it, and by persevering in such courses I really think he shortened Crowe's life. " Can't the man realize," Crowe used to say, " that long after he has gone home in his Rolls-Royce, I have to catch a No. 11 bus for Elm Park Road and sup off sardines or cold sausages before dealing with the evening's telegrams ? "

I passed five years very congenially in the Northern Department diversified by two interesting journeys. The first of these was to Copenhagen whither I accompanied a representative of the Supreme Economic Council, Mr. E. F. Wise, in order to see whether an agreement on economic questions could be made with the Government of the Russian Socialist Federation of Soviet Republics, as it was then named. This Government was represented by Messrs. Krassin and Litvinoff, and with these we carried on ineffectual negotiations for several days ; later proceeding from Denmark to San Remo in order to report the result of our conversations to the Supreme Council then in session there. At San Remo, the meetings of the Supreme Council were being held in the Villa Devachan, which was perched on the hillside overlooking the sea and embowered in April flowers ; and when we arrived, this body was considering what steps could be taken to induce a more compliant attitude in the German and Turkish Governments, the occupation of the Ruhr and of the territory surrounding the Sea of Marmora having been proposed as means to this end. As one day I was waiting in the *foyer* of the Council Chamber, Mr. Lloyd George and Signor Nitti came out together from a meeting at which the military subcommission had been expressing its views, and the latter pointed to a large group of donkeys, executed in Dresden china, which embellished the hall. " Tiens," said Signor Nitti, nudging the Prime Minister, " les experts militaires." Presently the military experts themselves issued onto the terrace where I had gone to watch the yellow-bellied Ligurian bees at work in the flowerbeds. I had seated myself by a small yellow tin table to which Foch, Beatty, Henry Wilson and Acton (the Italian naval Commander-in-Chief) proceeded to pull up their chairs. No one

paid any attention to me and I saw no reason to move away.
It was clear that Foch and Beatty were barely acquainted,
but though Foch spoke no English and Beatty no French,
they entered at once into conversation, Henry Wilson inter-
preting. Foch wanted to know what had happened at the
Battle of Jutland, and from his questions his ignorance of
everything connected with fighting at sea soon became obvious.
" Tell me," he said at one point, " how do ships at sea communicate with each other ? If an action takes place in thick
weather, how does the Commander give orders to the ships
under his command ? " Beatty gave the necessary explana-
tions, adding that in the last resort wireless telegraphy could
be used. " Ah," said Foch, " that is very interesting. So
you can use wireless telegraphy at sea, can you ? " Beatty
went on to explain by request with the aid of pencil and paper,
the tactics employed at Jutland, and the Marshal had no
difficulty in following his account of events down to the
position which had been reached by about half-past five
o'clock in the afternoon of May 31st, 1916. Although, of
course, Foch was poorly informed about the crisis of the engagement, everyone in British official circles was by this date
familiar with the controversy between Beatty's supporters and
Jellicoe's supporters as to whether Jellicoe was right in ordering
the deployment of the Grand Fleet to port or whether he
would have done better to deploy to starboard on his western
division. This conflict of view was very much in Beatty's
mind at the moment of which I write ; and consequently he
was embarrassed when Foch began to question him closely as
to exactly what had happened at 6.14 p.m. on that murky
afternoon when the main forces of the British and German
fleets at last made contact. " Oh, hell ! " whispered Beatty
to Wilson, " tell the old boy that there was lots of fog, and
that nobody quite knew what was happening " ; and turning
to Foch he said : " Bocoo de brewyard, bocoo de brewyard."
Wilson then said to Beatty : " Now you'll see the old chap
will make you sign those scrawls and he will put 'em with
his collection. He has drawers full of that sort of stuff."
Sure enough Beatty, Henry Wilson and Acton were asked to

put their signature to the diagrams which Beatty had drawn ; and when they had done so they all returned to the villa, leaving me seated alone with the Frenchman at our little tin table. I was quite burned up with desire to say to him : " Sir, I am sure you have many mementoes of this nature, but I have none. I beg you to add your own signature to the paper which will then become an heirloom of priceless value to my family " ; and I now bitterly regret that an exaggerated sense of propriety prevented me from doing so, reflecting how high a value I should have placed upon it, supposing Nelson had lived to draw a plan of the Battle of Trafalgar, get it autographed by Wellington, and give it to my great grand-father.

The second of the two journeys to which I have referred was undertaken in November 1922 when I went again to Constantinople as a King's Messenger, passing through Milan on the day when the Blackshirts set out for Rome. I anticipated that three clear days would be available to me in Turkey before having to start back to London ; and these I proposed to spend in visiting Gallipoli, if the letters which I had addressed to various friends in the Embassy—or High Commissioner's Office as it then was—should have borne fruit and have procured for me the necessary permits. Thanks to the kindness of one of the secretaries—Hal Mack [1]—I found on arrival that the way had been well prepared, and that we should be able to get a passage to Kelia on a military transport which was then on the point of departure.

The political situation was at this time very uncertain in spite of the Mudania Convention ; the Turks claimed that only the presence of British troops in Turkish soil and not the " occupation " by them of Turkish territory was per-missible ; and in order to lend force to their point of view Mustapha Kemal had despatched an emissary, accompanied by a considerable body of gendarmerie, to Constantinople. It seemed possible that we might have to defend our position at Chanak by force, and the transport on which Mack and I embarked in fact carried a number of British staff officers on

[1] Sir Henry Mack, K.C.M.G., H.M. Ambassador in Buenos Aires.

the way to investigate whether in such circumstances the
British Army could advantageously be based on Gallipoli
behind the protection of the Bulair lines.

We reached Kelia early in the morning and enquired for
means of transport to Anzac Cove and Suvla Bay.   Only one
horse was available, which Mack insisted I should have since
I had come two thousand miles to see these battlefields and
should certainly not have another chance of doing so.   My
feelings about horses have always oscillated violently between
admiration and affectionate disappointment.   I am moved—
who could not be ?—by their nobility and courage and by
the great shining pistonlike quarters that carry us so much
faster and farther than our own crawling feet : on the other
hand I know very well that the sensitive lips and eyes turning
this way and that, conceal an infantile mind and inhuman
obstinacy, which in a dog would be intolerable.   Nevertheless,
I was exceedingly grateful to the animal put at my disposal
by the War Graves' Commission, and together we spent a long
day of alternating sun and thunderstorms exploring the west
coast of the peninsula.   Anzac Cove, I found, was a small
shingly bay bare of all signs of war but a few wrecked barges ;
Shrapnel Gulley, a steep narrow sticky cleft in the hillside
shaded by arbutus and myrtle ; Sari Bair, a rounded hill
more suggestive of a Thracian goatherd and his pipes than of
a mighty feat of arms.   Seven years had caved in the trenches
and covered signs of battle with lavender, thyme and heath,
and partridges rose in front of me as I climbed the famous
ridge where shells from H.M.S. *Queen Elizabeth* had fallen
among the Gurkhas and men of the Warwickshire and South
Lancashire regiments on that glorious and disastrous ninth of
August 1915.   I carried John Masefield's *Gallipoli* in my hand
and read his words again :

" There was the storm, there was the crisis, the one picked
hour, to which this death and mangling and dying misery
and exultation had led.   Then was the hour for a casting off
of self, and a setting aside of every pain and longing and
sweet affection, a giving up of all that makes a man to the
something which makes a race, and a going forward to death

63

resolvedly to help out their brother high up above in the shellbursts and the blazing gorse."

From Sari Bair I turned downhill to visit the cemeteries. This township of the Glorious Dead lies between the shore where they prepared their adventure and the hill where they died. Women now well on in years whose treasure was buried here during those burning August days may be well content with the peace and dignity of this place where they lie who were their sons or husbands or lovers.

Satisfied with having accomplished this pilgrimage, I returned to Kelia and asked the L.C.O. where and when I could make contact with the destroyer which the Navy had promised should convey me back to Pera. He had no orders and advised me to get across to Chanak. At Chanak the R.T.O. said " There is great excitement in Constantinople. The Sultan is in flight, and leaving Turkey tonight in a British cruiser. All fleet orders are cancelled. The fleet is moving to its bombarding stations. You should report to O.C. 5th Hussars." Here was a pretty kettle of fish ! These inconsiderate monarchs and generals were going to make my immediate return to Constantinople impossible ; and if I missed the London train, I should get into trouble for delaying the arrival in London of a bag which no doubt contained despatches describing the dramatic turn which local events had taken. The 5th Hussars were established in a little tumbledown timber house in Chanak and received me with the greatest hospitality, saying that dinner was at eight o'clock and that I could sleep in Naylor Leyland's bed if I didn't mind his retriever sleeping with me. On explaining the imperative necessity of getting back to the Embassy without delay, it was suggested that I should get into touch with H.M.S. *Benbow*, then lying in the narrows ; and accordingly I went down to the shore and explained by signs to three old Turks that I wished them to take me across in their petrol-driven caique to the flagship lying a mile or so away in total darkness blinking with her Aldis lamp. I was unused to the ways of the Royal Navy, and in some doubt as to the correct procedure for approaching in semi-hostile waters so formidable an object. However, when we came within hailing distance I summoned up my courage and bellowed " Benbow ahoy ! I want to come aboard and see the Flag Captain ! " Instantly a most sympathetic voice answered through a megaphone " All right ; come alongside the after ladder and don't scratch the paint." The Officer of the Watch was not at all put about to see a muddy and bedraggled civilian with a suitcase stumble onto the quarter-deck, and the Flag Captain—Phillimore, I think it was—having given me sherry and biscuits, explained as if it was the most natural thing in the world that he would stop an Italian liner, the *Adria*, due next morning, and see that I got passage on her. These arrangements were later duly carried out, but in the meantime I returned to spend the night with my hosts at Chanak, who related to me the following incident :

A few days previously a Turkish officer bearing a white flag had come across to the British from the Turkish lines to seek an interview with the Officer Commanding this sector of our Front. The Turkish officer said that he was expecting shortly to receive a visit of inspection from his General and was anxious, in order to make a good impression, to show that his trenches had been well protected with barbed wire. While his own authorities had been very niggardly with this, he was impressed with the profusion of wire employed by the British, and wondered whether he might without impropriety suggest the loan to himself of a few rolls, which he promised faithfully to return as soon as the General had completed his inspection. Both sides knew, of course, that they might at any moment get orders to begin hostilities, but the British O.C. was anxious to maintain friendly relations with his Turkish opposite number up to the last possible moment in order by mutual goodwill and forbearance to prevent the occurrence of some minor incident which might have had very grave results. Accordingly he loaned to the Turks some of his barbed wire, and it was this very day that the wire, neatly rolled up again, had been brought back by a Turkish fatigue party. The Turkish officer said that his dispositions had obviously made a most favourable impression on the inspecting

65

General for which his warmest thanks were due to the British military authorities.

At the end of my fifth year in the Northern Department I went for a much longer and more exciting voyage of discovery all through Russia in Europe, but in order to make it clear why I should have sought and received permission to undertake this journey I must refer to relations between the United Kingdom Government and the Soviet Government during the years which followed the conclusion of the war.

These were hopelessly obscure and confused. We were not at war with Soviet Russia but our fleet in the Black Sea had orders to attack the Bolshevik Forces. We were not at peace with Russia but it was our declared policy actively to promote trade with her. Nevertheless British subjects were not allowed to go to Soviet Russia nor Russians admitted to the United Kingdom. Goods were not allowed to be exported directly to Soviet Russia from the United Kingdom but there was no obstacle to indirect trade through European countries. There was no postal communication between the two countries but no prohibition or censorship on indirect correspondence. The blockade of Soviet Russia had been publicly declared at an end but the Customs were giving no clearances to Soviet ports. All these anomalies arose from the divergence of view in England as to how Russian Communists should be treated which persisted from 1917 till 1947. I wrote a memorandum about this in 1920 which was printed and circulated in the Foreign Office, suggesting that we should stop trying to upset the Soviet Government and do everything reasonably possible to get into normal relations with them. Crowe said he did not think such efforts would succeed but that he agreed with the course suggested. Maybe that was why I was made a member of the British Delegation, led by Mr. Arthur Ponsonby —which was instructed to try and make a comprehensive treaty with the Russians in 1924.

These negotiations took place in the Foreign Office and were remarkable both for other things and for having included what I suppose to have been one of the longest single sittings of a conference which ever took place in comparable circumstances, namely, the crucial debate of August 4th, 1924. This was preceded by a meeting of the British Delegation at 9 a.m. ; the plenary session began at 10 a.m. and we sat continuously until 7.30 a.m. on the following morning. During negotiations at the Peace Conference in Paris we had sometimes found it possible to get a tactical ascendancy over the French by ourselves first taking a heavy breakfast and then dragging out a meeting till half-past two or three o'clock in the afternoon— till well past the hour, that is to say, at which the Frenchmen are accustomed to take their midday meal. But let no one think Russians can be made to yield a point by hunger and exhaustion. They are of sterner stuff than this ; indeed, they are the sternest stuff I have ever met when it comes to long-drawn-out discussions. Mr. Gregory was also a member of the British Delegation. He and I did our best. We had sandwiches and coffee made ready in a neighbouring room, to which Ponsonby and he and I but not the Russians had access ; and we took it in turns to go out of the conference room and lie down for half an hour on one of the red leather sofas. But it was all in vain. Neither Joffe, the Chief Soviet Delegate, Rakovsky, Scheinman nor Tomsky batted an eyelid, and they looked perfectly fresh when the conference broke up without result in the morning of August 5th. However, Joffe subsequently committed suicide so perhaps our efforts to wear him down were not altogether wasted.

After the conference I wrote an immense memorandum about it all for Mr. Ramsay MacDonald, but while it was with the printer the Labour Government went out of office. Mr. Austen Chamberlain, who then took over the Foreign Office, circulated it to his Cabinet colleagues with a very flattering minute attached to it. " This remarkable memorandum," he said (to the best of my recollection), " had given him many new ideas." I was excited and pleased, and thought to myself that I was now getting on in the world. So I was, for the Secretary of State's commendation was no doubt one reason why I easily got permission early in 1925 to see this terrible place, Russia, for myself. One February morning I went into Crowe's room and suggested that it was high time that some member of the Foreign Office itself should explore what was to us *terra incognita* and that I hoped he would think I was the person to do the exploring. Crowe wasted no time.

" How long do you want to be away ? " he asked.

" About three months."

" How much do you want to spend ? "

" About £150."

" All right. Write a letter to the Treasury saying you have been sent and why."

As I was leaving the room, I added : " Oh, and by the way, there has been some sort of hostilities between the Russians and Persians down Bujnird way. Do you mind my going into Persia if I don't tread on Percy Loraine's toes ? "

" No," he said, " that will be all right. Goodbye and good luck."

And so I set out on a most memorable journey, little thinking that I should learn on the front-door steps of the Legation in Tehran that Crowe was dead.

I was not to see his like again.

CHAPTER 10

RUSSIAN JOURNEY

THE most convenient way to Leningrad from London was through Warsaw where I spent three or four days. One of the Legation chauffeurs drove me round to see the sights, among which was the battlefield where the Bolsheviks had been turned back from the gates of the city in 1921. It seemed to have been a protracted engagement. " About ten days, sir, it lasted," said the chauffeur. " I generally used to bring the General (i.e. the military attaché) out in the morning, and then we'd go back and have a bit of lunch, and the Naval Attaché used to watch it afternoons." But there were no signs of belligerancy to be seen in 1925. Only scrub pines, the long sandy curves of the Vistula and the storks circling wide and high. I went on to Kovno, where I was entertained by the Lithuanian Government whose respect for their vanished greatness I sympathized with. The amenities of Kovno were exceedingly limited, but in the President's modest dwelling a couple of dozen very modern and wholly imaginary portraits by peasant hands of bygone Lithuanian princes had been affixed to all the walls with touching artlessness. It was difficult to remember that in the fourteenth century the biggest state in Europe was Lithuania.

From Kovno I went on to stay with the British Minister in Riga and with the Consul-General in the delightful town of Reval, and on Friday, April 10th, I left this place in a Russian train drawn by an Esthonian locomotive, in charge of Esthonian personnel and filled for the most part with Esthonian peasants and shopkeepers who got out at the stations between the capital and the frontier. By eleven o'clock at night we had reached the bridge which carried a single track across the Narva and here the last traveller but myself alighted. Some ten miles further on, it being now about midnight, the train pulled up in the open country and starlight showed me a sentry-box, some striped poles, barbed wire and five Russian militiamen standing with piled arms in the snow. A Russian crew and guard, with whom I could not communicate except by signs, boarded the train and took me in charge. Being by nature timid, and Russia being to Western eyes at this time still half-obscured by the fume of revolution, I had the impression, so agreeable in retrospect, that I was entering upon an adventure. Having shared my supper of cold chicken with the agents of the Cheka [1] and set up on the little table provided in these old Belgian-built *wagon-lits* the photographs of my nearest and dearest, I composed myself to sleep in a huge sheepskin coat I had drawn from War Office stores catalogued as " Goat, furlined, M.T. Driver's, North China, one ".

The Consul, Mr. Preston, looked after me in Leningrad and showed me the sights of the town which exhibited much dilapidation in all directions. This was depressing, but what was much worse was the general appearance of the inhabitants who from four o'clock onwards seemed to have no relaxation but to slouch up and down the main streets. Ten and twenty deep on each side they slouched, badly dressed, sullen-looking, with averted eyes. These inward-looking eyes seemed to be the clue to the situation of the populace and confirmed the overwhelming impression which never left me till I left Russia, that I had entered what in the language of today might be described as a spiritual gas-chamber, a sinister, unnatural and unholy place. Mr. Preston said that most of the walkers in the streets were preoccupied with the question of where tomorrow's breakfast or next week's rent or next winter's boots were to come from ; that in a country where the very children were employed to spy on their parents, safety lay in obscurity and that all contacts with neighbours, even a greeting in the street, might be involved with some unrecognized danger. The head Bolshevik in the town was a little Jew called Weissman or some such name, and I tried to liven things up by teaching him to play ping-pong. But it was not much of a success and I was not sorry to leave for Moscow where I was

[1] The political police were so called in 1925.

received with the greatest hospitality by Mr. Hodgson, our Chargé d'Affaires.

In 1925 Lenin was, of course, dead—pickled in glycerine in a glass case in the Red Square. I was, however, taken into the Kremlin to see Monsieur Chicherin who was in charge of foreign relations. It was not an impressive interview. Mr. Chicherin had tooth-ache and his face was tied up in a coloured handkerchief with the knots on the top of his head. He made some agreeable remarks in his usual grating voice, but it was never the intention that we should talk politics. That was Hodgson's business, not mine.

As soon as possible Hodgson and I started on a peregrination of southern Russia. We left by train on April 24th for Nijni Novgorod and there boarded a steamer for Tzaritzin, or Stalingrad as it is now called, a town at the head of the Volga delta. Our steamer trip was very agreeable ; at every meal we ate the really fresh caviare so seldom met with outside Russia, with hard white butter and finely chopped onions. One of our fellow passengers used to play on the piano tunes distinguished by a haunting sadness. " These," he said in answer to our enquiries, " are the songs we used to sing when we were being marched across Siberia to the quarries as convicts." Many peasants seemed to be migrating from one province to another, for at every little pier whole families crowded onto the boat and settled themselves down between decks on their bundles and bedding to sleep, play the guitar and catch lice. The smell of Russians is much less offensive than that of English people. Instead of our own sweaty badger smell, Russian peasants have the same dry sweet-sour smell as the Chinese, though the Chinese when one gets them away from their garlic are so much given to hot baths that they hardly smell at all. We passed barges being hauled upstream by the famous Volga boatmen and our musical friend assured us that the song we are all familiar with is really and truly the song of the hauliers. It should, however, be sung as men sing when each note corresponds with the measured tread of a team of men bowed under the strain of a heavy towrope. Besides the musician there were only two other first-class passengers—

a Trade Unions Inspector and a Railway Inspector, both members of the Communist Party. They were always ready to talk and their conversation was fresh, sincere, intelligent and extremely ill-informed. Additionally, there was the Cheka agent who had been sent to keep an eye on us and eavesdrop ; a clean well-dressed man in an engine-driver's peaked cap, red beard, black drill blouse and blue serge riding-breeches. He did not seem at ease in his profession and refused to be drawn into conversation. Poor fellow, we gave him the slip at the end of the steamer journey and the punishment for his carelessness must surely have been death. The steamer in each case stopped long enough to give us a sight of such famous towns as Kazan, Simbirsk, Samara and Saratoff. They must have been untidy, graceless, dirty places at any date. In 1925, grass was growing in the streets, roofs were falling in and long-nosed pigs were wandering through the principal boulevards.

At the end of the third day and eighthundredth mile we approached our destination—Stalingrad. Here the prairie grass was interspersed as far as the eye could see with red and yellow tulips. At this point also, I saw for the first and only time in my life a camel and a donkey in double-harness. There was no train with first- or second-class carriages in Stalingrad station when we arrived, which no doubt was why our sleuth thought it safe to let us out of his sight for a short time. That was when he made his mistake. Hodgson and I bundled ourselves into a peasants' train and were shortly on the way to Tichoretzkaya, some three hundred miles to the south-west. Strange to relate, we were never afterwards followed by the Secret Police.

It was a very crowded peasants' train which we had boarded, with wooden seats, a few small windows and, for illumination at night, one or two candles ; and in this for some thirty hours we crossed the edge of the Kalmuick Steppe. A high wind obliged us to keep all windows shut, entailing a certain degree of discomfort, for lavatory accommodation was very limited and the peasant children had not been taught not to piss in a railway carriage. At night I rolled myself up in my sheepskin

coat with a view of testing the theory that bugs cannot walk
across fur, and found that it would not hold water.   I was kept
busy all night with a flash-lamp and a tin of Keatings.   My
bag was twenty-seven.   No food was available, not a blood
sausage nor a slice of sucking pig.   I made tea and boiled eggs
on a little Primus stove which I always carry with me everywhere.   Such trifling hardships could not detract from the
interest of the landscape which is flat with an uncompromising
and geometrical flatness such as I was not to see again till I
got to the Hortobagy in Hungary in 1939.   The plain is unbroken by hedges, trees or scrub, irrigated only by infrequent
and shallow streams, uncrossed except by rare and faintly
marked paths.   There are flattish districts in East Anglia,
Holland and Germany, but until this day I had formed no
conception of what an ocean of earth would be, or known that
the beauty of an unrippled sea could be manifested in dry land.
Kites, kestrels and white-headed eagles rose now and then from
the telegraph poles, and countless hamsters whistled and
plunged into their holes at the train's approach.   The tiny
stations and villages, boldly marked upon the maps, are lost
in this vast plain where once Tamberlaine had ranged and
ruled ; and the only beings who appeared at home in it were
a few families of nomads, sheltered at night by felt tents from
the intolerable wind, and moving by day to greener land
behind their grazing herds.

We arrived at Tichoretzkaya at one o'clock in the morning
of May 1st and settled down to wait for the seven-o'clock train
to Bezlan and Vladikavkaz.   The station, like all Russian
stations, was in a state of the utmost degradation.   During the
night beggars and diseased people crowded into it for shelter,
lay in rows on the floor, snoring and scratching, and when the
buildings were full, joined forces with the pigs rooting on the
platforms.   Nothing ever made Hodgson tired, but as I got
very tired sitting at a tin table with my head on my arms and
my back aching we decided we must get soft instead of hard
seats on the train for Bezlan.   All these being already engaged,
we applied for help to the station commander of the Cheka.
This magnificent individual in a full-length beige military coat

heard us with polite contempt and promised to turn out two of his fellow countrymen to make room for us. He was as good as his word and the incident passed without notice by fellow travellers accustomed to seven years of capricious tyranny at the hands of the political police.

We reached Vladikavkaz at 2 a.m. on May 2nd and put up at the only place resembling an inn. It was a half-ruined mansion with wrecks of old iron beds to lie down on. The custodian brought me tea the following morning on what appeared to be a silver salver with I.H.S. in Roman characters engraved upon it. To be served with early morning tea on a paten was interesting and I was tempted to carry the thing off in my luggage, but decided this was too dangerous. On May 2nd we rose early in hopes of engaging a motor-car to carry us over the Georgian Road to Tiflis, but the preceding winter had been exceptionally severe in the Caucasus and we learned with more disappointment than surprise that recent avalanches had rendered the road impassable. Availing myself therefore of Crowe's permission to enter Persia we decided to travel to Baku and thence to Tehran, intending to return from Tehran via Tabriz and re-enter the Soviet Union at the southernmost point of Armenia. On the afternoon, then, of the same day we retraced our steps to Bezlan and took the Baku train which carried us during the remaining hours of daylight through Cossack country alongside the river Terek ; through country more sweet and green than any we had yet traversed. To the south of the railway and about fifty miles away there appeared to us mile upon mile of white peaks and ridges pencilled faintly on the skyline. This was indeed one of those occasions memorable to every traveller when his eyes at last rest upon some desired mountain or river or shore, for who could look at last unmoved upon the frosty Caucasus ? The next morning found us between Petrovsk and Derbent exposed now to a strong wind blowing from the Kara Kum, and to a sun reflected from the pink ridges of Daghestan. The inhabitants of this area very closely resembled Japanese. At Derbent the remains of an enormous wall run down from the mountains towards the shore of the Caspian Sea. It was built by the Crusaders, and the only comparable thing I know is the end of the Great Wall of China where it runs into the sea at Shanhaikwan. After being entertained by the local Soviet we left Baku as soon as the necessary formalities had been completed, and on my birthday, May 4th, boarded the S.S. *Polwya* for Enzeli ; a clean and seaworthy vessel, built in Dunbarton in 1895.

When I went on deck early next morning the mountains of Daghestan were patterned like mother-of-pearl against the western sky, and presently the Persian coast appeared as a line of emeraldine green just above the southern horizon with poplars standing like ninepins on the swampy foreshore. The Caspian Sea interposes a very marked division between the natural features of the Persian province of Gilan and those of the Baku promontory which is covered not with poplars but with the thickly-grouped derricks of the oilfields ; but it was also the disparity between two forms of social life which made our landfall notable. When I left Russia and entered Persia I felt as I used to do at the end of a school term when the mental tension and physical discomfort of a lower classroom at Hillbrow or Radley could be exchanged for the freedom and comparative luxury of life at home at Denton. Consequently, as we drew into Enzeli over the pale silky waters of the Caspian the depression was lifted which had weighed upon me ever since I crossed the Narva bridge and I could wholeheartedly enjoy the prospect, so long looked forward to, of mounting onto the inner uplands of Asia. My spirits continued to rise as we later entered the environs of Resht and met a shepherd boy in tall black taboosh piping and singing to his sheep. He wore a wild rose threaded behind one ear, and as we passed him in our decrepit Ford car, I felt as I was to feel long afterwards in Indo-China between Tsang Bang and Soai Reang that I was again in a sense among my own people. This seems a whimsical and far-fetched idea, and so in a way it is, because, of course, this shepherd lad was not at all like old Hicks whom we used to see setting up hurdles for his folded sheep on the cold sticky fields of rape above Denton. Old Hicks never put a dog-rose behind his ear. Nevertheless, Hicks and this

Persian herd had this in common, that they were—unlike the
unfortunate Russians—free to be themselves within the narrow
circumstances of their lives ; and it was this which made me
feel that Persia was more like South Oxfordshire than was any
place I had seen in the R.S.F.S.R.

Leaving Enzeli for Resht we passed through sub-tropical
jungle, sweet even at midday with the voices of innumerable
nightingales. From Resht next morning, at 4.30 a.m., in
another old Ford car we drove up through plantations of acacia
and box and entered a stony defile bare of timber and nourish-
ing herbs, but clothed in May with alpine and desert flowers :
vetch, thyme, poppy, thrift, rockrose, stonecrop, lupin and
borage in many varieties. A great distance below and to the
east the Safid Rud flowed in spate towards the Caspian in its
rocky bed and on the other side of it the lower slopes of the
Elburz range were extended. Beyond Mangil the road
climbed to the plateau of central Persia, and in the afternoon
in great heat we reached Kazvin and continued our journey
after only a short rest in the hope of reaching Tehran before
dark. It was clear that this was still an important highway,
for we were never out of sight of a caravan and as evening drew
in we observed every caravanserai to be filled with travellers,
merchants and muleteers whose cattle grazed or chewed the
cud in scores about its walls. So we retraced the steps of the
innumerable men and beasts who had marched from the
uplands of Asia to the Euxine and Aegaean coasts ; and camels
passed us in the dusk, tied nose to tail, carrying in their contemptuous eyes and lips the secrets of a thousand tribes and
miles and years. I had been quite right in what I thought
when Harold Nicolson and I found ourselves in 1912 on the
road from Scutari to Bagdad. These experiences on the road
from Resht to Tehran were indeed a fulfilment rather than a
mere projection into the unknown. This indeed was Asia, and
this was one of the oldest greatest roads in the world. Just so,
I thought, looking at the passing traffic, did Abraham journey
from Ur of the Chaldees ; thus came Melchior, Balthazar and
Caspar to Bethlehem ; this is just what life should be like ;
this is the fruit of all those expeditions from Denton, and of

my endurance at Radley and of the unutterable boredom and exertions of preparation for the Foreign Office examination ; this, at last, is what I have really wanted to see and to do.

At eleven o'clock in the evening we reached the Legation in Tehran where we were to spend a week as Sir Percy Loraine's guests.   He had motored out for twenty or thirty miles to meet us, and I thought this very civil of him.   All Legations and Embassies have something in common.   Outside, they may well differ ; in one case the building may conform to local architecture ; in another His Majesty's Government may have constructed a residence more appropriate to St. John's Wood or Woking.   Inside, though imitation Hepplewhite furniture from the Tottenham Court Road will certainly have been provided by the Office of Works for every room, the decoration will vary with the taste and income of the head of the Mission. But in all Missions the offices resemble each other closely ; here are the same stationery, the same filing cabinets, the same pencils and punches and calendars and the same Foreign Office List and " Who's Who " on the same tables and desks. In the residential part of the house too, though the servants may be white or black or yellow, there will be the same order and kindly discipline, the same Lux, Ronuk, chintz, potplants, water-colours, large bath towels and Bromo, which the Englishman carries round the world like a snail its shell : which form indeed the temple and fortress of his soul.   In nearly but not quite all Missions, too, there will be the same welcome from the host for the visiting colleague, the same preliminary exchange of service news and scandal and, for the guest, the delightful relaxation from the fatigues of his journey.   All these pleasures were mine on the evening of our arrival, hot, tired, dirty, but well pleased with ourselves, in Tehran.

The week passed all too quickly and on May 13th we prepared to continue our journey.   After a dinner-party at which Reza Khan was present we said goodbye to our kind hosts at one o'clock in the morning, breakfasted at three, and at half-past four o'clock set off for Tabriz in a Buick car from the Haifa-Bagdad service which had been fitted to carry ninety gallons of petrol. The distance from Tehran to Tabriz is rather less than four hundred miles of which only the first hundred and ten and the last thirty-five could, in 1925, be traversed by road. The two hundred and fifty intervening miles were described on the map as " main road unmetalled ", but this description conveys no idea of the difficulties which many sections of it presented to wheeled transport. These difficulties varied with the nature of the soil, the configuration of the country and the weather, and they were greatly enhanced by the Persian custom of leading water across all obstacles in trenches fifteen to eighteen inches deep and two to three feet wide. I have already referred to the character of the Tehran–Kazvin road which we now traversed for the second time. From Kazvin we followed the Hamadan road for some thirty miles, and, as we then turned towards Urmia and Ararat, I thought with regret of the famous cities of the south, Shiraz and Isphahan and Yezd which must be visited some other day. Leaving the Hamadan road we mounted towards the north-west the gradual slope of a fertile strath some twenty miles wide, bounded on either side by rocky ridges 8,000 or 9,000 feet high and rendered lovely during these May weeks by innumerable short-lived flowers. Time was too short to stop for most of these, but at least once I made a determined effort to dig up with this knife which now lies on my table what must, I thought, surely be the mandrake. The ground was like concrete and the wretched plant would neither groan nor bleed nor yield its roots to me ; so I decided that it must be an Eremurus, and to push on towards Zinjan which we hoped to reach before dusk. By six o'clock in the evening we were making our way through the tangled streets of this town towards the house of an Armenian employee of the Indo-European Telegraph Company where we spent a night disturbed only by many Persian fleas. At three o'clock the next morning, to the sound of camels' feet padding through the dust, we got up and took the road again for Mianeh, down the valley of the Zinjan Chai. The ground on both sides of this valley, composed of the detritus of rapidly disintegrating rock, is bounded by the serrated crests of more enduring and many-coloured hills, and for half a day we lived in a world of vermilion glens and cliffs diversified by streaks of white, slate green and blue. Very little traffic was met with on the road ; indeed, I can recall but two parties of travellers threading their way like us over the rosy spurs and through the verdant water-courses. The first consisted of a number of Persian ladies, veiled in black *chuddas* and shod in foolish high-heeled slippers. They were crowded into two decrepit broughams, from which their heads and hands projected like feathers from a worn-out cushion ; the second was composed of a Persian family travel-ling to Kum upon donkeys. The first animal carried the leader of the expedition, armed with scimitar and lance ; the second bore his veiled wife, the third his servant. Our curiosity and pity were alike aroused by the sight of the fourth donkey, which bore in panniers two small coffins or boxes of bones destined for burial in the Holy City. Were the thoughts of this couple, we wondered, occupied during their long pil-grimage with the timely death of parents, or had sickness robbed them of both children at a blow ?

About midday we reached the foot of the pass over the Kaflan Khu and at two o'clock slid down its northern face to Mianeh. I can hardly expect to be believed when I assert that short stretches of the track over this famous hill are at an angle of one in two, but a British Vice-Consul had surveyed it with a plane-table and assured me that it is so. We did not carry sufficient spare tyres to risk putting the engine into reverse during the descent, so the wheels were locked and the car allowed to slide. By keeping its head straight and heaping stones under the wheels to form a kind of shoe, we got it safely to the bottom. The day was exceedingly hot and we were glad to rest for an hour in Mianeh, a village noted not only for its heresy but as the headquarters of a celebrated bug with blue spots—*Argas persicus*—whose bite is sometimes fatal and always the cause of protracted and enervating fever. Although, therefore, there was little prospect of reaching Tabriz that day, we preferred the certainty of a night in the open to the risk of illness and pushed on along a track which, after wandering irresolutely between tortuous walls and through irrigated fields, climbed onto rocky ground where darkness overtook and obliged us to bivouac.

The night was very cold ; rain fell in torrents and it blew half a gale. Mr. Hodgson slept peacefully in the *tonneau* and I crouched sleepless beside the driver. Though we did not know it we had bivouacked in the country of a rather lawless tribe famed for their horses, called the Sachshevan. Some years afterwards Hodgson heard from Mikoyan—one of the bosses of the Azerbaijani Soviet in 1925—that this Soviet after having entertained us in Baku, had decided that it would be a sound political move to get Hodgson and myself murdered by bandits. Later they got cold feet and called the plan off, but if they had not done so it was probably in the Sachshevan country that we should have been attacked. I am easily alarmed by physical danger of any kind and, even if there is none, often imagine that there is. Perhaps it was because, all unknown to us, such sinister designs had been under discussion in Baku, that it was apprehension of danger as well as cold which made me shiver during that uncomfortable night, lost in the Persian uplands.

At three o'clock in the morning, to restore the morale of myself and our servants, I made tea on my little Primus stove. From four to six we worked at the engine which would not start, and from six o'clock, when it did start, till noon we drove and pushed and pulled the car over a succession of downs turned by rain into deep and sticky mud. In this heart-breaking task we received much assistance from a roadguard who accepted a passage on the running-board, and com-mandeered the services of peasants, obliging them to heave and haul with shouts of " Allah help ! " and " Call upon the name of Allah ! " In the course of the morning we came within a very few inches of losing the car over the side of a gulley together with the lives of the less cautious members of the party who had remained seated in it ; but the afternoon brought sunshine, drier ground and at last a metalled road by which we reached Tabriz in time for dinner. We had been on this arduous road for forty-seven out of the preceding sixty-four hours, and food and rest at the Vice-Consulate were exceedingly welcome. This was the only day in my life on which I have been so tired as to be barely able to speak or walk. Mr. Hodgson was as fresh as a daisy.

After resting for a day, our journey was resumed in more comfortable circumstances, and on the afternoon of May 18th we reached the banks of the Araxes in a hired car, and crossing the International Bridge to a village called Russian Julfa, sought a house where the night could be spent. It was the tragedy of this unfortunate place to have been a battleground in the secular struggle between Armenians and Tartars, and no single house had escaped partial destruction. Formerly it had held a mixed population, but when the strong hand of the Imperial Government was removed and before the Soviet authorities had undertaken the work of pacification, the two sections of the population had fallen to fighting, and here in this forgotten corner of the world they had struggled continuously by night and by day from house to house with explosives and knives and sticks and stones until the last Tartar had been destroyed and his body cast into the river. Here the survivors, without industries or amusements, still lingered like bees round an overturned hive, clinging to the now purposeless life for which they had fought so hard. That night we secured for ourselves a kind of cubicle or loose box in a ruined inn and with a lamp to keep the bugs at bay slept for some hours on bare planks. At half-past five in the morning we got up and breakfasted, but before breakfast we had climbed to the top of a small hill overlooking the village, and from this point had seen the sun rise over the snowy mountains of Armenia and the yellow waves of the Araxes. No contrast more sharp can be imagined than that between the miserable condition of the inhabitants on the one hand, and on the other, the rich history of the Pass in which we stood, the imposing character of the scene and the flashing beauty of innumerable swifts wheeling and screaming above the village street.

The train from Julfa to Erivan, the capital of Armenia, emerged suddenly from the umber rocks of a gorge through which the Arazes here flows, and stopped long enough for me to pick passion-flowers from between the sleepers and take a good look at Ararat. It is at once obvious why Noah is said to have landed upon Ararat, for the mountain rises solitary to a height of nearly 18,000 feet from the flat Armenian uplands, and must therefore, more than Kazbek or Elburz or Demavend, always have embodied for Eastern people the very idea of mountain. The railway line described an arc round its base through rice fields where storks, egrets and glossy ibis were busy, and brought us that evening to the capital of the Republic. My diary records that during this part of the journey I speculated upon the possibility that " things might some day require us to protect a chain of British interests extending from Duzdab and Meshed, through Tehran, Khanikin, Bagdad, and Palestine to the Suez Canal " ; but little did I foresee in 1925 the circumstances which later were to lay that heavy task upon us.

From Erivan we proceeded to Tiflis, delightful capital of Georgia, whence we made an expedition up the Georgian road which joins Tiflis to Vladikavkaz in company with the President of the Republic, the Commander-in-Chief and many other notabilities all armed to the teeth, all steeped in the blood of their compatriots. We lunched on the summit and enjoyed target practice with our revolvers at the milestones. I had a revolver concealed on my person but thought it well not to disclose this. I borrowed the President's revolver but did not shoot as well as he did. We were entertained in the afternoon to a gargantuan meal at Passnour. It is a Georgian custom to circulate a drinking horn containing a whole bottle of wine in turn to each person, who is expected to empty it and make a speech. In our case the horn went three times round the table before we reached the moment for brandy and songs. Mr. Hodgson got through this test with credit, but in this as in other great crises of my life I cut a poor figure, for I have a very indifferent stomach. We rose unsteadily from the table at half-past four and went on to Mshket where a halt was made for vodka, red and white wine and brandy. The President and the Commander-in-Chief had now reached a stage at which they ate with their fingers, but it was not till nearly seven o'clock that the innkeeper, a noted entertainer, gave his celebrated imitation of a nursing mother, kissed us on both cheeks and allowed us to get back to Tiflis. All the local characters in this story have long since passed out of the political scene—indeed have passed very violently and quickly out of the world altogether—but in case the present inhabitants of the country should consider my allusions to their former governors disrespectful, I must say that I liked Georgia and the Georgians as well as any place or people in the world I have ever visited. It and they are all too little known in England. Their country is lovely beyond compare ; the women are justly famed for beauty and the men for spirit. Always shall I remember the arcadian sweetness of the hill villages through which I rode during my brief visit : hardwood forests and forest paths horse-high in azaleas and rhododendrons ; a melodious company gathered in the evening under the village walnut trees ; high alps, leading up to glaciers and precipices, where armed shepherds guard their long-eared sheep ; and flowers all the way.

I never was in any country which I wished so strongly to explore as the Caucasus, for this district is remarkable for a combination of things to be found nowhere else in the world. Immense mountains, luxuriant vegetation, picturesque villagers, and game of many descriptions can all be found elsewhere ; but only in the Caucasus can they be found in conjunction with a white population whose manner of life and customs are as strange to English people as the manners and customs of England before the Norman Conquest would be to the present generation. Something like this might have been found in High Tartary a century ago, but the Tatra only runs up to about 9,000 feet above sea level and has lately become a holiday resort for neighbouring town-dwellers. Something like it exists in Bosnia and Albania today, but here also the mountains are on a smaller scale and the railways and telephones are easier to reach. In Europe, only the recesses of the Caucasus range provide the perfect setting for the highest excitements and adventures of exploration among people of our own race.

It is certain that the Caucasus shelter the descendants of a great variety of migrants and " broken clans " who, on passage between Europe and Asia or in flight from their enemies had sought there a refuge which later became their permanent habitation ; but I do not know if it be true, as I was told, that at least seventy distinct languages and scripts are here in use. Offspring of the Crusaders are alleged to be among these lost tribes, and a friend of mine told me that he had got proof that this was indeed the case. The possible survival of such people had been mentioned to him before he set out on his journey, and on asking how to recognize a descendant of a Crusader he had been advised to look out for big men with curly hair and deep voices. Having diverged with his interpreter for some distance from the road over the Mameson Pass, he observed one evening working in his fields a man of unusual stature who on closer inspection turned out to have a mass of curly hair. When addressed by the interpreter he gave back a greeting in an uncommonly rich deep voice. Not yet satisfied that he had found what he sought, my acquaintance, when friendly contact had been established, bethought himself of a further indication which, however little he expected to find it present, would be conclusive proof of the peasant's origin ; and begged through the interpreter to be allowed to take off the rough jacket or zouave which the man wore. The pleasure can easily be imagined with which he saw that the white shirt under the jacket was emblazoned in front with a broad red cross extending across the whole width and height of the body. Asked why he wore a shirt of this description, the man replied that it was a custom in his family and had always been so.

Hodgson and I stayed in Tiflis from May 21st to May 28th. The cheerful account I have given of this town and its environs is warranted by the bright gay busy life which surrounded us and contrasted sharply with the macabre and gloomy cities of Russia proper. But there was another side of the picture described to us by reliable local residents. In August of the preceding year a sort of counter-revolution had been planned and discovered and suppressed. Our informant described how from the very window where we sat he had watched for five nights in succession the lorries of the Cheka summoning suspected persons—which meant all persons of superior education or upbringing—from their beds. These were stunned, tied head to foot and piled into the lorries. When a lorry was full, planks were laid cross-wise on the bodies, the firing party mounted and all drove off to the grounds of the Agricultural College at Mshket where trenches had been prepared into which the bodies, conscious or unconscious, were thrown. Each victim was shot through the cervical vertebrae, the trenches were filled in, and the lorry ran back to Tiflis for the next load. Since those days we have all got so used to photographs and first-hand descriptions of man's brutality to man, that events of this kind and accounts of them hardly stimulate a flicker of interest anywhere. But for me in 1925 it was something quite different to learn that there in those very houses and through those very doors, before the eyes of my informant, these revolting scenes had been quite recently enacted. And the same sort of thing was still going on all round us. My informant took me down the street past the Cheka prison. " Do you see those little windows down in the area ? " he said. " They are the corridors of the upper cells. There are two storeys of underground cells, below them without light or air. Those cells, about sixteen feet below where we are standing, are now at this moment filled with acquaintances of mine undergoing torture, whose only offence is to have bourgeois antecedents. You cannot see them or hear them, but they are there quite close to you and about to undergo abominable things." To approach so close to such obscenities was useful education for a young man shortly to return to the Northern Department of the Foreign Office.

The counter-revolutionary movement to which I have referred had had its focus in a village called Guimeni, a couple of days' journey up in the surrounding mountains ; and as there was still resident there the Scottish engineer of what had been Messrs. Forwood and Sellars' manganese mine, I determined to go and see this place for myself on the way home. Accordingly we went by train to Chiatouri up the valley of the Quirril, past the bridge built by Pompey, and still called by his name, to the junction at Sarapan where Hodgson left me to return to Moscow. After a day or two in this place, also notorious for its atrocities, I continued alone on muleback to the manganese mine of Guimeni which lies some thousand feet higher. Here I spent a week and collected a good deal more information about local conditions and politics. It was pleasant enough, but the time to return to the Foreign Office had arrived, and I must rather ashamedly admit that the horrible feeling of being alone and in the power of these revolting barbarians was beginning to get on my nerves. It seemed difficult at first to get out and away, but after the lapse of a few days I heard that a British tramp steamer was shortly due in Poti, the manganese port on the Black Sea, and I made arrangements to join her. I left Guimeni at 1.30 a.m. on June 18th, rode down to Chiatouri, took the train through Kutais which bears upon its arms the Golden Fleece, descended the valley of the Phasis, reached Poti where the Argonauts drew up their ships, and went on board the British S.S. *Janeta*.

As the moment of departure approached—of another escape from the oppression from which I had suffered while in Soviet jurisdiction—I need hardly say that I felt excited. At last the Commissar came on board who was to check off the names of the crew and give us clearance. There were two absentees and someone called through the engine-room grating : " Jock, will ye come on deck now ? " The Chief Engineer and his mate presently appeared, stripped to the waist, their chests covered with red fur. The Commissar said : " Mackintosh ees eet ? McSporran ees eet ? " The Chief Engineer crossed his arms and scowled and said " It is not then, I'm Lenin and this is my mate Trotsky." I thought that this was a dangerous game to play but the joke went down quite well, particularly with me to whom the Clydeside accent was familiar music. The Commissar went off with the pilot and at last—at last !—we were at sea. That night, stretching myself out in my bunk and listening to the gentle pulsations of the engine, I surrendered myself with unutterable contentment to the ship and to the sea which in a sense and wherever it is, is Home. Being in manganese, the *Janeta* rolled like hell for two days and nights. We got lost in a minefield off Sinope, but nobody worried much. In sixty hours from Poti I was in Constantinople and a week afterwards in London. It had been a grand journey but a long one, though I had not been away more than two months and had not spent the whole £150.

It was very pleasant to get back to Bridgend.

CHAPTER 11

PEKING

O N returning to the Foreign Office I wrote a very long account of my journey which had great success. In due course it was printed and circulated to the Cabinet and the Service. Ambassadors whom I had never met wrote to say how much they had enjoyed it and Cabinet Ministers stopped me in the street to express appreciation. I was at this time professionally ambitious and hoped that my enterprise would secure my advancement. It did ; and I had not long to wait.

In the autumn of 1925, Mr. Gregory, the Head of the Northern Department, came down to Bridgend for Sunday and told me that he had been commissioned to ask whether I would like to go as Counsellor to Peking. The proposal was being made to me tentatively—instead of the necessary orders to proceed merely being issued—since I was one of those who had never contemplated service abroad, having entered the Foreign Office before its amalgamation with the Diplomatic Service. Technically a civil servant held his position at His Majesty's pleasure and enjoyed no contractual rights, but in practice Clerks who had joined the Office before amalgamation were being kept at home when they desired it and where it was consistent with the public interest. Gregory pointed out that if I went to China I should gain six years in seniority and become the youngest Counsellor the Service had ever known but added that it would not be counted against me if I decided against going abroad.

All this was very flattering, but, nevertheless, my first impulse was to avail myself of the permission to decline his proposal which we debated for a whole afternoon, walking round the 140-acre field and sitting in the evening sunlight in the stack-yard at Corsair. A sudden interruption of Bridgend life would not be congenial ; three children, the eldest eleven years old, must accompany me and would be exposed to risks I could not measure ; my parents were aged, respectively, eighty-three and seventy-eight and it was unlikely I should return to find them both alive ; a wide circle of close friendships would temporarily be broken up ; I should have to sell the flock of pedigree chicken to which I had devoted so much labour ; the garden would go to ruin, and who would look after the bees and the bullterriers and the tortoise I had brought from the Embassy garden at Constantinople ? I drove to Denton the following Sunday thinking that a right decision would come to me in the Chiselhampton lane or as I got to the top of the green road which drops down to Chippinghurst. In fact it came to me when I stopped for a few minutes under the beeches by Nettlebed, and I hope I shall be believed when I say that it was only from a sense of duty to the Service that I decided to do what the Office had asked me to do. My mind being made up, I told the authorities that if they meant all they said, I would go to China, but I took the precaution of asking at the same time whether my promotion to the rank of Counsellor was really to be substantive or merely promotion to acting rank. Mr. Gregory gave me satisfactory oral assurances. " There was to be no hanky-panky of that kind about it," said he. Nevertheless, I must here regretfully record that when I reached Peking I was told that there " had been a misunderstanding " and that I was only to enjoy acting rank. I met with a similarly souring experience near the end of my official life.

The P. & O. steamship *Karmala* which we joined at Tilbury on December 17th, 1925, was one of the old 7,000-ton well-deckers long since scrapped ; and we got very fond of her by the time we reached Hong Kong, and of her Commander, Captain Griffen, who had been brought up in sail and used to tell the children what it had been like in the Roaring Forties or rounding the Horn, with fingers split to the bone at every joint and dressed with tar and oakum. Ocean travel being a new experience to all of us, we all thoroughly enjoyed ourselves except perhaps Baker, half lady's maid half nurse, on whom as well as on the governess, Miss Bumpstead, fell much of the responsibility for seeing that none of the children fell overboard. What should my wife and I do if one of them did? My heart never would stand up to swimming in cold water; she did not mind what the temperature was. We could not both go after the child. Should I, the bread-winner, behave like a perfect gentleman or should I stand and watch my wife dive after the child with a better chance of saving it? Captain Griffen said it would be silly for either of us to go into the water and demonstrated with a biscuit box that a child falling overboard would infallibly be killed by the screw! I hope that will settle the question for any other couples who have been plagued with it. I do not know how it is nowadays, but in the 'twenties and 'thirties of this century people used to criticize the P. & O. Company for the discipline, rather stricter than in the case of other Lines, to which passengers were subjected. We had no complaints. I have travelled in a number of P. & O. ships and never had anything but pleasure from it; splendid food, nice company, companionable officers. All this we enjoyed on our journey to Hong Kong. Additionally the P. & O. Line, in the days of which I write, carried a majority of the Service men and Government passengers travelling to the Far East; and we had a dozen Naval Officers on board who greatly added to our entertainment, though Captain Griffen called them seamen not sailors. Sailors, he said, were not merely navigators or mechanics, they were men who could hand, reef and sail by the wind.

It had seemed to take an eternity to get the *Karmala* away from the dockside at Tilbury. My father looked very small and old as he stood and waved us away on a journey he had made often himself. *Partir c'est un peu mourir.* So we were separated from him and Bridgend and Denton and Skipness and every-thing that was familiar by yard after yard and then mile after mile of water; but as it seemed an adventure, our thoughts were ahead and not astern of us. Each day was good in its own individual way: heavy storm off Ushant, strong sun off St. Vincent, warm airs in the Mediterranean, intense heat, noise and coal-dust at Port Said. Every day I learned to

share the life of a big ship, and best when I was alone. In
the Bay of Biscay, when not too sick, I watched the reeling
bows and the seas coming on board over the forward well-
deck ; in the Red Sea I pulled my mattress on deck and lay
all night feeling a strong hot wind blow between body and
shirt ; in the Indian Ocean, where the sea was calm with a
long swell, I leaned at night over the rail under the bridge
and watched the ship's nose sawing and snoring through the
water, and the foremast swinging like a slow pendulum across
the stars. At such times I shared the brave purposeful life
of the *Karmala* which gave me confidence to meet what was
going to be quite a new kind of life for me and my family ;
but I felt closest to the ship when, after spending some hours
in port, hot and dirty, tied lifeless to her bollards, she at last
put out again to sea and the beat of her engines was again
perceptible. Considering that to make a landfall and come
safe to port is the fulfilment of her destiny, it is strange that a
ship should so manifestly rejoice to be again at sea ; but in
this she resembles the mariner who hates the sea when he is
afloat and despises the land when he is ashore. One cannot
participate in the wonderful life of a ship without submitting
to this contradiction.

Since at Colombo the children had been exposed to measles
I telegraphed to the Governor of Hong Kong asking him to
make the necessary arrangements for them to live in quarantine
for ten days on arrival. The steps taken by the Colonial
Government to this end were as ample as the reception given
to me when the *Karmala* eventually picked up her moorings
in Victoria harbour. I was met by the Colonial Secretary,
the Governor's A.D.C., the Principal Medical Officer and his
assistant, the Consul-General from Canton and a considerable
following of minor officials, porters and servants from Government House and the Governor's office. Two steam launches
took us ashore, and three motor-cars and two trucks carried
us and our gear up the Peak road to a point where about fifteen
rickshaws awaited the party. In these we were whisked along
paths contouring the mountain to a house called Tanderagee
which had been completely fitted out for our reception and

provided with six servants. Like all Chinese servants, these not only understood and fulfilled to perfection their various duties, but behaved as if our sudden influx and the steps taken to meet it were the most normal thing in the world. I was of course full of gratitude to the Governor, Sir Cecil Clementi, for his overflowing kindness to us, but I was soon to discover that all the practical arrangements for life in our Far Eastern colonies and dependencies were similarly conceived on what, if it were in England, would seem a princely scale. This endeared the Far East to me at once, for I like prodigality and luxury and convenience, and innumerable perfectly behaved and very efficient servants. I like these things for their own sake ; I like to see others enjoy them if I cannot ; but above all I like to be myself the object of consideration and centre of attraction.

It was no doubt this as well as the happy termination of my first voyage across the great oceans, the wonderful climate of the Peak, the novel and manifold beauty of the colony, the first sight of a " Flame of the Forest " tree and of butterflies six inches across, the absorbing glimpses of Chinese life in Victoria and the many new friendships formed, which gave to myself and my wife a strong and enduring affection for Hong Kong. My father had been Attorney-General there from 1880 to 1886 and had lived for part of the time in Government House. I cannot be certain of it, but I think the No. 1 Boy at Government House knew when he welcomed me that he was welcoming the son of an old friend. Nice as it would have been to have spent the ensuing fortnight bathing at Stonecutters and exploring the island, I was impatient to get into China proper and accordingly invited myself to spend ten days in visiting Canton and patrolling the delta of the Pearl River in H.M.S. *Cicala*, Commander Alleyne, R.N. In *Cicala*, drawing so far as I remember only about three feet of water, we explored numerous shallow and remote channels through the delta ; chasing pirates, shooting snipe, drinking gin and showing off our armament to villages where, except for the Royal Navy, Europeans are never seen. One day we landed to shoot snipe in paddy fields surrounded by bunds or embankments rising ten feet or so above the deep mud in which the rice plants are bedded out. As we were having lunch at an intersection of these bunds we observed advancing towards us simultaneously from all four quarters small parties of Chinese dressed only in loincloths and armed with rifles and revolvers. No road for retreat was open to us nor any other course than to sit still and look unconcerned ; but although the inhabitants of these delta villages combine piracy with agriculture and live beyond reach of the law, my fears for the safety of myself and my friends proved unfounded. The villagers decided we were harmless, and after an exchange of mutually unintelligible compliments left us to finish our meal and go on shooting. A year later I met the First Lieutenant of *Cicala* in Shanghai who reminded me of this incident and enquired what impression it had made on me. I confessed to having felt some alarm. " Yes," he said, " so did I, and what is more I loaded both barrels of my gun, taking jolly good care you should not see what I was doing." " That," I answered, " was just precisely what I did too." All this brought vividly to my mind how far I had travelled from the Northern Department of the Foreign Office and lunch at the Oxford and Cambridge Club.

From Hong Kong my family and I went in the R.M.S. *Rawalpindi* to Shanghai in the company of the Consul-General Sir Sidney Barton, and I had three clear days in which to get much instruction and stimulation from that gallant and talented man who, although we did not always see eye to eye, was to be my steadfast and lifelong friend. There was plenty to discuss, for China was in a ferment ; at any rate such parts of it as were accessible to foreigners. For several millennia the country had evolved, within as it were a closed alembic, institutions and forms of life peculiarly its own and in many respects of the highest value. The alembic had been shattered by the arrival of Europeans on the China coast and the virus of what is called progress had been introduced into the blood-stream of the race ; now China was a mass of political abscesses and neither the Chinese nor the foreigners knew what to do about it. All the officials and merchants and missionaries in

China were spouting and bubbling with political controversy, and the Foreign Office in London and its pundits, Sir Victor Wellesley who had never been to China, and Sir John Pratt who knew it very well, did not find it easy to make the British Government give clear directions on the main lines of policy or on the way in which British interests should be adjusted to the fluid local situations which were different in all the eighteen provinces of China. No wonder. Nobody could have done such a thing. No wonder nearly everybody in China had a different answer to every question. It was all very confusing for an ignoramus like myself but gave me plenty of material to turn over in my mind, first sitting in the hydrangea-filled garden at Tanderagee, now listening to Barton in the saloon of the *Rawalpindi* and later when I had at last arrived in sight of the great walls of Peking and reached, as it seemed, the extreme end of all ordinary travel.

The voyage from Shanghai to Tientsin had been continued in one of Butterfield and Swires small ships and had not been without incident. It was intensely rough and cold. Deck and rigging were sheathed in ice which the spaniel we had picked up in Shanghai found most disagreeable. In sight of the lee-shore of Shantung we blew the head loose of the high-compression cylinder and rolled for two hours miserably in the easterly wind. However, we arrived eventually and safely at Taku, and by the next day were in an uncomfortable train between Tientsin and Peking, the children staring glumly at a Chinese soldier with an umbrella under his arm and an executioner's broad-bladed sword on his back or looking out of the windows at the frozen and featureless fields. The visitor from overseas is told that everyone reaches Peking in tears of disappointment and leaves it with tears of regret. Our arrival confirmed the truth of this. We saw as yet little that was romantic or enticing in the view, and even when the train had passed through the outer wall of Peking there was not much to please the eye, for what was called a city seemed for the most part to consist of stagnant pools and waste land and impoverished steadings. Nevertheless, as after a few days we began to explore our surroundings, we found

WINTER PALACE, PEKING

GREAT WALL OF CHINA

that the general appearance of dirt and desolation was deceptive, and that sinister alleys and blind walls concealed many
delightful houses and courtyards and gardens ; and when in
due course we visited the great palaces and temples it became
clear that this was a place we were going to like. As spring
quickened the willows bordering each evil-smelling canal the
surrounding country took on the beauties for which Chinese
pictures and porcelains had prepared us. When the roses and
peonies of May followed the cherry and peach-blossom of
April, the gloomy and forbidding prospect encountered on
arrival in January was quite forgotten ; and by the time
November came round our eyes had learned to find beauty
even in the dun austerity of a northern Chinese winter.

The British Legation compound, 1,908 yards in circumference, accommodated a Minister, Counsellor, First, Second
and Third Secretaries ; Chinese Secretary and Assistant
Secretary ; Consul, Vice-Consul, Commercial Secretariat,
Accountant, Doctor, a double company of the Durham Light
Infantry, sergeants, clerks, students, servants of every degree,
stables, *manège*, dairy farm, central heating, electric-light and
sewage-disposal installations, tennis courts, chapel and hos-
pital. Located in the Legation Quarter, it was a city within
a city within a city. Two thousand souls went to sleep in it
every night. We were surrounded by other foreign Legations
and the whole Quarter was contained within a loopholed
wall and *glacis*—a relic of the Boxer Rebellion. Outside the
Legation Quarter lay the Tartar city surrounded by walls some
forty feet wide on which the children took their afternoon
walks. The walls were pierced by great gates strictly closed
at sundown to the passage even of privileged diplomats.
Beyond the walls and the outlying suburbs lay the yellow
fields, interspersed with numerous villages and temples and
farms ; and through these we used to drive most days past
the municipal shambles, past the thieves' graveyard, past the
yards where night-soil was made into bricks of manure to
the racecourse, and on to the Teichman's villa[1] where we

---

[1] Chinese Counsellor, later Sir Eric Teichman, of the Far Eastern
Consular Service.

picked up our ponies. Beyond the fields to the north and west the hills began which stretch away to Shansi and Mongolia. Here we could find ourselves in country wholly unaffected by foreign influence ; and, if we behaved with discretion and escaped the notice of brigands, could closely observe the life of the people wherever we chose to go. Such was the environment in which we settled down in the spring of 1926.

One of the first things that was borne in upon us was that though the Quarter which contained foreign Embassies and Legations was two or three miles in circumference, we foreigners were a very small and unimportant part of the life of the city ; that Peking was a completely Asiatic town and that it was not a mixed life as at Shanghai but a purely Chinese life which went on all round us, so closely encompassing us that in the evenings the whole air was filled with an enveloping murmur of Chinese cries and voices not to be overcome even by the pulsating stridency of the cicadas in the garden trees. It was therefore desirable and inevitable that we should learn as soon as possible to speak a few words of Chinese, and should accommodate our behaviour to the tastes and habits of the people of the country.

The best way for a foreigner to start to do this is to observe closely his own domestic servants. The Counsellor had eighteen menservants. The commander-in-chief of these was my butler—or No. 1 Boy—Niu. He engaged or dismissed the subordinate servants, and if a stranger brought me my early morning cup of tea, it was no matter for surprise ; it was a nephew or cousin, a *peng-yu* of Niu's who had been temporarily taken on to substitute my valet, the No. 2 boy. Better servants could hardly have been found. They were dignified, genial, competent and attentive and had memories like elephants. Our private lives, I would almost say our thoughts were an open book to them. My No. 2 boy, Li, for instance, would nearly always know, without anything said, which of the five books I happened to be reading was the one I should want on my bedside table, and if he had found it lying open, he would before taking it to my bedroom put a marker in it. This meticulous knowledge of their masters extended throughout the whole body of Chinese clerks and servants in the compound. The Legation accountants being Chinese, the income of every official was accurately known, and on the basis of this figure every member of the British staff had to pay a differential price for everything he bought. A corresponding increase in the price of food was noticed shortly after the Foreign Office had granted us a small increment in our foreign allowances. One of the British officers stationed at the Legation was a man of fortune ; his wife had to pay twice as much for chickens as anybody else. It would have been foolish as well as quite useless to try to escape from this system which, like many other Chinese customs, we soon came to accept as ingenious and sensible. What we had to do was to find out what, to Chinese minds, was the equitable rate of " squeeze " to be levied on the O'Malleys and not to allow ourselves to be squeezed unduly. Besides " squeeze " the second regulating factor in our domestic life was " face ". As this is not the place for a long essay on Chinese manners and customs I will confine myself to two imaginary and one true example of this. If I had severely reproached Niu in front of one of his sub-ordinates he would have disappeared for ever at once from Legation service ; he might even have committed suicide. On the other hand, if a silver spoon had disappeared, no one knew why, from my dinner service, Niu would have got an exact replica at his own expense. His " face " was involved in everything in my house being perfect and, no matter what the cause, his self-respect suffered in the most intimate way if anything went wrong. One day my secretary invited the guests for two dinner-parties of ten persons each for the same instead of for two successive days. When the mistake at the last moment became apparent, Niu produced the necessary extra food, silver and china from the pantries and kitchens of my colleagues without any of us having to give the matter any thought. When the crisis broke he just said " I fix ", and he fixed. The dinner party was a success and his " face " was saved.

Here are two more sidelights on Chinese behaviour and then I will have done with the servants :—Some months before

the details of my journey home from China were settled I
told Niu that I contemplated returning by caravan to the
frontier of Chinese Turkestan, and thence by Leh or Gilgit
to India. I explained shortly that the journey, entailing some
risks and many hardships, would take about six months or
even nine, and enquired whether he would care to accompany
me. He looked at me quizzically for a minute or so and
then said quite simply that he would like to do so ; and what
is more, he meant it. I am quite sure he would have come,
and that he would have made no fuss about it all, would
have carried out my orders with his usual impassive efficiency,
and would have left the question of what was to happen to
him when we got to India and to his dependants in the meanwhile more or less in my hands. Niu was a family man,
and had not previously travelled further than Shanghai, yet
he had acquiesced with little hesitation to a suggestion which
would surely have staggered any European servant, it not
being a normal part of an English butler's duty to walk or
ride on donkeys or camels for half a year across the roof of
the world.

The second story is about my No. 2 boy, Li. When the
time came for my family to go home, my wife asked him
to accept a number of toys and small possessions which Patrick
would be obliged to leave behind and which might have been
of some use or pleasure to Li's only son, who was about the
same age. In response Li, with the deprecating smile which
good manners in China prescribe for such occasions, asked
leave to refuse the offer on grounds which he seemed reluctant
to state explicitly. My wife's curiosity was aroused but gave
place to consternation when Li under her gentle pressure
revealed the fact that his son was dead. Now to lose an
only son is, God knows, as harsh a test of courage and con-
stancy as any parent can be called on to endure ; but for a
Chinese it has an added significance, which may be roughly
expressed by saying that a father's own immortality is involved
with the life of his male offspring, and that if he leaves none
behind him, he loses in the same moment his hope of felicity
in the next world and in this. In great distress therefore, my

wife enquired the circumstances of this tragedy and why we had known nothing of it at the time : why Li had not even asked for a day's leave to spend by the child's sickbed or to commit the small body to the grave. Li's explanation left us at once humbled and aghast. When his son fell ill, Li told her, Patrick, our only son, had himself been in mortal danger with double septic pneumonia ; and, still with the deprecatory smile exacted by perfect conformity to Chinese standards of behaviour, Li went on to explain that "small master" being very sick, he had not liked to bring his private distresses to our notice or add in any way to our preoccupations. Accordingly, without a word to us, he had supported the agonies which we by a hair's breadth had escaped. My conversation with Niu showed that spacial and temporal dimensions are not the same to the Chinese as they are to us and our conversation with Li illustrated the importance to the Chinese of good manners, of the control of emotion and stylization of behaviour in all the circumstances and accidents of life. Such episodes were trivial in themselves, but there was much to be learned from them, and in this manner, from day to day contacts with servants and coolies and shopkeepers, we began to build up a modest understanding of the Chinese way of life in the light of which larger political questions could be studied.

China inspired in me so high a degree of affection and respect that I got to understand very well why the Chinese had traditionally regarded Europeans as barbarians ; and never better that on one very hot day in the summer of 1926 which I spent wandering through the old streets of Canton, no more than ten or twelve feet broad and thronged by Chinese, chattering and chaffering, carrying and hauling or sitting impassively among the smells and flies. There was something venerable in the busy poverty of most of them, and much refinement of gesture and address in children as well as in very old people. I was particularly attracted by the humblest class of coolies who, dressed only in smallclothes, displayed beautiful hairless chests and shoulders coloured like a Sheraton table when the mahogany has been sun-bleached to the lightness of pale sherry. I hardly saw a European all day until I met an English businessman who was returning like myself to the British Concession at Shameen. He was an ordinary type with pale freckled skin, scrubby moustache and irregular teeth, dressed like myself in white drill on which, as in my case, patches of sweat showed under the arms and on the back; and, although I could not see it, I realized with distaste that his chest and thighs, like mine (but unlike the Chinese), were covered with hair. We should both of us have passed unnoticed in the grotesque ugliness of an ordinary London crowd. I was glad to see this Englishman because great animosity was being shown at the time by the populace towards the blameless foreigners, who were in consequence living behind barbed wire and sandbags in Shameen; but though the man, whose unpleasing appearance I shared, was allied to me by race, interests and sympathy, though he was a personal friend of mine, though he represented (as I hoped I did also) a cultural tradition of great excellence, yet the contrast was shocking between his crudity and mine on the one hand, and, on the other, the patina of an ancient and static civilization which gave dignity to the unwarrantably hostile population of Canton. It was not easy to bring such conflicting thoughts and feelings into an orderly pattern in my mind.

Anybody must be very hard to please who could not find plenty of agreeable occupation for his leisure in and around Peking as it was in our day. Our leisure was occupied for the most part by exploring the town, by horses and by expeditions into the country.

At all times of the year it was a pleasure to wander round the Forbidden City or poke about in the markets and antique shops, for we never knew what was going to happen. One day I bought a small vase for ten shillings—and I don't suppose it is worth more than that anywhere—which is to my eyes one of the most perfect examples in the world in shape, colour and texture of the potter's art. Another day, walking with the children round the Temple of Heaven, we found pasque flowers (*Anemone pulsatilla*) in full bloom, growing fifteen inches high between the paving-stones. Another day we met the public executioner going to the execution ground in the Temple of Agriculture with the condemned men trussed up in a cart behind him. On the way there he was playing with the cord which is used to pull forward the kneeling victim's head and make it easy to cut off. On the way back he was chewing dough-nuts. On many days we would spend an hour or two bargaining with the proprietor of our favourite curio shop called The Court of Miracles, drinking tea and admiring his goldfish and lotus blooms. With all this and much more at our doors we never lacked entertainment inside the city walls.

The principal sources of pleasure outside the city walls were horses and weekends in the Western hills. Our Mongolian ponies cost £10 each, stood 13.1 hands and could carry my 165 lb. for nine miles and over twenty-four jumps in the point-to-point races which took place every Sunday afternoon. They were rather wicked and very brave and it is a wonder to me that no army has used them in Europe since the days of Ghengiz Khan ; for I have known a mounted Chinese regiment march fifty miles in twenty-four hours and fight a battle at the end of it. The weekends in the summer were often spent in remote monasteries in the Western hills. I would say to Niu " Sunday we go T'an Chêh Ssū. Seven man. You fix donkeys, beds, food." This was all that was necessary to ensure that every conceivable arrangement was made for our comfort. We would drive eight or nine miles to the end of the motor road, meet the donkeys and servants and tramp all the long hot day through glens clothed in peach-blossom. Having reached the monastery and exchanged courtesies with the Abbot we would dine and sleep on terraces under the pine trees[1] and among the peonies ; retracing our steps on Monday morning full of tranquillity drawn in from the beauty and remoteness and silence and peace of a conventual establishment which appeared superficially to be in the last stages of spiritual decay.

I shall not describe all these Peking experiences in detail

[1] *Pinus Bungeana.*

because this has already been done very accurately in my wife's books and because this chapter is already too long. Moreover, no catalogue of Peking experiences, however long, however varied, would explain why to us who have been there, even a short residence in China seems in retrospect to be such a wonderful and enriching thing. When we got home again to Bridgend, we felt we had got two worlds instead of one to live in. Short of going to the moon, we did not see how anyone in any other way could similarly enlarge their universe. I cannot rationalize this ; can only suppose that the Chinese people—in spite of their shortcomings—are so old, so numerous, so self-sufficient, so complicated, so artistic, so intelligent, so experienced, so patient that the total is much more than the sum of the parts. Anyhow, the result of it was that when younger men later came down to Bridgend and asked me should they accept the offer of a Chinese appointment, I always answered : " Of course you must accept, you will then have two worlds instead of one. I cannot quite explain this. It is like the religious experience : you cannot understand it unless you have it. It is true that all my three children nearly died, but you must not worry unduly about this ; this risk, for the English, is the price of Empire. So go ; and go with a good courage and a receptive mind and heart, and you will see when you come back that I was right."

The Counsellor is second-in-command of an Embassy or Legation and stands outside but alongside of the ladder up which papers go to the Head of the Mission and instructions descend to the staff. When the Head of Mission is absent he takes full charge of it, but so long as the Ambassador or Minister is at his post, the Counsellor is a fifth wheel to the coach, and consequently has the opportunity to travel, visit Consuls, study general questions, supervise the preparations of the annual report, and generally take over any special subject deputed to him by his chief. My first year in China was occupied in all these ways. Official conversations with the Chinese were not carried on by the diplomatic staff who only stayed in China for from two to four years, but by the Chinese

Secretaries, who were Consular Officers, trained to speak and read Chinese and destined to spend their whole careers in the country. Except therefore for a few social contacts with prominent Chinese personalities, my knowledge of the people was derived from our servants, as I have already described, from coolies, from shopkeepers, and from the villagers whom we encountered on our expeditions. All were polite, helpful and hospitable. There was no anti-foreign feeling to be met with anywhere ; even when a patriotic crowd was howling outside the Legation Quarter gates for the blood or expulsion of all foreign devils, a pathway was made through the press, not by the police, but by the rioters themselves, for a British nurse and perambulator returning from a morning walk on the walls. Things were different in the centre and south of China. There there was a certain amount of real animosity. My own and rather unorthodox explanation of the tolerance and friendship we enjoyed in the north is that it was an indirect consequence of the brutality with which the European soldiers and sailors had sacked part of Peking after the Boxer Rebellion in the year 1900. The Chinese are not averse to brutality and violence. They are familiar with and understand these things. They are apt to respect and consequently —though the word is perhaps a little too strong—to like those who have strength and use it violently in their own interests and when they have a good reason for doing so. With this sort of thing they know where they are. What they cannot understand and despise and consequently dislike is people who command force but do not employ it. What was called the " gun-boat " policy had a good long run for its money. It might have had a longer run if invariably employed with resolution and on adequate grounds. What was quite hopeless was a " gun-boat policy " pursued after the English had begun to lose their self-confidence and sense of mission—after the English, or a large section of them, had been enfeebled by the first world war and had begun to feel that sweet reasonableness without readiness to use force where requisite was a right and useful guide to the conduct of foreign relations. Once this " rot ", as the old China hands would have called it, set in, the Chinese began to feel that the English were mad or afraid or both, and the " gun-boat policy " had to be reversed. I had a lot to do with reversing it as I shall relate in the following chapter.

CHAPTER 12

HANKOW

WHEN I arrived in China the Minister was Sir Ronald Macleay, with whom my personal relations throughout were warm. While he was in charge I was suitably employed, as explained in the previous chapter, in travelling ; and accordingly I went for a journey in the summer of 1926 for the purpose, besides my own education, of discussing Chinese relations with the Governor of Hong Kong, Consuls, Admirals, the internationally administered Customs and Salt officials, banks, merchants and any others with whom it was desirable that the Legation in Peking should keep in close contact. As a result of this journey I got into the most appalling row and, most of the principal participants in it now being dead, there is no reason why the story of it should not be told.

As the fruits of my journey I put my ideas about China into the form of an informal and unofficial memorandum and, with Macleay's consent, sent this home from Hong Kong to a friend in the Far Eastern Department of the Foreign Office. I do not know whether they were good or bad ideas, but my friends in the Office wrote to say that they provoked reflection from a new angle on Chinese relations, and that was quite as much as I desired or my memorandum deserved. Now at this time Lord Willingdon, lately Governor of Madras and now Governor-General designate of Canada, was in Peking as leader of the Boxer Indemnity Commission and making in that capacity an intensive study of the situation in China. As such, he and the other British delegates were naturally treated by the Legation as *fils de la maison* on a basis of the most complete confidence and intimacy. Some of the delegates—Dame Adelaide Anderson and Sir Sidney Peel—lived in my house and of course Lord and Lady Willingdon were in and out of it all the time. While I was in Hong Kong my wife in all good faith told Lord Willingdon that I had plenty to say about China and that I had in fact committed my reflections and speculations to paper. Lord Willingdon wrote to me and asked whether on return to London he might see what I had written, and in response I asked my friends in the China Department of the Foreign Office to tell him that he could get my unofficial memorandum from them if he so wished. Then the storm broke. The Foreign Office told Macleay that no one in London had the slightest wish to know what I thought about anything, that they did not like " being addressed in the language of Gibbon " and that my " literary productions were perfectly futile " through which it would be " sheer waste of their time to wade ". They went on to say that Lord Willingdon was neither the most discreet nor reliable person in the world ; that his Lordship was criticizing the Government's handling of Chinese affairs and that Sir Austen Chamberlain (then Secretary of State) was much embarrassed by the fact that Lord Willingdon knew that I had written something on the subject which he (Chamberlain) had felt obliged to withhold from him. All this Macleay passed on to me in the kindest and nicest possible way, but of course to my utmost dismay ; and my good friends in the China Department wrote a series of sympathetic letters to me saying that I was in most frightfully hot water and that terrible things would happen to me if I did not back-pedal very hard and very soon.

Every knowledgeable person would today agree that these aspersions on Lord Willingdon were totally without foundation, and we must suppose that by an oversight they were allowed to issue from the Foreign Office without Sir A. Chamberlain's personal approval. But of course it would have been very unwise of me to have tried to excuse myself or to have expressed astonishment that the Foreign Secretary was reluctant to discuss unreservedly Chinese relations with so eminent a man as a Governor-General of Canada designate who had been sent to China for the express purpose of studying them ; and so I went through all the appropriate motions of humility and repentance, and it all blew over without lasting damage to myself. Macleay told the Foreign Office they were making a mountain out of a molehill ; and the Foreign Office presently wrote and begged me to put " the little matter " of my indiscretion out of my mind. My literary style, Gibbonian or otherwise, remained such as it was. The whole incident would be hardly worth recording, except perhaps for a lesson it may convey to younger members of the Foreign Service which is that if they want to get on in the world they should remember that they must, above all things, make themselves agreeable and convenient to the higher officials in the Foreign Office and to the ruling politicians to whom their loyalty is pledged. From the point of view of professional advancement this is more important than loyalty to the truth as they see it.

Sir R. Macleay was succeeded towards the end of 1926 by Sir Miles Lampson (now Lord Killearn) and at the moment of Lampson's arrival in Peking occurred an incident at Hankow in the middle of China which eventually led to the despatch of a British army to Shanghai. On January 27th, 1927, armed Chinese assaulted and overran the British Concession at Hankow [1] ; British sailors were landed and some of them wounded ; local feeling rose to fever pitch ; British women and children were evacuated to Shanghai, while the men fortified themselves in the largest and strongest block of flats on the embankment of the Yangtse-kiang ; and so the two sides settled down in the posture of gladiators while the Chinese Nationalist authorities and the British Government exchanged disagreeable and minatory communications. I was told to go to Hankow where the Consul-General seemed to have lost his nerve, find out what was happening and make recommendations. It seemed, then, that my reputation for discretion had been restored ; but considering how recently and how narrowly I had escaped disgrace, the prospect made me quite dizzy. It was like the switch-back at the fair—down one minute and up the next.

[1] Viz. a part of the town reserved for the British and exclusively under British administration.

I left Peking by train for Nanking in company with Teichman, the Chinese Counsellor, at the beginning of February.
At Pukow, the railway terminus on the opposite side of the
Yangtse-kiang to Nanking, we embarked on a river steamer
for Hankow ; but a destroyer—H.M.S. *Wishart*, Commander
Church, R.N.—overtook us, and in the middle of a wet and
windy night we hurriedly dressed and transferred to her,
drank much hot cocoa in the wardroom, and so continued
up river. It was not the first time I had been entertained
by the Royal Navy. I had spent, as I have already related,
a week in *Cicala* in the Canton river delta ; and I had on a
visit to the south of China in the summer of 1926 persuaded
Despatch, Captain Le Motté, R.N., to take the Governor and
myself on a pirate-hunting expedition to Bias Bay on the
mainland just opposite Hong Kong. Nobody, I should have
thought, could have been more out of place than myself in
a man-of-war, but such is the Royal Navy that I have imperishable and extremely agreeable memories of all the many
occasions when I have been their guest, and not least of this
short journey in *Wishart*.

Hankow lies about eight hundred miles up the Yangtse
and it took me about a fortnight to get there from the day
I got my orders in Peking. Here I was now in a position
of great prominence. A glance at the newspapers of that date
will confirm that the eyes of the world were not only directed
at China but focused on the British Concession at Hankow ;
focused more particularly on the Counsellor from Peking now
living in Admiral Cameron's minute flagship, H.M.S. *Bee*, and
only able to communicate with the outside world through *Bee's*
newly-invented short-wave long-distance wireless machine.
And I was not only in a position of great prominence but,
for the first and last time in my life in a position of great
power ; for my remoteness and the rapidly moving course of
events and the great excitement both of Chinese and of public
opinion everywhere put me for a few days and nights in the
glorious position of holding peace in one hand and hostilities
in the other. That was what it felt like in 1927, and looking
at it soberly at this distance of time, that is what I think it

in fact was. I visited the men sitting behind their machine-guns and sandbags in the Asiatic Petroleum Company's dominating concrete building, and consulted the leaders of the British community—experienced, long-headed men. They asked : " Do you want prestige or trade ? " It was no time for discussing the action and reaction of trade and prestige upon each other, so I said : " Trade " thinking to myself that I should know better in a day or two whether the odds on trade were shortening or lengthening, and that if they lengthened I should still have time to back prestige for a place. " Very well," said the business men, " we'll now discuss what sort of accommodation we can hope to get " ; and so we did, and they were very sensible and helpful about it.

The British Government, as well as the public, were justly incensed by the turbulent and unlawful behaviour of the Hankow mob and upset by the fact that some marines had been pelted with brick-bats and wounded. The whole of the British community in Shanghai and elsewhere had had its pride or " face " wounded in the most sensitive place, and demanded that force should be met with force and the Navy instructed to supply that protection for British life and property which the Chinese Government had so conspicuously failed to provide. It was natural therefore, that the first instructions I received from the Foreign Office should have been full of fire and resolution and quite strong enough to cover me if I had decided to turn the Chinese out of the Concession by force. But in my somewhat lonely situation I reflected how difficult it was to know when one started something where it was going to end ; and, transporting myself in imagination to the familiar atmosphere of Downing Street, I remembered how intensely reluctant, how wisely reluctant any British Government always was to force any issue which timely con-cessions could possibly resolve. Brooding on this as from the windows of the Consulate-General I watched the mob painting insulting messages on the garden walls, I found it difficult to believe that in the course of a few days I should not see the Foreign Office putting a lot of water in its wine, or that the

Opposition, under Mr. MacDonald's leadership, would have any sympathy with the use of force until every conceivable alternative had been explored.

What finally decided me to show the greatest restraint and patience and to recommend conciliation even at the expense of our dignity was this : it was not only Hankow but Shanghai that was in question. The probability was that the same sort of situation that had arisen at Hankow would soon arise also in Shanghai. It would be fatal in Shanghai to leave unrequited the same sort of injuries which we had received in Hankow ; in Shanghai force must at all costs be answered by force. But I could not see how the Tory government could take a strong line successfully at Shanghai unless they enjoyed the support of the Opposition at home, and I could not see any means by which Opposition support for a strong line in Shanghai could be enlisted unless the party in power had already demonstrated in the most unambiguous manner its patience and pacific intention. Hankow offered the only opportunity for such a demonstration, and I therefore determined to treat the Chinese in Hankow with so much indulgence that the Opposition—if and when the crisis in Shanghai occurred—would already have been convinced of the Government's sincere intention to preserve peace to the last possible moment, and would, therefore, be ready to lend Mr. Baldwin their support if it should eventually in his opinion be necessary to employ force for the defence of a major British interest. I determined, in fact, to make a tactical withdrawal for strategic reasons. After the lapse of a few days I found, as I expected, that Sir Austen Chamberlain was very anxious for a compromise settlement at Hankow ; and later, when things got worse at Shanghai, my hopes that the Government would get full support from the Opposition were also fulfilled. One of the most curious aspects of the working of the British constitution which I had several times seen in operation when I was in the Foreign Office, is the way in which when some major British interest in the international field is in jeopardy the Prime Minister of the day consults informally with the Leader of the Opposition, both of them suppressing, for love of England, old animosities and suspicions, forgetting for the moment invective and provocation exchanged in the House of Commons and studying conjointly the reports received from officials abroad and from the admirals and generals. I think it is only the English [1] in the heyday of their experience and power who could have invented so nice and valuable a form of political conduct, and it was this which I hoped to bring into operation by my manœuvres in Hankow. I do not know whether I did or not, but I hope so.

The details of a compromise settlement between myself and Mr. Eugene Chen, the local representative of the Kuomintang, were ably worked out by Mr. Teichman ; and I am happy to think that the constitution of what presently replaced the Concession and became known as the " Special District " of Hankow worked admirably during the years which ensued, and that Monsieur Borodin, the representative of the Soviet Union deputed to make trouble between us, was soon afterwards sent packing by the Chinese. At the time, however, I was covered with obloquy by the mercantile community in China who feared, not without good grounds, that we had lost so much " face " in China as to put all our vested interests there in danger of destruction.

During the events which I have related Hankow was a very " rough house ". It was full of wild and disorderly regiments from Hupeh who had never been in contact with Europeans. Curiosity impelled me from time to time to skulk alone through the streets to look at them, and they certainly did not inspire confidence. Knowing all this my wife and Mrs. Teichman in Peking used to crouch along with the operator over the little W/T receiver in the Legation hoping for news of us. Short-wave W/T being in its infancy, messages received from Hankow were few and far between. At the height of the tension, however, they were delighted one night when the machine gave *Bee's* call sign and began to tick out its message. The message was :

[1] Scotsmen may censure me for using the word " English " instead of British, but I think the root of the phenomena I write about lies in the English and not the Scottish character and history.

" Please send our woollen drawers and vests. It's damn cold here.

TEICHMAN."

And after that silence. Warm pants are very material to international negotiations. For lack of them I got a kind of dysentery which made my last ten days in Hankow a misery. I was glad then when after eight weeks or so up-river the time came to go down to Kiukiang. At Kiukiang I made a second agreement with the Chinese, surrendering to them the relatively unimportant Concession in that place which had been overrun and partially sacked when the British Concession at Hankow itself was attacked. Then I went on downstream to Shanghai. I well remember the night I and my typist spent listening to Chinese bullets pinging through the river-steamer's sides : a demonstration not so much of Chinese hostility as of the Chinese idea of fun. At Shanghai, where a division of British troops, including part of the Brigade of Guards, had recently arrived I joined up with Admiral Sir R. Tyrwhitt, who besides being a splendid man and a great sailor, shared my tastes for gardening and joinery. I had to face drum-fire from the British community in Shanghai but could not explain to them that it was in their interests that I had yielded Hankow and Kiukiang to the Chinese. Meantime in London, in the Press and in the House of Commons I had become a public figure. Who was this O'Malley, they asked, who had pulled the contending parties together in Hankow? Mr. John Jones, M.P., asked why I pronounced my name to rhyme with Bailey instead of Sally, but of course no one in the House knew enough about Mayo or the Irish language to answer the question. Mr. Campbell, M.P., suggested that the thanks of Parliament should be telegraphed to me but the Secretary of State said he had already done all that was necessary in this line. All this was very flattering and amusing, but I had no time to pay any attention to it. Immediately after my return to Peking my small son, Patrick, fell desperately ill of septic pneumonia. When he was sufficiently recovered, I sent my wife and family back to England and prepared to follow them as soon as possible.

When I got back to London in the autumn of the same year—1927—I was not invited by the Secretary of State to give any further account of the events I have related. The Far Eastern Department of the Foreign Office were equally incurious. In December I went into the room of a friend of mine in this department and found him writing a memorandum on China for the Secretary of State in the course of which he speculated on the reasons for which I had taken a certain course at Hankow. " Mr. O'Malley," he had written, " may have thought . . . or on the other hand he may have considered . . ." " Would it not," I asked him, " have been simpler to refer this particular question to me, since you knew I was available in the Office ? " " Well," he answered, " you have been here all your life. You know what the Foreign Office is like."

My efforts in Hankow were rewarded by a C.M.G. and the offer of a substantive Counsellorship in the Diplomatic Service which I refused as the children's health made it necessary that I should, for the time being, remain in England.

CHAPTER 13

INDO-CHINA

THE final paragraphs of the preceding chapter record my return to the Foreign Office, but I must now go back to my journey home from China which afforded many interesting and delightful experiences.

This journey was not simple to plan, because owing to the general exodus of foreigners from China consequent upon the disturbances described above, all passenger steamers were fully booked up. The best course for me, and the one I followed, was to go to Yokohama and take my chance of getting spare berths to Shanghai and Hong Kong and ultimately Penang. It was now mid-August, and the first opportunity of getting on from Penang would not occur till the S.S. *Khyber* left that place on October 7th. This suited me very well, since it looked as if with reasonable luck I should have time to visit French Indo-China *en route*, and satisfy a long-cherished wish to see the great temple of Angkor Wat in Cambodia. But nothing could be definitely settled till I got to Hong Kong and accordingly, instead of the prolonged and detailed anticipation of a journey which often provides almost as much pleasure as the journey itself, I was to have the excitements and surprises of unpremeditated opportunities and decisions.

The way from Peking to Japan was through Manchuria and Korea, and as on August 23rd, 1927, the train rumbled along towards Mukden through the fields of the ripening millet I had leisure for some serious reflections and for indulgence in an orgy of sentimental recollections of everything that had happened since the frozen and colourless day two years earlier when the O'Malleys had arrived in Peking. I gave thanks to God, and with good reason, that we were all still alive, for some or all of the children had had scarlet fever, diphtheria, amoebic dysentery and septic pneumonia ; and my wife and

I had spent nights and days watching them oscillate between life and death. I enjoyed with, I hope, modest pride the publicity which had attended my recent activities and the approval with which the Foreign Office had crowned them. And besides all that I had my golden memories. Peking was not, as two years earlier, merely a place on the map or an appointment offered by the Foreign Office ; it was a bit of life and of the world that had become part of me for ever ; new knowledge and new friendships ; the pride of walls and gate-towers and palaces ; the beauty of lotus and willow ; the serenity of temple terraces and not least the memory of our little horses, of their courage and foolishness, of their light feet on cold December fields and of soft eyes and breath in dark sweet-smelling stables. It was all over now, all these memories were slipping behind me as the train plugged on into Manchuria and I started to make my way round the world and back to Bridgend and Denton. By the time I get home, thought I, the dahlias will be frozen and the last swallows almost gone ; and at that thought I realized how homesick I really was, and how much I thirsted to drink again among English fields and meadows at the well-springs of my beliefs and strength. But it was an agreeable homesickness, because my feet were now set upon the homeward path which, the goal being clearly in view, I had no wish to shorten by a mile or an hour.

After a week in Japan and four days in Shanghai I approached Hong Kong again and for the last time on the evening of September 16th. As we passed through the Limoun Channel a flaming sunset illuminated the shining islands and the terraced rock and as the sun sank innumerable lights started out from beach to peak. I dined in Government House, and after dinner one of the governesses to the Clementi children took me for a moonlit drive, swishing silently along the pale ribbon of road alongside the phosphorescent sea, through the fragrant undergrowth and past brightly lighted Chinese homes with men, women and children clustering in them like bees on a honeycomb. She was a big woman, very agreeable. I have forgotten her name as she no doubt has forgotten me. It was a good thing I could not foresee the agony and indignity Hong Kong was going to suffer during the late war. Considering all the nonsense that is talked nowadays about British Imperialism I am glad that I cannot now foresee the future of that gallant and enchanting island.

Owing to a complete lack of information about Indo-China in Tokio and Shanghai, I had been obliged to rely upon Sir C. Clementi's kindness for such arrangements as were necessary for the next stage in my journey. My idea had been to go direct to Saigon, to make arrangements there for a few days' shooting somewhere in the surrounding country and then to cross the peninsula to Bangkok by road in time to catch the *Khyber* at Penang. On arrival in Hong Kong, however, I was told that no means existed of getting directly to Saigon in the time at my disposal, but that a passage had been booked in the French S.S. *Tong-King* due to leave Hong Kong for Haiphong on the next day, September 17th. Haiphong lay in the extreme north of French Indo-China and was connected with Saigon by eighteen hundred and sixty-two kilometres of motor road, partially duplicated by two sections of railway, two hundred and twenty kilometres and one hundred and ninety-six kilometres, respectively, in length. It might well have been that the expense and difficulty of travelling by this route would be considerable but no time for enquiries under this head was available, the S.S. *Tong-King* was sailing in twenty hours' time and I was obliged to make up my mind at once whether to trust to fortune and the French authorities to facilitate my journey between Haiphong and Saigon or to abandon my projects altogether. I took a chance on getting into trouble with the Foreign Office for being too long on the road home and left Hong Kong on the evening of September 17th.

Sunday, September 18th, was a day of strong sun and northerly wind, and most of it was spent in the Hainan Straits. The navigation of this channel is difficult and the scenery un-exhilarating. About nine o'clock in the morning of September 19th we entered the estuary of the Red River and at about half-past ten o'clock tied up to the quay at Haiphong, where I was welcomed as a local celebrity by the French authorities. The Red River is properly so-called for it is as red as a new red brick. Where it meets the sea low mud banks covered with vividly green scrub form a network of channels and lagoons in which Tong-Kingese and pelicans live an unlaborious life, fishing in the warm and ruddy water. The road from Haiphong to Hanoi stretches for a hundred and fifty flat kilometres over the cultivated section of the delta through which we now drove. So far as the eye can see on both sides of the road the richest rice land in the world is clothed with a green so vivid as hardly to be imagined or remembered. Two abundant and unfailing crops a year support as many as two thousand inhabitants to the square mile, living in villages surrounded by tall bamboo groves which have developed out of the stockades erected in the past against Chinese pirates. The railway to Yunnan Fu runs alongside the road and beyond the delta stand the hills.

There is no consistency about the way human beings look at mountains ; some are feared and avoided, some visited and worshipped, some regarded with horror or veneration by different communities at the same time or by the same community at different times. I could not know, of course, how the Tong-Kingese now making their way back along the dusty road after the day's work felt about these mountains of theirs, but to me at any rate their beauty is memorable and seemed at the time full of assurance of good things. Since the intervening country was quite flat and the sun now dropping behind them, they were not much more than a pattern of uniform opal cut out against the sky, from which, beyond the steaming land, they seemed to be suspended. Seen like this, they gave a tender grace even to the hard and muddy labour of the rice fields.

The night of September 19th was spent at the *Résidence Supérieure* at Hanoi and the preceding afternoon and evening in an inspection of the town and its environs. Although the French colonial style of architecture owes nothing to native art—the governing authorities having laid out their boulevards and mansions in the style of Cannes or Nice—Hanoi was neither inelegant nor pretentious. On the contrary, the yellow stucco façades, the shaded streets and a general look of cleanliness and good order combined with an appearance of prosperity in the suburbs and of fertility in the surrounding country to make it an agreeable place. The inhabitants of Tong-King, Annam and Cochin China are distinguished from each other by language and history but no sudden differences are to be seen between them, so that the casual visitor would not easily discover by the use of his eyes where one country ended and another began. The appearance of the Indo-Chinese is known to most people who have lived under French jurisdiction where soldiers or policemen recruited from the Union are generally to be found, and familiarity with Annamite troops in Peking had led me to think that the Indo-Chinese possessed more beauty and at least as much courage as any other yellow race. I soon found, however, that the native regiments which I had remembered had consisted of carefully selected peasants who had responded generously to the strong diet provided by the French military authorities. The average native of the peninsula and particularly the average town-dweller is small and mean looking and betrays in face and manner that inferiority which had enabled the Chinese for long to lay the coastal districts of the peninsula under tribute. The people of Indo-China—excluding Cambodia—resemble the Tibetans rather than the inhabitants of the Liang Kwang or Hainan ; but they are smaller in stature, the eyes are nearer together and the bridge of the nose is often sunk in a way which suggests, and often rightly suggests, the possession of a certain cunning and disingenuous obstinacy. The inhabitants of Tong-King, Annam and Cochin China are equally at home on land or in the coastal water. They are cleaner in person and habit than the Chinese. The women do not bind their feet, and do most of the hard work in the rice fields. The men plough and the children mind the stock at grass. Houses are built of bamboo and palm wattle rather than of stone or clay ; they stand upon the ground except where fisherfolk have built on piles as the Cambodians and Siamese do. Their diet is primarily rice and fish. Ancestor worship is universal and from it spring reckless procreation and an underfed population.

The young women of Tong-King are dressed in a plain gown of russet cloth, homespun and home-dyed, worn over a short skirt of white or black. Eyes, jaded by the unchanging blue cloth of China, find relief in the harmony of this rich brown with the green rice fields, and the contrast with China is accentuated by the more graceful figure which this uniform covers rather than conceals. The Tong-Kingese girls are carriers from childhood and on every road a file of six or more will always be in sight half running and half walking with short steps steadily beneath the balanced carrying-pole, one arm raised to steady it and the other swinging and half crooked. Continual exercise of this kind has made their bare calves and ankles tough and supple and seems to have developed neck and shoulders so that their breasts are braced up and carried high and firm until age or much use have pulled them down. Many, however, make themselves repulsive by chewing what is called betel nut, but is in fact an areca nut wrapped up in a leaf of the betel vine on which shell lime has been smeared. Whether betel-nut does, as the classics affirm, prevent the accumulation of uric acid, enrich the blood, check the secretion of milk or cure the phlegm is uncertain, but what is beyond doubt is the effect on the face of the addict. The teeth seem to turn black and project monstrously, the lips assume the colour of blood and the whole mouth hangs square and open so that the process as well as the results of mastication are exposed.

On Tuesday, September 20th, I arrived in Vinh, two hundred and fifty kilometres to the south, and received here a more definite impression of French colonial administration that had been possible in Hanoi. It had been to some extent modelled, I was told, on the Indian Civil Service, and throughout French Indo-China and irrespective of the technical difference between the position of the French authorities in its various parts, the French civil servant was the father and mother, the administrator, the tax collector and the judge of the people committed to his charge. The district officers carried out their duties so far as I could judge with firmness, sympathy and rectitude. All the French officials, except one, with whom I came in contact showed signs of what is sometimes called Nordic rather than of Alpine blood. A considerable proportion of them came from Gascony, Provence and the south of France. The round-headed black-haired Frenchmen to be seen in every Paris bank and stockbroker's office were wholly absent. Owing to the difficulty of learning the native languages an officer would probably have been required to spend the whole of his service career in the country to which he was first appointed ; and of all those of whom I made enquiry, there was not one who wished for transfer to some other part of the peninsula, who did not say that he would choose the same career if he had to live life over again, did not express interest in his work and his people and did not do his solid eight or ten hours of work a day.

The government of Tong-King, Annam and Cochin China had so far presented no serious difficulties. Economic development had been universal and rapid—perhaps too rapid. The Union balanced its own budget and made no claims on French Government funds. The administration was securely based on the road system and the colonial police. These were so efficient that brigandage had ceased altogether to exist and no demonstration of force was ever required. An expanding educational system was producing an excessive number of restless, ambitious and irresponsible students for whom no employment could be found, and these were too apt to employ their leisure in political agitation and intrigue. The great majority of the population, however, had not forgotten the years of subordination to the Chinese ; valued the relative comfort, riches and security enjoyed under French rule, and were, according to my hosts, reluctant to exchange their present advantages for the speculative and illusory glories of complete independence.

These impressions are written down here just as I recorded them at the time, and look rather silly in the light of the so-called war of independence which has been going on for five years in French Indo-China. However, I think they represent

the truth as it was in 1927 and I can assure the reader that
they are free from any pro-French bias for I have always
been disposed to be critical of the French because they are
more civilized than the English or the Irish.

Doubts about the means by which I should reach Saigon
were to some extent removed by the assurances which I received in Hanoi that the *Résidents* along my route would put
motor transport at my disposal ; and this in fact they did. I
was, however, never quite free from fear that the further I
got from Hanoi the less help I should get ; and so, at the end
of each of the ensuing eight days, I projected myself into the
arms of a French official sweating, hungry, and exhausted
but determined to purchase with an evening's conversation
entertainment for the night and transport for the ensuing day.
This technique was only partially successful at Vinh where
the *Résident* was unable to take me into his own house, his
wife having been delivered of a son on the previous day.
Accordingly, after dining with him and his staff, I went
early to bed in the local hotel in some fear that a sultry night
would have turned to bad weather before dawn. These fears
were justified, and when I got up at three o'clock the next
day it was to find that a tornado was going on and had already
put all electric light out of action. I had difficulty in the
pitch darkness and heavy wind in attracting the attention of
the night watchman, but eventually candles were produced
and shutters put up, and at four o'clock I set forth for Hué
in the *Résident's* car. Telegraph wires and branches bestrewed
the main road but did not prevent us from getting through
the rather mountainous country round Vinh at about 70 m.p.h.
without running over anything more important than two dogs
and some hens. By ten o'clock in the morning we had cleared
the edge of the storm and reached Dong Hoi where lunch
was eaten. By four-thirty I was at Hué having tea with the
Résident Supérieur of Annam. Four rivers had been crossed
en route by ferries, the largest of which was about a quarter
of a mile in width. The distance from Vinh to Hué is
three hundred kilometres.

The latter part of this drive had afforded a view of many

kinds of attractive scenery. The mountains of Annam stood
in range upon range on the right hand, and to the east the
sea constantly came in sight. The recent passage of a storm
had set up a heavy swell, and upon many lonely bays and
headlands the long Pacific rollers broke with incomparable
dignity upon the heat and silence of the day. Between the
mountains and the sea all such land as was not under water
or cultivation was covered with jungle and full of many strange
and beautiful birds and flowers which time did not allow me
to watch or examine with proper attention. Had I possessed
a good memory or a travelling library I should now be able
to exasperate my readers with a formidable list of the generic
and specific names of exotic plants but, as it is, I can only
ask them to recall the surprise of delight with which they came
for the first time upon, say, *Orobanche* in a Dorsetshire spinney,
or *Helleborine* in a Berkshire beechwood, and to imagine the
excitement with which I noticed innumerable unfamiliar
shrubs, creepers, meadow plants and more particularly water-
flowers : blue water hyacinth ; pink and white lotuses ; a
pink water-lily with a yellow heart similar in shape to, but
smaller than *Victoria Regia*, a carmine variation of the same
species ; two white water-lilies one half and one quarter respectively of the size of those just described, and a yellow
Villarsia smaller but in every other respect like that found on
the middle Thames. These are the buttercups and daisies of
the ricelands.

Hué, the capital of Annam, was a town of considerable
size and distinction, and headquarters of the native government which still administered most public services (exclusive
of foreign affairs and defence) subject to the advice of the
French authorities. It possessed a palace situated in a walled
and moated fortress several square kilometres in extent, and
it was revered as the burial place of former emperors whose
tombs were scrupulously repaired and respected. These monu-
ments to a past independence are built in the Chinese style, but
without the taste shown by the craftsmen of Peking in interior
and exterior decoration. Nevertheless, the old city was dignified and well cared for, and the more modern parts of it

made a favourable impression. The French take a serious aesthetic interest in the lay-out and embellishment of their colonial towns, and Hué, like all other cities in the Union, bore witness in one way or another to this Gallic sense of propriety and grace. As I drove through the streets to the *Résidence Supérieure* I thought how surprising it was that all this should exist without my ever having even heard the name of Hué before. From my conception of the world Hué had been left entirely out of account ; and if Hué, was it not probable that a hundred other cities in other parts of the world had also been overlooked ? And countries too perhaps, and rulers and entire races—whole worlds of thought and feeling and tradition and beliefs ? These reflections caused my thoughts to fly back again as they so constantly did to our desks and telephones in the Foreign Office, and to the little procession of black-hatted officials crossing the Horse Guards Parade for luncheon. How small were the windows from which we officials in the Foreign Office had looked out at the world, how limited the knowledge which dictated the minutes which we ceaselessly turned out ! It was a terrifying thought that one of my friends in the Office, chewing the end of his pen in Room 92, might even now be drafting a memorandum about some remote country, which would eventually affect the lives of populations of which he had no direct knowledge whatever. I seemed to see these minutes and memoranda running, like the cables that carried them, to the far corners of the world and arriving clothed with the authority of the Government before the dismayed eyes of Ministers and Consuls. How often had not telegrams arrived in Peking which seemed to us to show insufficient acquaintance with the local situation ! How unfruitful our efforts to explain this to the Foreign Office had often seemed ! Here in Hué I resolved afresh to remember the extent of my own ignorance when I should have returned to London.

The *Résident* at Hué kindly substituted his Delage for the Hotchkiss which had brought me from Vinh and on September 22nd I started for Dalat, a highland resort some way from the coast, where I hoped to shoot a tiger or a gaur. I made a later start than usual for I had gone short of sleep for two nights, was to go short for two more, and had already found the fatigues of continuous motoring under a tropical sun to be severe. After clearing the outskirts of Hué, the main road, which is in fact the old Chinese *route Mandarinaire*, drops gently in and out and down and round a tangle of small hills, crosses a ferry at Ha Trung and then rises steeply to the Col des Nuages which forms the boundary between the provinces of Quang Nam and Thua Thien. Between this and Quang Ngai the mountains abut upon the sea at numerous points and are clothed throughout with larger trees and a more luxuriant undergrowth. Since the district was mountainous there were few people on the road, and since the sun was not long up, the birds were tame and still afield. The commonest *accipiter* resembled the white-headed eagle of North America. Kites, falcons, buzzards and hawks were conspicuous by their absence. A common and attractive bird was like the magpie in shape and the blackbird in habits, had back and wing coverlets the colour of burnished copper and was elsewhere black. The common bee eater, always associated for me with the road from Resht and Tehran, was everywhere to be seen in open country. Besides these I noticed a blackbird with a kite's tail, kingfishers with cinnamon head and breast and the ubiquitous blue jay. Butterflies of all kinds were everywhere.

I lunched at Quang Ngai in a clean and comfortable hotel where the landlady was a Spaniard by birth, forty years old, who had travelled extensively. We got into conversation and she discoursed to me from personal experience on the Indo-China peninsula, Siam and the Malay States. Having discovered that she was also familiar with the Polynesian Archipelago, Australia and New Zealand, we turned to Japan and China where all the eighteen provinces were known to her. She had also visited Chita, Omsk, Kazan and other towns lying along the Siberian railway and had been not only to Persia and Arabia but to the Khanates of Bokhara, Khiva and Merv. Russia proper and all the countries of Europe were much more familiar to her than to me. Unlike me, she had also travelled throughout Africa and South America, and on the North American continent was equally at home in New Orleans, New England, St. Louis, Hollywood, Quebec, Ottawa and Vancouver. Surprised to find so much experience collected in so remote a place, I tried to puzzle her by reference to England and Scotland, but here again her encyclopaedic knowledge was not at fault ; she had visited Brighton and Luton and Bath and Rugby and Carlisle and Fort William, and in London could have found her way without help from the Elephant to the Swan and Pyramids. I hardly know whether to be glad or sorry that some impulse prevented me from enquiring for what purpose so much travel had been undertaken or why such a wandering life should have come at last to rest at Quang Ngai. Here was just one more subject of speculation to add to all the others. Refusal to indulge my curiosity was a symbolic act—a kind of acceptance of the limitations of knowledge and tribute to life's mysteries.

To get the best out of the sort of journey on which I was engaged it is a good thing to get up at about four o'clock in the morning and take only a very light breakfast. If milk is available, so much the better ; but a cup of raw tea or coffee and a crust to chew is quite enough. In this way one can get on the way well before the sun is up and put past the greater part of the day's road before sitting down to a regular meal at, say, eleven o'clock. After resting, one should try to reach the place where one intends to sleep not later than four ; then drink but not eat, and at six or half-past six o'clock sit down to eat as much as one wants. This régime is calculated to keep the traveller in good health and spirits. The afternoon hours of great heat will be trying, but compensated by the imagination's activity during the first two or three hours on the road to which an empty stomach contributes, and by an abnormal acuity of perception to which discipline of the body is essential.

With these ideas as usual in mind, I got up the next morning at half-past three o'clock and breakfasted off a piece of bread and black coffee after passing the night in a very dirty inn at Qui Nhon. After crossing the Col de Cumong we reached the big ferry at Tuy Hoa at eight o'clock, contoured the mountains at about five hundred feet above sea level as far as Ninh Hoa, then dropped to sea level again and passed through sandy country where the heat and glare were almost intolerable. I stopped at Nhia Trang for lunch and reached Phan Rang about three o'clock with another hundred and fifty kilometres still to do. Here I parted for good with the people, vegetation and scenery of Tong-King and Annam after completing the fifteen hundred kilometres from Hanoi. From Phan Rang through Krongpha to Bellevue the road strikes up, into the highlands among which Dalat lies, and at Dalat I put up for the night in an expensive and pretentious hotel. It had been a day of contrasts. The morning had been very quiet and the sheltered valleys reaching down to the Pacific shore had been filled with white mist. Sky, sea and sand had been all white and I had picked what looked like white passion flowers on the beach where jungle growths had given place to coconut palms, holding their plumed heads breathless in the morning air. This serene and comforting landscape had been succeeded in the afternoon, as we turned uphill and inland, by views over the tops of immense trees stretching in every direction as far as the eye could see. At other times I had looked down onto other forests such as the Ardennes, for instance, and the Black Forest, and from a point near the head of the Mameson Pass on the Arcadian beauty of the Caucasus ; and, of course, I had known every mood of oak and ash and beech and thorn, and was very familiar, as the reader already knows, with Oxfordshire elms meditating upon their cattle and their harvests and the returning rooks. But the prospect which now met my eyes had nothing at all in common with these ; there was an arrogance and aloofness about these monstrous and majestic trees likely to discourage anyone sensitive to the unfriendly influences of nature. This inhospitable forest seemed to exclude all affinity with the labour or imagination of men, brooding only upon its own sinister and purposeless regeneration. I can see no reason why Ninh Hoa should have consoled and Bellevue have dismayed a person like me to whom both were new and dissociated from any earlier experiences. Perhaps such contrasts take their origin only in our own dispositions; but I do not think so. Whatever the reason, this kind of assault which nature makes upon our moods adds much to the interest of a journey in a new country and serves to keep our memories of things seen only once and long ago for ever green.

At Dalat I called upon the *Résident* and M. Millet, the local game warden, and we made preliminary arrangements for passing the nights of September 26th and 27th under canvas somewhere in the neighbourhood of Djiring, and for spending those two days in search of a *gaur*. M. Millet discouraged any attempt to shoot a tiger. At Dalat live bait is not used for this purpose. The tiger's sense of smell is so poor that a buffalo some ten days dead is found to be much more attractive to the quarry. When the stench is sufficiently strong and the tiger has begun to feed, the hunter conceals himself behind a bush and at the appropriate moment fires a charge of number four shot from a twelve-bore gun into the animal's ribs; but this, M. Millet explained, was murder not sport and, anyhow, the time at our disposal was not enough to make the prospect of success at all good. Hunting the *gaur* on the other hand was sport in the best sense of the word—sport for the *gaur* as well as for the hunter. The local variety of the species in question (*Bos gaurus*) must be the largest member of the buffalo family for of the heads displayed in M. Millet's house one belonged, I was told, to an animal that had stood twenty-one hands at the withers. These beasts must be walked up with the assistance of native trackers —the Moï—and they do not, like nearly all other game, move away at the first scent of danger, but, on the contrary, stalk and attack the hunter with skill and courage. Consequently, as M. Millet said, " *il faut être très prudent* ".

On returning to the hotel I began to make further enquiries about the journey which was to bring me to Penang on October 7th, and found that it was much less easy to make the connection that I had supposed; indeed, the more information I collected the more probable it seemed that unless I left Dalat almost immediately I should either have to abandon my visit to Angkor or risk losing the *Khyber*. I was determined to do neither and was consequently obliged to cancel the arrangements made with M. Millet and to prepare to leave Dalat on the following day, September 25th. This decision was forced upon me by events but, truth to tell, my disappointment was mixed with relief. On the one hand, never having consciously stood in danger of my life, I was anxious to know how in such circumstances I should behave. There was something unfair about having all my life killed large numbers of small and harmless animals with great enjoyment : the balance might be redressed were I now to offer the animal kingdom an opportunity of taking its revenge, and to find that I did not shoot any worse when my life was at stake than otherwise. On the other hand, to find myself separated by only a few hours from an attack upon a cunning and vindictive animal in wholly new country in company with a stranger, and with a weapon I had not previously used, was a disturbing prospect. Perhaps it is as well that I have no buffalo's head to hang in the hall at Rockfleet. It might have created the illusion that I am not easily frightened.

CHAPTER 14

ANGKOR WAT

BY September 25th I was in Saigon and on the afternoon of the following day I was on the road to Cambodia, having no reason to think that an important point in my journey was at hand ; yet so it proved to be. The road on which we were travelling was carried at this point on a causeway between waste lands inundated during the autumn months by the heavy rains which fall at this season on the eastern side of the watershed between Siam and Annam, and we had passed the ferry at Sang Bang and were about to cross a second river at Soai Reang when I observed patches of brilliant and unexpected colours on the road about half a kilometre in front of us. As we rapidly approached them, I saw that the objects of my curiosity were men and women dressed in tunics and *sampots* of brightly dyed cloth : saffron and purple, scarlet and indigo, orange and emerald green. These people were in other respects besides the brilliance and neatness of their clothing wholly unlike the inhabitants of Tong-King, Annam or Cochin China. They were more tall and shapely and betrayed no trace of Mongolian blood ; their bodies, it is true, were hairless but their skin was brown not yellow and their features marked them as members of a different race. Among the first groups to pass me was a funeral procession. The emblems of solicitude and remembrance were not the garish and laughable paper models of Peking. The ritual and habiliments of the mourners showed a sense of propriety in marked contrast to the tawdry callousness of a Chinese ceremony. A tune which caught my ear was sung in a familiar mode and as the eyes of these unfamiliar folk were lifted to mine, our looks met, as it seemed to me, in a kind of embrace, and I found running through my head the words " My own people. I am among my own people."

This was my first meeting with the Cambodians. Now so great had been my ignorance of this part of the world that I had supposed the Cambodians to be sprung from the same stock as other Indo-Chinese peoples ; but, in fact, I had actually crossed one of the most important of ethnological frontiers without realizing that I had parted for good from the Mongoloid peoples amidst which the preceding eighteen months had been spent. When I later described the singular experience I have just related to the representatives of the *École de France* at Angkor, they assured me that the phrase that had run in my head was not so fanciful as might be supposed, for they themselves described the Cambodians as Indo-Polynesians and asserted that they were affiliated to the same stock as ourselves. The Cambodians were perhaps of the whole Indo-European family the branch most remotely connected with my own, yet the recognition of our kinship had imposed itself upon me with unmistakable force. I now first fully realized across how great a gulf communication between ourselves and the Chinese must be carried on.

The Cambodians never build houses of stone or brick like the Chinese or of clay like the Malays. Their dwellings are invariably made, as the Annamites make them, of bamboo and palm leaf, and always raised on stilts. Their canoes, some eight spans in breadth, are cut out of tree-trunks and not built up like a sampan. They are a cheerful and easy-going people, working no more than they need, responsive to good treatment at the hands of their employers or rulers and too simple-minded to succeed in commerce which is entirely in foreign hands. Their homes seemed no cleaner than they should be, but were not unduly dirty. The people have a passion for washing their persons and their clothes ; and wherever the water is breast high these operations are carried on by both sexes at the same time with perfect propriety. The women wear a cloth tightly bound under their armpits and over their shapely breasts. Both men and women are covered below the waist with what the French call a *sampot*— a plain web hardly as broad but longer than a sarong which is wrapped round the waist and drawn up between the thighs so as to look like knee breeches. They are fond of bright colours and can invent and carry out, indeed seem unable to restrain themselves from continually inventing and carrying out in silver, silk, wood or stone, decorative designs of astonishing grace and variety.

When I arrived at Pnom Penh, where there are first-rate hotels, it was already too late to get a night's lodging from the *Résident Supérieur* ; but on the following morning when I explained to him my wish to travel overland from Angkor to Bangkok without avoidable waste of time he at once made all the necessary arrangements with the *Résidents* at Angkor and Battambang. My difficulties were briefly as follows : The motor road terminated at Angkor. In the dry season the traveller could continue along a sand track through Sisophon for some two hundred kilometres till he arrived at Arroya in Siam, where the Siamese railway begins. The rainy season, however, which has just begun on the east coast of the peninsula, was approaching its end in the gulf of Siam and on the Siamese frontier, with the result that the Sisophon route was quite impracticable. There was a hard road— just completed—from Battambang, which lies about a hundred kilometres WSW. from Angkor, to a point on the frontier only eleven kilometres from Arroya ; but Battambang was unconnected by any road at all with Angkor and unless I could somehow cover the ground between the two, I should have been obliged at a great waste of time and money to return from Angkor to Pnom Penh and there hire motorcars to take me three hundred kilometres to Battambang and a further one hundred and fifty kilometres to the frontier. The *Résident* settled these difficulties for me by putting at my disposal a small government launch, the *Sisophon*, which was to meet me at the head of the great lake, Tonlé Sap, and convey me through channels navigable at this time of the year to Battambang, whence a government car would take me to the frontier whenever I wished.

The omnibus on which I was to continue my journey started at six o'clock the next morning and our road ran alongside the west bank of the Mekong—the tenth largest river in the world. The weather was fair and the waters reflected the pale light of dawn. A canoe passed beside us paddled by eight young men in the saffron gowns worn by priests. There was nothing remarkable about all this, but I remember very well that I then experienced one of those moments of what, for lack of a better word, I will call trans-lumination. Such experiences, apparently fortuitous, light up a normally dark and untenanted cave in the very middle of our labyrinthine consciousness. They are unself-regarding and incommunicable, distinguished from all the rest of life in that the perception of something appears momentarily to be of overwhelming significance ; though what it signifies is un-known and—as it feels—unknowable. This thing had hap-pened to me among other occasions when as a child I was leaning on the bridge over the Thames at Clifton Hampden looking at some Aylesbury ducks ; and it happened one day in the year 1914 when I was walking back from luncheon to the Foreign Office across Horse Guards Parade ; and it was to happen to me again on a drive down the road to Burgos which I shall describe in Chapter 18. It was this thing which happened to me as I watched a canoe load of priests or novitiates in their yellow gowns paddling down the Mekong. If the Spaniards had not appropriated the words to the bull-ring I should have called it a " moment of truth " ; but what the truth was or is I cannot say.

The bus went on and on. At the thirtieth kilometre from Pnom Penh I saw a woodpecker bigger than a yaffle and coloured like a ruddy sheldrake ; at the fiftieth, monkeys appeared in large numbers crashing through the branches ; and at the eightieth, parakeets rose by twenties and fifties from the bushes on each side of the road. At five o'clock in the evening I reached the resthouse at Siem Reap where visitors sleep who come to see the great temple of Angkor Wat, and as I ate my supper and watched the *geckos* catching flies on the ceiling, I was very much pleased to have brought my pilgrimage to a successful conclusion. One thing that has made pilgrimages of all descriptions attractive all through the centuries to people of various races and religions is that, apart from the benefits to be received, a pilgrimage as a rule requires the pilgrim to show a good deal of resolution and ingenuity and self-discipline in order to reach his goal. This makes the journey and its completion more stirring than mere vagabondage. I had had to use much exertion and ingenuity in order to get to Angkor and this enhanced the satisfaction of safe arrival and the pleasurable anticipation of what I was going to see on the following day.

The golden age of the Cambodians or Khmer, a people of reputed Indian origin, covered the ninth, tenth, eleventh and twelfth centuries of the Christian Era. This period witnessed the foundation and aggrandizement of the realm ; the thirteenth century saw successive invasions and the severance of Cambodia from the parent India ; and the last six centuries have been occupied with its decay. During the time of their greatest prosperity the reigning dynasty had covered the central parts of the kingdom—extending as it then did to the mouth of the Mekong in the east, to Malacca in the south, and well beyond the present borders of Siam and the Laos country to the west and north—with numerous palaces and temples of great size connected with each other by a network of roads and bridges. Many of these had by 1927 been discovered, and conservancy work was in progress on them, but none exceed in magnificence or had received more care and study than the great temple of Angkor Wat to which the account which follows is confined. The construction of this edifice is attributed to Souryavmarne II, who reigned from the year 1112 to the year 1145. Like all the rest of his family he was a Brahman, and though traces of Sanscrit Buddhism are found as early as the sixth century and never disappeared from Cambodia, the worship of Siva preponderated there, and it was to this divinity that the temple in question was apparently dedicated.

Angkor Wat is, in a manner of speaking, the biggest building in the world. The following figures will give a rough idea of its dimensions : perimeter about two-and-a-half miles ; width of exterior moat, faced throughout with dressed stone, two hundred and six yards ; perimeter of inner cloisters,

about one-and-a-half miles (the buildings between the inner
cloisters and the sanctuary have disappeared) ; perimeter of
the sanctuary or central structure, about eight hundred and
fifty yards ; height of central tower, two hundred and eleven
feet.   The sanctuary consists of three superimposed concentric
squarish blocks of solid masonry diminishing in size and each
raised about twenty or thirty feet above the one below.   The
outer walls and each storey of the sanctuary comprise intercon-
nected cloisters, courts, tanks, staircases, chambers, pavilions,
chapels, gates and towers geometrically integrated into one single
immense architectural unit.   The builders did not know how
to support the thrust of a vault with a result that no interior
spaces are larger than can be roofed by oversailing courses
of stone.   Consequently, whereas St. Paul's Cathedral is a
hollow structure inside which people move about and worship,
Angkor is a solid lump of about six million tons of stone (en-
crusted with small rooms) on the exterior surface of which
people move and worship.   This difference imposed aesthetic
problems on the builders with which we nowadays have
nothing to do, and the principal interest of Angkor Wat lies
in the extraordinary skill with which these problems have
been met.   I will give a single example of their ingenuity.
In St. Paul's Cathedral reverence in the worshippers is induced by the proportions and groupings of internal architectural features which focus eyes and mind upon altar and
crucifix.   In Angkor Wat reverence is among other things
induced by building the staircases which lead storey by storey
to the central shrine at angles first of 45° and finally of 66°.
The result is extraordinarily successful.   A second elementary
bit of building technique undiscovered as yet by the Khmer
was the bonding of stones by alternating headers and stretchers.
The Angkor builders placed their immense blocks more or less
one on top of the other with the result that dividing lines
often ran vertically in a straight line for many courses.   They
tried to overcome this weakness by shaping each block of
stone to fit very tightly against its neighbour, and to this end
each stone—weighing, say a ton—was, so I was told by the
French custodians, hung in a cradle from a sheerlegs and rubbed

BRIDGEND

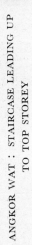

ANGKOR WAT : STAIRCASE LEADING UP
TO TOP STOREY

to and fro till abrasion had produced a tight fit. No wonder the temple was centuries in building! A large proportion of the entire edifice is covered with an astonishing wealth of bas-reliefs depicting every aspect of the life of Cambodians and their gods, set off with geometrical and naturalistic designs of great beauty and sophistication. An almost unrivalled elaboration of intricate patterns is still the outstanding character-istic of Cambodian art today and I know of no other people than they who have succeeded in using such profuse decoration without prejudice to the general appearance of their buildings.

Having read this fragmentary and dry-as-dust description of Angkor Wat, some intending sightseers may ask themselves whether the place really justifies the expense and bother of getting there and the fuss that others have made about it. I say it does, or anyhow, that it did in my case. A person like myself, brought up in the Thame Valley, and familiar from childhood with Magdalen and Salisbury and Chartres must not expect to find at Angkor anything reflecting in the re-motest degree the aspirations which began in Bethlehem and ended at Bethany because temples are not built with hands alone, and Our Lord Jesus Christ was not at all like Siva, nor the jungle like our meadows and gardens, or even the sand and sun of Palestine. But a large part of the world is covered with the intolerable exuberance of the jungle and of the growth and destruction over which Siva presides; and about all this it is surely proper to be curious. I had been curious about it, and by going to Angkor I had now, I thought, discovered something—a very little—about it. I had been lucky; it was not the tourist season and I had been alone. Climbing every evening to the very highest terrace of the temple, I had watched the sun withdraw its fervour from the tragic splendour and elegance of the purple pinnacles and walls, yielding the temple precincts to innumerable bats; and I had been filled with wonder not far removed from worship.

I left Angkor at six o'clock in the morning of September 30th in the *Résident's* motor-car and, after passing through Siem Reap and along the picturesque banks of the river on which it stands, joined the launch which had been put at my disposal by M. le Fol at the head of the great lake some forty kilometres distant. A comfortable day was spent in crossing the headwaters of the lake and following the winding course of a stream as far as Battambang. For some twenty kilometres below that town its banks are thickly populated, and the yellow waters afford to the peasants and fishermen and to their children every opportunity to indulge their passion for bathing. The life of the river, as of the town which stands upon it, seemed full of gaiety and colour. At Battambang I put up with the *Résident*, who despatched me at about four o'clock in the morning of October 1st in his Hotchkiss to the Siamese frontier. Before the sun was up we had killed two cats and eleven owls and collided with one wild boar in country consisting for the most part of moor and grassland. By six o'clock I had reached the frontier where the Siamese Government had obligingly provided a pony, two Ford trucks and a team of coolies to convey myself and my hand bags across eleven kilometres of boggy track along which the Siamese railway has not yet been carried. A Hungarian innkeeper at Arroya, the railhead, gave me a breakfast of porridge and fried eggs. At half-past eight o'clock we left the station and at about six o'clock in the evening reached the Legation at Bangkok. Here I was entertained for three days, and called on the Emperor's sacred white elephant, visited His Majesty's snake-pits and on October 5th left in the mail train which carried passengers three times a week in comfort to Penang.

By October 9th the *Khyber* was among the uneasy waves of a south-west monsoon which tossed, like jostling steers, the sunlight from their streaming horns. Presently, for three days and nights in the Arabian Sea no breath of wind at all disturbed the surface of a sea moved only, as the ship crushed the water from her hollow bed, by the undulations of the bow-waves despatched like the humped backs of buffalo to march in echelon across the watery plain. By October 30th I was on the terrace at Denton where the flycatchers nest in the ivy and the blackcaps in the syringa. It had been a very wet summer and there would be little fruit the following year.

Since for nine weeks I had been more at liberty to think,

speak and act as pleased myself than had been the case for many years, and since I had been virtually alone, I had had a reason and plenty of time to think about freedom and solitude. In adolescence many of us hope to escape from solitude into the companionship of other people ; but in maturity we learn that there is no escape, and that solitude is a quality of our own nature with which we must come to terms. A solitary journey had done a good deal for my education in this respect. Freedom, like intimacy, is early an object of passionate desire, and frequently pursued onto wrong ground. I had also now gone some way towards learning that true freedom is not to be found in any accident or adjustment of the circumstances of life, but only in a willing acceptance of the conditions under which life is carried on. Although I did not know it yet I was very soon to stand desperately in need of whatever fortitude such reflections give.

CHAPTER 15

THE FRANCS CASE

BY the time I got back to England my mother was dead. I found that my wife had had an operation for appendicitis and that Patrick was still suffering from the effects of pneumonia and dysentery. Bridgend was still in the hands of tenants, and of course, we were short of money. These preoccupations were, however, soon to be overshadowed by what became known as the " Francs Case ", which created a deal of political excitement at the time. Not only was I closely involved in it, but it presented certain features of public interest on which at this distance of time I may properly comment.

Broadly speaking, the facts were as follows :—an action came before the High Court for the recovery of a debt incurred to a firm of exchange brokers by a lady who had used them extensively over a period of years for the purchase and sale of futures in French francs, which were at that time a speculative market. It emerged in the course of these judicial proceedings that she had been closely associated in her dealings with one particular member of the Foreign Office ; and also that some other members of the Foreign Office and Diplomatic Service had, either independently or in consultation with the defendant, speculated in francs. Of these I had been one, although I should add that my transactions had taken place between 1922 and 1925 and that we were now in the year 1928. The political world was much agitated by these revelations, supposing both that public servants had made improper use of their official position for private gain, and that their speculation in francs might disturb relations between His Majesty's Government and the French Government. The Cabinet took the view that a *prima facie* case of misbehaviour by civil servants existed and appointed a Board of Enquiry to go into the whole matter. The Board was composed of the Permanent Secretary to the Treasury, Sir Warren Fisher, Sir Malcolm Ramsay, the

Comptroller and Auditor-General and the Treasury Solicitor, Sir Maurice Gwyer, all now dead. Its findings were laid before Parliament and accepted by Mr. Baldwin, the Prime Minister, Mr. Churchill, the Chancellor of the Exchequer and Sir Austen Chamberlain, the Foreign Secretary. The Board found that no one " had used or endeavoured to use any official information for the purpose of their transactions ", but that three members of the Office " acted in a manner incon-sistent with their obligations as civil servants ". To these, Ministers accordingly dealt out punishment ; and of these, again, I was one.

While civil proceedings were in progress in the High Court and before the Board of Enquiry was set up, I was warned privately by one of the other members of the service who had bought and sold francs that our operations were likely shortly to attract a great deal of official and public attention ; but, though many people have since expressed surprise at the fact, I was not uneasy about my own position. Since the dismay which my punishment later caused me is very material to the results of the whole business on my own interior life, I must briefly indicate the reason why I was not at first uneasy, begging the reader, however, to remember throughout this chapter that I have no intention of arguing the " Francs Case " afresh or of justifying anything which at the time I thought or said or did ; my object being only to tell a story truly.

In the first place all my transactions had taken place four to five years previously ; secondly, more than one senior member of the Foreign Office had long been aware of the facts —some had been aware of them at the time they were actually taking place—but nothing like a warning or remonstrance had ever been addressed to me or to any of the other parties concerned ; thirdly, my transactions had been few and for relatively small amounts. Like many people with only a few hundred pounds to invest I had tried to increase my capital by Stock Exchange dealings, and in the course of 1923–24 had bought and sold a variety of securities without much profit or loss. Additionally, I had on five or six occasions during that

period bought or sold futures in francs, which, when the transactions were closed, left me the poorer by about £100. I took
the view that, provided my official position and knowledge
were not used or rather misused, it was no concern of the
Government what I invested my money in. It was obvious,
though contrary to general belief, that official information was
useless in the exchange market ; indeed I believe the professional dealers in exchange considered the idea ludicrous that
any amateur, however politically well-informed, could foresee
the course of exchange. The difference between investment
and speculation seemed to me in 1923 to be a tenuous and
subjective one ; though after all that occurred in 1928 I saw
that I had wrongly estimated the importance attached to the
distinction by the public, and to this extent was to be blamed
for indiscretion. Previously, I had taken the line that I was
just as free to buy a share in a copper mine or indeed any
commodity and sell it if I could make a profit, as I was to buy
eight weeks' pigs in the village and sell them a fortnight later
in Guildford market if I could turn an honest penny by so
doing. What I had bought and sold in this case was a document of title to the delivery of so many francs on such and such
a day. French War Bonds were similarly promises to pay the
holder so many francs on such and such dates, and the Government itself had consistently urged us to buy them. There
did not, therefore, seem to me to be any grounds on which my
transactions could be gravely censured ; and the preliminary
rumblings of the " Francs Case " did not much disturb me.

In due course I learned that a Board of Enquiry, on which
the Foreign Office were not represented, had been set up ; that
two of my colleagues had been suspended from duty and that,
while I had not been suspended from duty and was not therefore a target for the Board's censures, the testimony of myself
and several others in the Service who had speculated in foreign
currency was to be called for. I was examined two or three
times, and learned afterwards that the " Board did not find
Mr. O'Malley a helpful or forthcoming witness " and that " the
manner as well as the matter of his evidence created an unfavourable impression. Nor did he appear to recognize that

he was, or might be, very directly interested in the outcome of the enquiry ". This very moderate language was, I think, an understatement. Without suggesting for a moment that the Board were anxious to be anything but scrupulously fair, I should hazard a guess that they were not only disturbed by my self-confidence, but felt intuitively that I was insensitive to the nicer obligations of a public servant. In the interests of historical truth, but purely in order to draw a true picture of things as they were then, I am bound to relate that the Board also made an unfavourable impression upon me. There was, so it seemed to me at the time, a note of irony, I should almost have said levity or what the Germans call *schadenfreude* in their language and manner : they seemed to me to assume the functions of prosecuting counsel, without, so far as I was aware, having any title to the position. And below the surface there was a deeper antagonism, which I cannot omit to mention if my story is to be fully intelligible, again reminding the reader that what I am describing is my state of mind in February 1928 and has nothing to do with my feelings today towards these eminent men, two of whom were later actually guests in my house and one of whom, Sir Warren Fisher, was till his death a close friend. In matters of taste I had always been only too readily disposed to think that if I did a thing it was right—almost that my doing it made it right. It was, for instance, a middle-class practice to pour milk into a cup before tea : I preferred the taste of tea when it was mixed with milk in this way : this, therefore, was the way I made my tea, and this was for me the right way to make tea, though for all I knew or cared the practice might be as socially distressing, where others were concerned, as to say " 'phone " instead of " telephone " or " pardon ? " instead of " what ? " In matters of duty and honour I felt similarly that my own instincts were the final authority. Who were these men, unconnected with the Foreign Service, to probe and pry into my personal motives and standards ? How dared they have the impertinence to appear to doubt my veracity ? I would give them all the relevant facts that concerned me, but I required them to accept my answers as final and sufficient. These feelings

were accentuated by the necessity under which I lay of keeping
my temper and by a growing apprehension, as my examination
proceeded, that for one reason or another these men might be
preparing some unpleasant surprise for me. I am far from
wishing to represent this attitude of mind as an elegant one
and I am not sure that it was not morally open to question.
What is certain is that it was from the point of view of my
own imperfectly understood interests highly prejudicial. There
were few situations in life in which such an attitude would not
have been very imprudent, and if, on this occasion my attitude
was " I am Owen O'Malley and you can take it or leave it ? "
I ought not to have been surprised that the Board—like many
other people before and since—would not only not take it, but
quite distinctly prefer to leave it. But how decisively the
Board preferred to leave it was not clear to me when I concluded my evidence ; and, unlikely as it may now seem, it is
the fact that I went back to Denton with the impression that
I had left them ruffled but without any serious grounds for
penalizing me. This impression was fortified by the fact that
even when my evidence had been completed I was not
suspended from duty as had been my two colleagues.

I heard nothing more of this affair until a fortnight or so
later when I was staying alone in Oxfordshire with my father,
now aged eighty-six. At about eleven o'clock one night the
servants were aroused by the back door bell—a most unusual
occurrence at Denton, which lies remote from railways and
high roads. I was summoned to see a Foreign Office messenger
who handed to me an official envelope. The house and garden
were plunged in their habitual deep silence, and all lights had
been put out but one oil lamp in the hall. By the light of this
I read a letter from the Under-Secretary of State for Foreign
Affairs enclosing first, a copy of the report of the Board of
Enquiry, and secondly a minute signed by Mr. Baldwin, Mr.
Churchill and Sir A. Chamberlain and containing their decision that one of my colleagues be dismissed from the Service,
one adjudged to lose three years' seniority and myself to be
permitted to resign. The report and the minute were to be
given to the Press in the course of the night.

Having thanked the messenger for the trouble to which he had been put in making his way out from Oxford at night, and expressing my regret that at so late an hour I could not direct the servants to give him any refreshment, I went into my own study to collect myself before going to my father's room to tell him what happened. When I did tell him he was very much upset, but I noticed at the time and have remembered ever since that the impact of this shocking news upon him was different from what it would have been upon a younger man. My father's brain was at eighty-six years of age still perfectly clear, but it seemed to me that he had moved so far from the strivings and passions and turbulence of middle life towards the peace and detachment which a singularly well-balanced nature and a profound sense of spiritual values had prepared for his old age, that he could accept in its true light as a mere modification of exterior circumstances a shock which I, for my part, found barely tolerable.

Few of those who read this narrative can have found themselves in a situation comparable to mine ; and to make what follows intelligible I must therefore enumerate the distresses which attacked me. The whole proceedings seemed to me unjust ; I had been given no opportunity to defend myself against any charge or to comment on a report which in my view and so far as it related specifically to me was generally misleading and in some elementary and factual respects demonstrably inaccurate. I could find no reason for the harsh nature of the sentence but either prejudice or stupidity or political opportunism. All three are dreadful things to contend with. I was to be cast out of a profession to which my working life was wholeheartedly devoted and classed socially with people who cheat at cards. It was not at all clear how I was going to support my wife and family. My disgrace was going to be attended by the utmost publicity ; it would shout at me and at all my friends from every newspaper. Humiliation is always hard to bear : public humiliation without possibility of redress is inexpressibly bitter. Worst of all, it was my honour which was impugned. The laws of honour present one of the most curious features of social life. In the light of cold reason a man admitting obligations to religion and society should place first in order of importance the laws of God and second the laws of the land, rating below these that somewhat vague and variable code which we denominate the laws of honour. In fact our conduct constantly shows that most of us place these standards of conduct in the reverse order ; so that while a police court summons leaves us emotionally unmoved, and we can accommodate ourselves without overmuch effort to a consciousness of sin, a dishonourable action can utterly destroy our peace of mind, and a general belief that we have acted dishonourably can render life itself insupportable. No moral or legal issue arose out of the report of the Board of Enquiry : it was a general belief that I had acted dishonourably which threatened me in the moments of which I write.

People frequently say that they have passed a sleepless night, but in fact a night wholly without sleep is very rare for healthy people. This night was one of the very few on which I have not slept at all, and it was indeed a very memorable and important vigil. For me the religious experience is to want nothing for myself, to be rid of myself, being in this way liberated and ready to be identified through worship with goodness and beauty. The blow which I had received had this liberating effect, so that in the same moment that I was assaulted by pain I found myself outside myself, and apprehended that pain and pleasure and personality were, so to speak, irrelevant to my true purpose, which was to be something not myself. Such a thing had never happened to me before, and I must add that it has never happened to me again. I knew at the time that the revelation would become dim, and so it has ; but I know quite well that what I think happened really did happen, that what I now see through a glass darkly then filled the whole range of my vision. My concern ever since has been to get back to where in those moments I belonged.

Something else of importance was brought home to me simultaneously which also related to the nature of suffering in general as much as to the " Francs Case " and my part in it. I felt that I had been selected for a particularly hazardous and alarming duty. Irrespective of the whole rather distasteful setting and of any real or imputed delinquencies on my part, I had been suddenly called upon to leave the ranks of ordinary people and put my faith and courage to the test. It was of overwhelming importance that in this I should not fail, for the spiritual wellbeing of others seemed for this brief instant of time to have been put in my custody. It was irrelevant that others did not know, and would probably never know of the struggle or of my part in it. If my fortitude now failed, the failure would recoil on the heads of others : if it did not fail I should have rendered them a real service. What little courage I myself had was inadequate to this end, but it was not my business to rely upon myself. My affair was to make myself a channel through which courage from some other source could flow ; to be a willing, almost a passive instrument ; to be poor in spirit. Nor was I alone in this emergency. I was surrounded by a great company who in their time had been exposed to anxieties and losses and humiliations and the relentless fatigues of pain. They rode beside me clothed in the panoply of fortitude and if I did not fail them now, if I made myself nothing, all would draw strength and increase from my fidelity.

My recollection of the course of events during the next few days is indistinct. The report was printed in the newspapers within a few hours of being handed to me, and I remember finding myself in the course of the morning of February 28th or March 1st sitting on a common near the Duke of Wellington's column at Strathfieldsaye looking at banner headlines in the cheap newspapers proclaiming my dishonour. This occurred, I think, when I was on my way to visit a very dear friend of mine in Surrey. Anyhow, I have a record that about four days after these events, on March 3rd, I addressed the following letter to the Under-Secretary of State at the Foreign Office :

Denton,
Wheatley,
Oxon.

Sir,

I have the honour to acknowledge the receipt of your letter of February 27th transmitting a copy of the report of the

Board appointed by the Prime Minister to investigate certain statements affecting Civil Servants made in a case in the High Court and of a Minute conveying the decisions arising out of it.

In accordance with these decisions, I tender herewith my resignation.

I profoundly regret that any action of mine should have embarrassed the Secretary of State or placed in jeopardy the reputation of the Service of which I have the honour to be a member. Without wishing to qualify in any way this expression of my regret, I beg leave to enclose a statement commenting on certain aspects of the recent proceedings.

I am, Sir,

Your obedient Servant,

OWEN O'MALLEY.

The following are the first four and last paragraphs of the enclosure. The intermediate paragraphs relate in detail to certain charges made against me of which I denied the truth. These intermediate paragraphs did not constitute a comprehensive answer to the report, but served to illustrate the sort of charges to which I was anxious to reply. The main object of my memorandum was to get leave to make a comprehensive defence.

" The procedure of most English courts provides that an accused person shall be charged with certain definite offences and shall be entitled to plead and to hear the evidence given against him. The procedure under which I have been condemned to leave the Foreign Office differs—and for all I know quite rightly differs—from this. It was comparable not so much to criminal justice or the exercise of justice in the army or navy, as to the procedure under which an unsatisfactory servant in ordinary civil life is removed from his employment. I have not now got the knowledge or desire to criticize this procedure, which was framed and applied with the most complete wish to ensure to me, among others, fair treatment. It is however the fact that no definite charges were brought against me by the Board of Enquiry, that no invitation was extended to me to plead, and that it was only subsequent to my examination that charges were formulated, verdict given and sentence pronounced without an opportunity being afforded to me to speak on my own behalf. In these circumstances it would seem to be not inconsistent with the ordinary principles of fair play that the statement I now make should be read by the Prime Minister and the Foreign Secretary, as well as by the Board on whose report they acted ; and to them I respectfully submit it.

2. " There is one sentence (paragraph 20) in that report, and that the most damaging to myself, to which I must demur, and its character is such that I can, in my own interest, only usefully express my disagreement with it now or not at all. It is this : ' in his (Mr. O'Malley's) case . . . we cannot doubt that he knew well what he was doing '. Whatever be the exact meaning of the Board expressed in those words, they will always be read by ordinary persons to mean that in the Board's opinion I did what I well knew to be wrong. That charge I deny. But if in future I apply for employment in some position of trust, I must expect to be refused on the grounds that I stand condemned of moral turpitude, and that by my silence—if I now am silent—I assented to the justice of the Report. It will be useless, in such circumstances, to protest my innocence, of that particular offence. ' Why ', I shall be asked, ' did you not protest to the proper people at the time, when all the witnesses were available, and the Enquiry was fresh in the minds of all concerned ? If your statements had then been explicitly declared to be untrue, so much the worse for you ; but you should at least have given your judges the opportunity of considering what you call an " injustice ". To resign in silence shows you had little confidence in your case.'

3. " I have not the slightest doubt that the sentence I have quoted was drafted with the most sincere desire for accuracy, but I deny that in dealing with francs as I did, I did what I knew to be wrong, nor so far as I can recollect, did I ever admit this in my evidence.

4. " Since the Report has been in my hands I have re-examined my recollection and my conscience on the point with all possible care. It is not an easy task at this distance of time for a somewhat disordered mind. But if those for whom I write will recall any experience which has shaken the foundations of their life, they will understand and forgive me if, of such cases, I say that, in the crucible of the mind, thought can be purged of self-esteem and fear by the fires of circumstances, permitting the conscience to speak with a singular detachment. Experience of this kind during the last few days allows me to

believe that what I have written in the preceding paragraph is the truth.

. . . .

9. " I do not for one moment wish to cast doubt on the desire of my examiners or my judges to be scrupulously fair to me, and I realize the great public importance that nothing should be done, if it can be helped, to keep recent events alive or to disturb public confidence in the issue. But if by what I have written, I have raised any doubt about the fairness of my treatment in the minds of those among whom rests the responsibility for the Report and the decisions arising out of it, I appeal to them to consider whether means could not be found, even if not immediately, to test the truth and if necessary qualify the damaging character of the words of which I have complained. I feel constrained to go further. Whether or not they consider that all the requirements of fairness have already been satisfied, I appeal to them for mercy. If they have been merciful already I appeal to them to be more merciful, to consider whether my sixteen years of service, filled with greater efforts to fit myself for that service than they can ever know, do not only, as the Report states, aggravate my offence, but also justify that appeal.

Denton.
2 March 1928."

A day or two later a friend of mine in the Office asked me whether I would like to see the Chairman of the Board of Enquiry privately—we had never previously met except in the course of the proceedings which I have described. I accepted the invitation and we met at luncheon in my friend's house and spent the whole afternoon in conversation. It was as strange an encounter as I ever took part in. Instead of his seeing the worst in me and I the worst in him, we each found in the other much to respect and like ; and the mutual respect and liking, though we still found plenty to criticize in each other, continued uninterruptedly till his death. There used to be a book of stories about ancient Rome in the schoolroom shelves at Denton, and I remember one tale was of an executioner and his victim who had been destroyed at the same moment by some cataclysm of nature. Together their " *manes* " had stood on the banks of the Styx and they had sat side by side in Charon's punt on their journey to that shadowy country where the spirits of dead Romans dwelt, exchanging with minds liberated by death from all earthly passions, reflections upon the execution at which they had just both been present. The author's motive had, of course, been to contrast contacts between human beings still subject to the limitations of mortality with intercourse carried on " *sub specie aeternitatis* ". That afternoon which I spent with the man who had been, so to speak, my executioner as well as Prosecutor, Jury and Judge, was certainly not free from much emotion on either side ; but nevertheless we were able to discuss with a sort of Lethean calm the events in which we had recently been involved. The Chairman of the Board had hardly expected to find this degree of detachment in one whom he had just condemned to professional and social disgrace, but this was because he had under-estimated (as anyone who had not had my experience must have done) the violence of the shock which he had administered to me. He had something still to learn about the effects of suffering.

The shorthand record of my evidence had been sent to me for correction immediately after my examination, and returned by me to the Board's secretary within a few hours. Towards the end of March I applied twice to be allowed to have a copy of this record, but my request was refused.

The letter and memorandum which I had sent to the Foreign Office on March 3rd remained unanswered for fifty-three days during which the authorities considered my case. On April 25th, however, in answer to a question from the Deputy Leader of the Opposition, the Secretary of State told the House of Commons that " an appeal for consideration had been received from Mr. O'Malley " and that Sir Austen Chamberlain " after full consideration and such consultations as appeared necessary " had " decided with the approval of the Prime Minister to give effect to that appeal " and that instead of being obliged to resign from the Foreign Service I was to be unemployed for one year and to lose five years' seniority. What underlay this decision to " give effect to my appeal " was never revealed to me. It may be that the authorities saw some disadvantage for themselves in standing by a judgment which stated what in certain particulars was demonstrably incorrect : it is certain that considerable efforts made in many quarters to secure a mitigation of the sentence had had some effect. In any case, the grounds on which this sentence was in fact mitigated are not, if I have told my story well, an essential part of it. There had never as far as I knew been a precedent for such a change of governmental heart, or shall I say, mind. The telegram from the Foreign Office communicating this news to me was brought down to Denton by Mr. Mitchell, the postmaster. It contained a hundred and sixty words, and was, I am sure, the longest message ever received by Cuddesdon Post Office. The under-gardener said " 'E was sure Mister Owen wouldn't 'a gone and done what was wrong."

It was only after sentence upon me had been modified that the authorities discovered that I had never been suspended from duty—the usual method for giving a Crown Servant notice that a *prima facie* case against him existed—but had been summoned before the Board of Enquiry only as a witness. Strong representations were made by the Chairman of the Board to the Foreign Office that this mistake in procedure— for it was so regarded—had vitiated the proceedings of the Board so far as I was concerned and called for the cancellation of the remaining disabilities under which I suffered ; but it was too late. In the Secretary of State's view " substantial justice had been done " and mistakes in procedure could no longer be brought into account.

There were two curious features about the whole business to which this chapter has been devoted. The first was that a servant of the Crown had been virtually cashiered—though the sentence was later reduced—without first being confronted with a charge ; without being told what witnesses before the Board had said about him or being allowed to contest their evidence ; and without being given any opportunity to reply to the Board's criticism on his conduct either before or after their report was drawn up. The second curious feature was the honest conviction that a just view of my conduct could be reached without any defence being made by me either orally or in writing or with or without the assistance of Counsel. The authorities were perfectly sure at the time the Report was issued that it was in every respect just. When later they learned that it was in at least one respect demonstrably inaccurate, they were again perfectly sure that their view of the case, revised in the light of fresh evidence (which was never disclosed to me) was perfectly just. When, later still, the mistakes in procedure referred to were revealed, a difference of opinion sprang up between one authority and another, but again both authorities were convinced that the view each severally took of the case in the light of this new fact, was perfectly just. Such a general conviction on the part of all the authorities that they could reach a proper comprehension of the whole matter without hearing me in my own defence would have been curious even if what was in question had been only the actions of myself and other people ; but it was even more curious in view of the fact that the motives and states of mind of myself and others had also been in question. The correct appraisement of the psychological background of a chain of events is always a matter of great difficulty not perfectly accomplished even in courts of law where judge and jury have the assistance of Counsel and are guided by rules of procedure drawn up with great care in the light of vast experience. It seems inconsistent with the teachings of jurisprudence to suppose that it can be better done by barring any defence from the accused and combining in the same group of persons, as the Board did, the functions of Counsel, Jury and Judge ; and inconsistent with common sense to suppose that, even if the Board's procedure was better adapted to this end than something more elaborate, a conviction that this was so would be generally shared by the public.

I happened to think the sentence passed upon me was unjust but that was unimportant, because no man is a good judge in his own case. But it was not at all unimportant that a lot of other people thought so too, because in all judicial or quasi-judicial proceedings it is vital not only that justice should be done but that the public shall see in no uncertain light that justice has been done. These reflections were all present in my mind when some years later I found myself Chairman of a Board of Enquiry into a not dissimilar affair, particulars of which are given in Chapter 19.

This chapter was written before my friend, Sir Warren Fisher's death. I submitted it to him at the time it was written and he told me that it was in his view factually accurate, and that if I ever wanted to publish it he had no objection whatever to my doing so.

CHAPTER 16

MIDDLE YEARS

I AM very fond of driving long distances in a motor-car. This is one of the ways of recovering equanimity after a trying experience. I begin to feel better as soon as preparations for the journey are in full swing. I make sure my car is in good running order and that all necessary tools are in the right place. I look out maps and arrange them in order. Sheets 25, 19, 14, 13, 9, 6, 4, 2 and others, if I am going up the Great North Road and across the Yorkshire dales and into Scotland. These maps are so delightful that I can hardly lay them aside to get on with my packing. I must find two thermos flasks, field-glasses, chocolate, fruit, a rug to sit on by the roadside, suitable books, dark spectacles. I get all in order the night before, since we must go three hundred miles on the first day and it is agreeable to start at dawn and break the back of the journey before even the milk lorries are on the road to the station. At four o'clock in the morning we go out into the mild air and through the sleeping village. We breakfast at Stamford and, having time in hand, stop presently in the middle of a village and have half a pint sitting on the churchyard wall. We go into the church and note that here is the burying-place of this or that family. I say to my companion that soon we shall see the middle townland of Stainmore or, it may be, Belford Moor ; and so indeed we do, and it is wonderful to see them, and at last the sea also, and wonderful to stretch and wash and drink and sleep again among foreign sounds and smells so well remembered. My memory is a library of such recollections of thousands of miles of English and Scottish roads, and I am sorry to think that when I die so great riches will die with me. A whole river of delightful memories takes its source in this stored-up knowledge of the counties of England, and, in those periods of desiccating boredom from which all diplomatists resident abroad must from time to time suffer, I have generally been able to console myself by getting out the Ordnance Maps of England and Scotland and following with my mind's eye the high roads and by-roads, reminding myself of this or that hill or river or bridge where I had been accustomed to stop and smoke a cigarette or drink some coffee out of a thermos flask, while reflecting on the perfection and self-sufficiency and indifference of Nature and admitting the image of the place unassailable and sustaining to dwell in my memory for ever.

All this being so, my wife and I drove up to Scotland as soon as the affair related in the previous chapter had reached its conclusion. This was to purge the poison it had left in our systems. It was June, and we drove by "A1" and up Wharfedale to Grassington and Kirk Gill, then over Stake Fell to Askrigg and away up by the eastern marches of Argyll and through Glen Orchy into Lochaber. The purge worked all right. When we got to Roy Bridge I got a letter from the Chancellor of the Exchequer, Mr. Churchill, suggesting that I should spend part of my year of enforced unemployment helping him with the preparation of a book to be called " The Aftermath " which was to form the fifth volume of his History of the 1914–18 war. This was generous, for Mr. Churchill had been signatory to the Minute under which I had been called upon to resign from the Foreign Office. I accepted at once, and the autumn and winter were spent by me in a room in No. 11 Downing Street or at Chartwell. I am therefore naturally in a position to write a detailed and colourful description of my vastly entertaining host. Naturally also I shall do nothing of the kind ; venturing only to say that as a man fourteen years younger than him I was now inspired to try harder than I had tried before to make of myself a loving husband, tender parent, constant friend, faithful servant, considerate master and magnanimous opponent. So far as devilling for his book was concerned I was ineffective, but it was out of regard for him and for the book that I was not more active to help him. I felt that it was better to do little or nothing as long as the composition of the book was going easily and well ; and in fact it went very easily and very well, and will probably be more read and more valued as time goes on than anything he has written about the Second World War. If I had been other than I was, my close association with Mr. Churchill might, I guess, have been made to contribute to my advancement in life ; but when in the spring of 1929 I again took my place in the Foreign Office, I trailed no clouds of glory from the important circles in which I had spent part of the preceding year. However, friendship remained and I am pleased to think that when fourteen years afterwards I went to Chequers to help receive members of the Polish Government in exile, it was into the bathroom that the familiar voice summoned me, where the Prime Minister of England was soaking on his back in a good deal more than the prescribed five inches of hot water.

I thought the Foreign Office behaved tactlessly on my return to the fold in putting me immediately below a man who had formerly been immediately below me ; but considering what a nuisance I had been to them in the " Francs Case " affair, they behaved very considerately in trying to push me up the ladder of promotion. In 1929 I was offered the Counsellorship at Moscow but the health of Patrick who had barely recovered from his illness in China and of Jane who had just undergone a very serious operation made my family circumstances far too precarious to allow me to accept it. In 1934 I was offered the Counsellorship in Brussels, but I refused this also because I did not at this time at all want to go abroad ; first, because life at Bridgend was so agreeable, secondly because I thought my children now at school imperatively needed me to be in England, and thirdly because, having become a Counsellor and head of the Southern Department in the Foreign Office, the move to Brussels did not constitute promotion. Shortly afterwards, Vansittart, always friendly, proposed that I should go as Minister to Bogota which he said would open the road to something more important ; but by this time the European cauldron was boiling up in a fascinating and dangerous way and I wanted to be in England if and when it boiled over.

During these years 1929–37 Bridgend life went on at a

spanking pace. It had started badly with the children's illnesses which I have already mentioned ; besides which we were very short of money and should have been in much worse case unless some generous person, whose identity I have never discovered, had paid £400 into my banking account after the " Francs Case ". In due course the clouds rolled by. Patrick recovered and Jane recovered and we resumed possession of Bridgend from our tenants. The bull-terriers had gone but the tortoise had survived. The big wisteria was dead but we replaced it with a *Clematis Armandi la Mortala* from Gertrude Leverton-Harris' garden at Little Compton, and we started up again the pig and poultry and bee industries. We had everyone we liked best to dine and sleep or to spend the weekends and to top it all up we got hold of some money.

I have no doubt that my wife, " Ann Bridge " will some day tell the story of her own life in her own way, and it is not for me to anticipate that in this book. However, since it had important results on our family fortunes, I must note that it was at this date that she tried her hand at writing a novel, having already had some small successes with poems and stories in the weekly and monthly periodicals. When " Peking Picnic " was nearing completion she submitted it to one of the best known publishers in London who specializes in travel stories. He offered her thirty pounds down for it and the usual royalties on sales in England, reserving exclusively for himself all American, foreign and film rights. A knowledgeable friend staying the weekend at Bridgend, said that this was not good enough and steered her into the arms of a reputable literary agent. With this man's help and before many months had elapsed " Peking Picnic " had won the Atlantic Monthly prize of ten thousand dollars in the face of competition from seven hundred and fifty aspiring authors, and brought in another five thousand dollars in film rights. It has gone on earning money for us from then to now ; and, on publication, it enabled us to rebuild Bridgend and raise our standard of living to a point which has kept the family on the verge of insolvency ever since. Authors would clearly have a hard life if there were no good literary agents.

AUTHOR'S WIFE : " ANN BRIDGE ". (1953)

AUTHOR, JANE O'MALLEY, AND PIGS AT BRIDGEND, 1937

These years were spent by me first as Assistant in the Central Department and later as Head of the Southern Department. In selective form the story of the very many important things which happened during this period in central and southern Europe is being slowly unfolded in volumes of documents edited under the auspices of the Government; but there is no one who sat in either of those two departments who would not feel that he could add much to these volumes that was either never recorded documentarily or is excluded from what the Government selects for publication. I was a humble participant in the debates which raged over the *Anschluss* and Hitler's rise to power and our relations with France and the Little Entente and the Italo-Abyssinian war and the Hoare-Laval agreement and all the other stirring topics which crowded in on us. Nothing would be more congenial than to fight the old battles over again, fill in the gaps which official histories inevitably leave open, describe the interplay of personalities, and the principles and passions and prejudices of those who shared in our official debates, selecting from stored-up memories all the less foolish and more percipient things which I said or wrote at the time. But, quite apart from the Official Secrets Act, that territory is barred to government servants. The efficient conduct of business in the Foreign Office depends almost more than anything else on complete frankness between the Secretary of State at the top and the latest joined member of the Service at the bottom. This would be shattered if any member of the brotherhood, high or low, had reason to fear that words spoken within this citadel of mutual trust and confidence might afterwards be made public. Accordingly I leave all that sort of thing out of this book. I miss a lot, and my readers, perhaps, a little fun; but I can assure them that it is all for the best.

Into the arguments which will no doubt rage for generations about the merits of the policies favoured successively by Mr. Arthur Henderson, Sir John Simon, Sir Samuel Hoare, Mr. Eden and Lord Halifax, I wish only to inject one observation on a matter of fact and one on a matter of theory.

The fact I wish to mention is the fragility of the intellectual foundations of policy or, in other words, the difficulty of finding out by a process of continuous thought what is possible or expedient or unwise. If anybody has got to make up his mind what to do tomorrow, he will certainly be thinking about what happened yesterday. He will say to himself " If only we had last year done this instead of that, the other would have followed " ; or " If only we had not said such and such a thing, the consequences would have been so and so." In nine cases out of ten in the political world such arguments based on the historical method have very little weight because in nine cases out of ten it is absolutely impossible to know what the consequences would have been of doing what was not done. It is, for instance, absolutely impossible to know what would have happened if we had followed Lord Lansdowne's advice in November 1917 to compromise with the Germans, or if we had closed the Suez Canal when Mussolini attacked Abyssinia. This is a great pity, because this process of thought which on the Stock Exchange is called " jobbing backwards " cannot be dispensed with. Our intellectual processes in the Foreign Office can also be looked at from this angle : suppose that four experts—equally well-informed, well-educated and honest men, joined together by identical loyalties and traditions, working upon the same documents—each give reasoned advice on the same problem. It is more than possible, indeed I have seen it happen many times, that they will recommend four totally dissimilar courses each with a wealth of plausible argument. It is all very like an " Alice in Wonderland " game of billiards. If a billiard-table is rectangular and flat, if the balls are round and there are only three of them, and only two players who play turn and turn about, a clever player has a chance of getting and keeping the balls where he wants them. In politics unfortunately, the table is not rectangular and has superficial excrescences and depressions, the balls are different sizes and there are perhaps twelve players all playing at the same time. This makes the game very difficult ; so difficult in fact that it is very nearly quite impossible to know what the ultimate results of any particular stroke are going to be. " But this line of thought," we indignantly exclaim, " is sheer madness ;

is the world of foreign policy like the inside of a lunatic asylum ? " The answer, alas ! is that the world of foreign policy *is* indeed very much like a lunatic asylum, and that we are lunatics unless we remember the extreme fallibility of our arguments and judgments.

My theoretical point was stated by Sir Edward Grey in the words : " What is right is generally the right thing to do " and by that wise man Headlam-Morley, Historical Adviser to the Foreign Office, in the words : " What in the international sphere is morally unjustifiable nearly always turns out in the long run to have been politically inept." The soundness of this principle follows from the fallibility of our knowledge and reason ; for surely most of us when in our private lives we are confronted by some intellectually irresolvable problem in respect, say, of a wife or a child, look closely to see whether some clear point of honour or ethics is involved, and if it is— as it generally is—we say to ourselves " I will stick to this line which honour or right conduct requires, and adjust all other interests and feelings and actions to it, hoping that thus every-thing will work out for the best in the long run." I should have thought most people could say that their experiences confirmed that this was common sense and that honesty was in fact the best policy. What amazes me is that governments and government servants so seldom use that kind of argumenta-tion. On this point I am not moralizing but speaking from exact knowledge. I spent nearly forty years in the Foreign Service and confidently assert that though millions of words were employed to show that something or other was expedient or advantageous, no one ever, or hardly anyone ever said or wrote : " We should do this because it is right and honour-able " or " We should not do this because it is wrong." " Right " and " wrong ", in the sense in which we use the words in church, are words for which one may search in vain in the masses of official documents now available to the public. This seems to me a pity not only because it is wrong but because it is imprudent ; or, if the alternative is preferred, not only because it is imprudent but because it is wrong.

The years 1929 to 1937 were now for me a straight road

across the watershed of life. So far as one stops anywhere between growing and dying, these were the years and Bridgend the place where I did just this. In 1929 I was forty-two years of age and no longer feeling young. If Skipness had not been sold and I had been invited to walk to the top butt on Laggan, there to await the glorious grouse roaring over from Monibachach and jinking in the wind, I should have tried to change places with the man in the bottom butt though he would only get them coming flat and low over the hollows. In 1936 I found that I could not ski any more ; I had to watch Roger Makins [1] and Michael Wright [2] go off the top of the Weissfluh to Küblis and myself crawl down with Esther Wright to the Parsenn hut to drink *glühwein* in her entrancing company, trudge home to Davos and take off my ski for the last time. By 1937 when I went to Mexico I had begun to be old. Apart from my wretched back this premature senile decay was mostly due to an infected gall-bladder which nearly killed me. It had been grumbling for years and an unusually bad attack overtook me when I was staying with Betty Campbell at Lennell near Coldstream in April 1934. I was walking along under the steep north bank of the Tweed when the pain started gently deep in my body. It was like a voice calling indistinctly and I listened for it to call again. It called again and then again more and more clearly, and I said to myself : " Yes, this is it. Now I am still my ordinary self but frightened. Now I am still myself, but soon I shall be ill and not myself. How strange," I thought, " that I can stand here still an inhabitant of the normal world but knowing, as I do, that in a few minutes or hours I shall not be my normal self at all, but shall be in a rigor with only a thread of memory leading from the me which walks alongside this river in full intimacy with the burdocks and the celandines to the me which will be sweating and squirming half-conscious in bed." And so indeed it happened, and it was only after I had had four injections of morphia that I passed out of spasms into poppy-laden twilight. When that was over I lay looking out of the

---

[1] Now Sir Roger Makins, G.C.M.G., H.M. Ambassador in Washington.
[2] Now Sir Michael Wright, K.C.M.G., H.M. Minister in Oslo.

window at a ploughed field across the Tweed, red in the next morning's sunlight, with the plough team creeping across and across ; and in imagination I felt the hales kicking in my hands and smelt the sweating horses and heard the peewits scream and wheel, knowing that I was separated, if not for ever, at any rate by many months and miles from bodily contact with these dear familiar things. A few days later Worth, the chauffeur, cleverly turned the Daimler into an ambulance and drove me over Sutra to Edinburgh where three days were spent in a nursing-home. Then I got myself by train to Bridgend and to London and into the London Clinic, there to undergo an operation.

While all this was going on I had a lot of time to think about being ill. To be ill was to be in a place by myself, curtained off from other people, but able to see and communicate with them because the curtain was transparent and transaudient. But this communication was not an exchange of equivalents ; for whereas I who was ill could fully remember what it was to be well, other people who were well could not completely imagine themselves into my separate world of illness. I had plenty of time also to think about what I ought to do if I got well again and had to look after someone else who was ill. It would not be enough, it seemed to me, to feel affection and pity and be cheerfully tolerant when the patient was fractious or some bedside duty called me from sleep. I could only fortify or heal the ill person by a very exacting self-discipline, by habituating myself to singleness of mind and, when the emergency arose, by subordinating myself wholly to a purpose which was in no way whatever self-regarding. If I can really empty myself of myself, I thought, I shall be able to pass on healing and fortitude through the curtain to the ill person, but not so if there is an inner conflict in myself. This was a tall order, but a thing I ought to think about seriously if and when I recovered.

By the time I entered the Clinic I had so far got over my latest attack as to be in a perfectly normal state of mind. There were grounds for uncertainty about the result of the operation, and I was in consequence, and as always when I have occasion and leisure to contemplate my own death, exceedingly frightened. My surgeon was delighted. " That's splendid," he said, " surgeons like patients who scream with fright. It simply shows a very strong desire to live and that is the thing which is going to make the patient recover. People who are not frightened are seldom quick healers." I did not find any specific for my panic ; I just had to put up with it quietly. But I got very tired of it as the last two days of expectancy wore on and was very much surprised and relieved when at six o'clock in the evening of the day before my operation my panic left me suddenly and completely. Thereafter the fatigue of being frightened disappeared and while waiting for what was going to happen to me I was internally as well as externally composed. The surgeons told me afterwards that even after the anaesthetic had begun to take effect, my body had remained motionless. I have no explanation for this curious episode, but the impression was that I had been taken completely in charge by some benevolent agency outside myself.

The nearest thing I know to heaven on earth is the state of mind to which the patient sometimes wakes on that day when his body has decided to live and not die ; when its counter-attack on illness has been crowned with success and nothing remains but to lie wrapped in blessed peace and feel the fact of being alive with an intensity unattainable in any other circumstances. I lay two whole mornings like that in the Clinic and watched the sunlight on the red brick wall outside my bedroom window, and thought without any resentment of the pain and weakness which for a week after the operation had afflicted me. From that point onwards my complete recovery was only a matter of time. It was a perfect summer, and day after day and by night as well as day I watched with the minute attention of an idle mind at peace the movements of plants and animals in the garden at Bridgend—lying in the loggia which I had built under the cedar tree and finding an unusual sweetness in smells and tastes and sounds. In five months I was at work again in the Office.

I wish now to recall in a serious mood what the experiences

I have just described and other troubles had taught me. The teachers at Denton and Belclare and Radley and Magdalen who made claims to universality and finality for the words and practices of their religion had only opened the door ajar to apprehension of the life of the spirit. Institutions and their regulations pushed it a little but not much further open. The masters of long words, as I said earlier, had no contribution to make. What trouble seemed to have taught me was first, that the life of the spirit was mostly a function of trying to be good, which, in brief, meant wanting nothing for myself; and secondly, that so long as I tried to do what was right, I should know what it was right to do ; not of course in its totality but always in sufficiency for the day and the hour. There was nothing new about this : it was obviously what King David meant when he said that " to fear God is the beginning of wisdom and to flee from evil that is understanding ". How lucky I was then ! for I was never in a situation where I could not see a choice in front of me between right and wrong conduct, and here was a tremendous promise that if I wanted nothing for myself—chose a dying life instead of a living death—this wonderful thing, " understanding " would be mine. The processes would of course be infinitely difficult and painful but that made no difference to their satisfying simplicity or to the validity of the promise. Having once, as I related previously, been momentarily released by humiliation from obsession with myself, I carried ever afterwards with me this awful knowledge : heavy as gold, heavy as a cross carried to the place of crucifixion.

CHAPTER 17

MEXICO

AS I mentioned in the preceding chapter I had, during the years 1929–37 three times demurred to being sent abroad. In two instances the decision was left to me, but in the third I was simply instructed to go to a certain post and had a good deal of trouble in getting the instruction withdrawn. In the ordinary way of things it would not have been open to me to resist a decision taken by the authorities in regard to my employment, but there were special circumstances why in this particular case I was entitled to do so, and after some difficulty I succeeded in getting permission to set them forth, and did so in a memorandum the preparation of which taught me a valuable lesson in draftsmanship. As this may prove instructive to others similarly situated, I shall tell the whole story at some length.

Needless to say, I devoted my best attention to the drafting of the memorandum in question, and I was not dissatisfied with the result of my efforts ; knowing, as I fancied, almost everything there was to be known about the technique of understatement and persuasion. I was therefore disappointed when a friend of mine outside the Service to whom I had submitted it told me that in his view it had too much " punch " in it, and that it would be more acceptable to the recipients if the tone were less personal and combative. Numerous alterations having been made in the sense suggested, I then asked one of our Legal Advisers to look through it, being anxious to get the best possible opinion on a document which was partly legalistic in character and might be submitted for a final decision to the extremely acute legal mind of Sir John Simon which at that time ruled all our activities. " There is no doubt," said my adviser, " that you have a goodish case, but if you take my advice you will make the whole thing less personal and contentious; and I shall, I hope, have helped you by making the emendations which strike me as desirable in pencil on your draft." Somewhat dashed, I again re-wrote my petition, embodying all my friend's suggestions; and, since he had by this time gone on leave, I asked another of the Legal Advisers to look through the second revision for me. My chagrin was great when he remarked in almost the same words that his colleague had employed "There is no doubt that you have strong points on your side, but the argument is too vigorous. I have cut out parts of it and toned down others." In the form to which he had now reduced it, my case seemed but a pale shadow of itself; many telling points had been cut out and irrefutable conclusions from unchallengeable premises presented as mere suggestions or afterthoughts. However, I decided wholly to subordinate myself to this detached and expert judge and sent in my memorandum in its now emasculated and etiolated form.

The instructive nature of this episode lies not so much in the fact that the departmental authorities, after dismissing my memorandum as unconvincing, told me that they had decided for reasons of their own not to send me abroad as in what Sir John Simon, the Secretary of State, said to me personally afterwards: for without in any way cutting the ground from under the official view of things he showed me that my arguments had not left him unmoved. "I see your point," he said, "I see your point; and it was, if I may say so, very well put, very properly put . . . I think I have made an arrangement which satisfies everybody . . ." Well, well, I thought, this has indeed been a valuable lesson in moderation; praise from this source on a matter of draftsmanship is praise indeed; and I recalled a story of his early life which my father used to tell. He was at the time appearing as a junior on the Norwich Circuit and his leader had just finished his concluding speech in a very important case. My father had expressed his astonishment and concern that in this speech the obvious and apparently unanswered conclusions from a series of powerfully argued premises had not explicitly been stated. "Young man," the silk answered, "I saw that the judge had seen the point. When you are sure a judge has reached in his own mind the conclusion you desire, break off as soon as you can."

When I first joined the Service a good deal of regard used to be shown to the predilections of members of the Service in respect to appointments but the consideration shown by the authorities had in some cases been presumed upon, and in others proved prejudicial to efficiency. Soon after the 1914 war therefore, it was decided that only in exceptional cases could a man be permitted to decline a transfer ; and accordingly, when the time came for my own promotion from the Office to be a Minister, I was not asked whether I would like to go to Mexico City but simply instructed to proceed. While this meant the end of Bridgend, and while of my family only Jane could accompany me, I had nothing to complain about. For a first Legation, Mexico was as important a post as most people could expect to get.

While the move to Mexico cost me about £1,000 out of my own pocket, the cost of the upkeep of a Legation made it impossible for us to continue in occupation of Bridgend, and so the decision was inevitable that we must part company with the lovely place where my three children had been brought up ; with the house and garden which was so much part of our lives, on which we had spent so much money, and in which we had entertained so many friends. I cannot recall the exact circumstances in which I drove for the last time away from its gates but, though the final liquidation of all our activities was supervised by my wife after my departure, I remember very well that when taking the preliminary steps in this direction I felt much the same as when I had had to destroy a dearly loved dog or cat, or to condemn poor "Bananas" to be shot after he had broken the big tendon in his stifle under me in a race at the Peking gymkhana. What a wealth of labour one puts into a place when one hasn't many servants ! There was the electric-light engine that always wanted so much loving attention, the Mirabelle hedge which was just getting into shape, the big plantation of flowering shrubs in the cottage garden, the laburnums and chestnuts that had been intended to make of our crossroads a thing the Sunday visitors from London would never forget, the " Pitmaston Duchess " which now covered most of the east gable, the henhouses where after a protracted struggle the rats had been finally defeated, the bower of honeysuckle outside the back door. It was too much to hope that anyone now would understand, as I had understood, the significance and importance of these things. Here where I had loved and sweated, the influences of man and nature would destroy the imaginings and graces which had filled the middle period of my life. But such regrets were foolish, for houses and gardens are not like statues cut out of marble which neither growth nor decay but only malice can destroy. They are like songs sung, which draw their substance from living hearts and throats, not less valuable because ephemeral. Nevertheless the goodbyes were hard, and I expect I and all my family will always feel the pang of leaving Bridgend, with the apple blossom hanging over the paddock wall, the white *Iris stilosa*, the little old gate between the Roughs and the Forest on the way to Blackmoor, the bees working in the great rows of Michaelmas daisies, and the vagaries of the outflow from the septic tank. I have got a good conscience about all of it except the tortoises. These tortoises were determined to walk uphill, and the big tortoise that came from the Embassy at Constantinople had spent fifteen summers trying to get through the wire netting into Strong's field. Once when we were in China he had got through and the blade of a reaper in the 140 acre had taken a chip out of his back ; but the farm hands had brought him back, and in 1937 he was still wandering purposefully up and down the fence. I blame myself very much for not having made proper provision, before my departure, for him and his small companion brought from Phil Nichols' [1] garden on the Janiculum in 1935. When on return from Mexico I went down to Bridgend, the fence was full of holes and all trace of those two enigmatic friends was lost.

[1] Sir Philip Nichols, K.C.M.G., lately H.M. Ambassador at The Hague.

It was all the harder to give up our home because Denton was also gone. My father had died in 1932 and the house had been sold. Skipness had been sold about the same time so that there was now no place of which I could think " *ille terrarum mihi praeter omnes angulus renidet* ". However, two things partly reconciled me to leaving Bridgend : the first was the appalling changes taking place in its environment, and the second was the acquisition of Rockfleet, of which more hereafter.

Since the end of the war in 1918 sinister developments had been going on all round the parishes of Ockham and Wisley which lie on either side of the Hut pond between Cobham and Ripley. Of these the most noxious was the construction of cheap six-roomed houses all along the new Kingston by-pass road from Esher to Wimbledon. In 1914 the Londoner by walking over Wimbledon Common and turning to the left just before coming to Kingston hill, could hear larks singing, see peewits wheeling in the spring, and in the autumn watch a plough team at work ; but by 1933 this was a thing of the past. The children of Wandsworth and Battersea had no doubt been made to read Shakespeare and perhaps part of the Bible also in their Council schools and could here in 1914 actually have seen with their own eyes the kind of husbandry which forms the groundwork of classical English literature. Now I suppose they will have to look in dictionaries and picture books for the meaning of such words as plough, furrow and harrow. This urbanization of the country close to London must surely be one of the worst crimes committed against the people of England since the enclosure of the commons.

Simultaneously, the villages surrounding Ockham were in the 1920's being rapidly vulgarized, and by 1937 many of them had become neither town nor country. Ockham itself was a favourite place for Sunday motorists from London ; and Watery Lane and Chatley Lane which, when we went to live there, were utterly secluded, were now thronged weekly with motor-cars drawn up head to tail. I dare say that if our circumstances had been different, if we had had to bring up a family in the unbeautiful streets of Lambeth or Putney, we should have devoted our savings to buying a motor-car and our weekends to visiting the quiet woods and meadows within reach of London ; but this is no reason why, being what we were, we should not have hated to lose the privacy and seclusion of our own village, to find our lanes full of motor bicycles, our coppices full of mating couples, and paper and glass everywhere defiling the hedges and ditches. It was rumoured also that the great high road which had been constructed through Red Hill and Dorking was soon to be linked to Aldershot and that a section of it would pass through our own parish. Whether this was true or not, it was clear that the Ockham which we had first seen on that snowy morning in 1919 would soon be a thing of the past ; and equally clear that a semi-suburban Ockham was no place for us. I had never meant to die there. I might as well go now as later. As regards Rockfleet I need only say that during the years preceding my appointment to Mexico I had several times revisited Mayo, and that the intention had been growing to return in retirement to live in my own country. I was already fifty years old, and it was therefore becoming a matter of urgency that I should set the transfer to Ireland in motion as soon as possible. The vague excitement engendered by this prospect could not overcome the immediate distresses of parting from Bridgend, but it served as a kind of counter-weight and enabled me to resist the temptation to cling to a home in England which I was no longer in a position to afford.

My daughter Jane and I made the voyage to Vera Cruz by Lisbon, the Azores and Havana in the Hamburg–American S.S. *Orinoco*. I was pleased to be in a German ship, for I am at ease among Germans whom in general I had hitherto liked. The voyage was without incident except that off Bermuda a man went overboard. It was about eight o'clock in the morning on a sunny windy day. He had been in a cradle painting the outside of the bridgehouse and must have dropped a good sixty feet. I shall never forget the urgency of the shout : " Mann über Bord." On the previous evening we had taken sherry with the captain, discussing cases of men lost overboard ; and in answer to my questions he told me that he reckoned he could turn the *Orinoco* through 360° in just over three minutes, little thinking that the accuracy of his statement was so soon to be tested. Having rushed on deck I followed operations with my watch in my hand and found that it was about 3½ minutes from the moment when the helm order was given to the point at which we were again parallel with our wake and about half a mile to the eastward with the sun behind us and all eyes now straining to pick up our man. A boat was got away, but the waves being high could not find him. Fortunately he was a strong swimmer and reached the ship unaided. In less than an hour we were again under way.

My First Secretary, Rodney Gallop and his wife met us on the quay at Vera Cruz and with them we drove up to Jalapa, there to spend the night. From Jalapa next day we traversed the mountains which at this point rise to 10,000 feet above the sea, and in the evening dropped out of the pine forests into Mexico City and drew up at the Legation House, a comfortable and uninspiring building in the 1900 Surbiton style.

My official work in Mexico consisted almost entirely in expostulating against the intention of the local government to expropriate, more or less without compensation, the oil properties and installations in which British investors had invested about one hundred million pounds. There was never any chance of preventing this by the use of words which was all I had in my armoury. I threw increasingly severe words at the Mexicans ending up with a note which was eventually laid before Parliament as Cmd. No. 5758 of 1938. This was too strong for them and caused them to withdraw their Minister from London. They were kind enough to tell me that they liked me personally and that it was out of consideration for me that they had taken this course instead of asking the British Government to withdraw me. Immediate instructions from the Foreign Office to return to London followed inevitably and thus it happened that I only spent seven months in Mexico. All this had seemed rather sensational to me and to the representatives of the Mexican Eagle Oil

Company but excited little interest in the Foreign Office where no one, on my return, wanted to see me or discuss what happened. In the spring of 1938 everyone in London was too preoccupied with Hitler and his doings to bother much about anything that happened in Mexico.

Considering that Mexico is fourteen times as big as England and comprises most kinds of country from snow-mountains to tropical jungle and an interesting mixture of peoples, I do not know why I do not want to write much about it. It is not for lack of material. There were the snow mountains, Popocatépetle, Ixtacsïwatle and Orizaba, forever near forever far; there was the all-surrounding untamed sinister *monte*; there was Acapulco with all its tropical extravagances of bird and plant and marine life; there were innumerable Indian tribes and villages as yet little affected by the colonists; there was the decaying magnificence of Spanish colonial life and lovely Spanish churches all forlorn; there was everywhere to be heard a slightly archaic variety of the Spanish language more melodious than anything spoken in Spain today; there were deserts and jungles and mountains and marshes all producing flowers of astonishing variety and luxuriance; and to all of these we made expeditions by motor-car over axle-breaking roads and on pony back up and down the roughest and steepest of paths. But I do not want to write about any of them except about Taxco.

This town—pronounced Tassco—lies some hundred miles from Mexico City in the state of Guerrero. It owes its origin to silver which is still mined there, and its unsymmetrical squares and streets and houses and churches lie tumbled on the rough mountainside. Whenever we could do so at weekends we dashed over to Taxco; up over the hill towards Cuernavaca, past the little group of wooden crosses where, in a recent revolution, thirteen officers had been shot (shot by mistake; contrary orders were on their way; it was too bad; but after all, what are thirteen officers more or less? anyhow it was their fault for being an unlucky number); down through pinewoods and sandy banks spilling waves of flowers onto the road as the lava had once spilled itself down

the hill ; 5,000 feet down to Cuernavaca with its *jacaranda*
and *bougainvillea* and Morning Glory ; down past the big
barranca, through the sugar plantations ; over the stony river
where the iguanas lived ; along the long hot shadeless miles ;
up and up and up the hill again where radiators boil and
little boys with tin cans shout " Agua, agua ? " ; into the
cactus belt : organ-cactus and prickly pear set off with yuccas
eight feet high ; round the sharp corners and at last, oh how
delightful ! pushing past the ponies with feet ringing on the
cobbles, pushing through the evening busyness of the twisting
streets, through the shady *plaza* among the towering houses
to the Taxqueno hotel for a bath and for many drinks, and
to Tamara's villa terraced into the side of a barranca and
furnished with loggia and courtyards full of a shrub with wax-
white trumpet-shaped calices nine inches long.

All round Taxco, all round the dry red-brown purlieus of
the town studded with banana trees and *poinsettias*, stand the
metallic mountains. When the sun is high they look hard
and brittle and blue-red like the freshly tempered points of
the pickaxes which we often see piled in London streets where
road works are in progress. But sunrise would turn these
ranges to pink gauze and summon us to a long hot day on
pony back among the painted gorges ; and I would follow
Tamara upright in her tight striped trousers and her Mexican
saddle, wondering that horses could climb like cats on such
declivities. In the evening we would get back to her verandah
and much Bacardi rum, to doze or talk or listen to Vicente
and Tito singing " El pescador de Vera Cruz " or " Panchita "
to their own accompaniment on the guitar. Towards midnight, Paco's bar being shut and the *paseo* almost concluded,
there was no sound to be heard but an occasional revolver
shot and the barking of dogs ; and so the town entered upon
the secret activities of the night in darkness and silence behind
closed shutters, the beggars slept on the cathedral steps, and
the racoons awoke to their saturnalia on the pantiles and
among the sweet potatoes.

So much for Taxco. My narrative now passes at once to
our journey home.

During the last stages of my negotiations with the Mexican authorities it became urgently necessary to send a bag to Washington. Carriage from Dallas, Texas, to Washington could easily be arranged, but the press of business was so great in my Legation that no member of the staff could be spared to take despatches from Mexico City to Dallas. Accordingly I sent Jane by air, appointing her thus to be the first female King's Messenger on record. It was in Dallas from the radio in a friend's motor-car that Jane learned of the rupture of relations and of course she hurried back to help with the frenzied packing which this sort of event inevitably entails. The archives of the Legation had to be partially re-sorted and destroyed, stores and wines to be sold, and the future position of my official and domestic staffs to be determined. Press correspondents, my foreign colleagues and British acquaintances called at all hours of the day and night. The cat and the canaries had to be provided for somehow. As is common in such circumstances, I was the recipient of many messages and letters, signed or unsigned, from all sorts of people ; and of these I can recall only one that was hostile. Some of my correspondents were moved to a pitch of absurdity or pathos which I cannot forbear to illustrate :

"Dear Sir, Minister," said one,
"My sorrow is deeply touched on the unhappy present diplomatic clinch between Mexico towards His Majesty's affairs, but my grateful hope rests in a hasty new handshake with wellfare to benefit both countries . . . Sire, I rise to heaven my prayers for England's Royal Splendour and His Majesty King's British Empire . . ."

and so on.

"*Adios,*" wrote another,
"*Mensajero Gentile de tierras lejanas . . . me encuentro desesperado ante el egoismo de los mios . . . Os iréis dejando melancólica a la Dama-Ciudad que con el beso de sus auroras os racibió y ahora con el bello espectaculo de sus crepúsculos os dice adios, hasta la vista . . .*"

A third sent me four hand-knitted ties, an embroidered

handkerchief and the image of St. Christopher, accompanied by the following letter :

" Excelently Sir, I am very sorry because you have to go from Mexico. I am anxious to let you know with this few lines that truly I have aprichiécheun of your country and you good person. Sincerley hope that you come back . . . With pleasure I send you a little present as a remembrance of Mexico City. Please I supplicate to you for your protection for my chailds."

At the last moment, when my tickets for the train journey via Laredo to Washington were taken, Mexico, in true Mexican fashion, sprang a surprise on me which necessitated a change of plan. General Cedillo, the Governor of the State of San Luis Potosi, had long been *en rebeldia* against General Cárdenas. He had a small private army and several aeroplanes and he had never even pretended to carry out the orders of the central government. Threatened with seditious activities from more quarters than one, President Cárdenas conceived the ingenious idea of anticipating a widespread and concerted movement against himself by throwing down the glove to an isolated antagonist. If, he argued, Cedillo capitulated without a fight, the prestige of the central government would be greatly enhanced ; if, on the other hand, Cedillo stood his ground, he could probably be crushed before any of the other discontented elements in Mexico were ready to strike ; and here, again, the result would be to reinforce General Cárdenas' personal position. I remember Mr. Winston Churchill saying during the Irish trouble in July 1914 that the proper prescription for revolutions was to " let them off at half-cock " ; and this, in fact, was what General Cárdenas now determined to do in San Luis Potosi. As a consequence of the sporadic hostilities which accordingly broke out in that state it came to my knowledge on the evening before my departure that the Ministry for Foreign Affairs had warned one of my colleagues not to start for Washington, as he had been intending to do, by the Laredo road. The Laredo Railway lies some two hundred miles west of the road and might well have been clear of disturbances, but there was no assurance that this

would be so and no means of getting any exact information
on the point. I decided, therefore, that it would be better
to steer clear of the possibility of trouble, to get out of Mexico
by Vera Cruz and the sea route, and to ignore whatever dis-
pleasure the Mexican Government might show at a change
of route which would be taken by the general public as
evidence of the serious nature of General Cedillo's rebellion.
Instead, therefore, of leaving Mexico in the train for Laredo,
I found myself on the evening of May 20th with the Deputy-
Manager of the Mexican Railways in his special coach on the
way to Vera Cruz. By that time, although I did not know
it, the railway from San Luis Potosi to Tampico had already
been cut, and by May 30th, although I could not have foreseen it, three bridges had been destroyed on the Laredo line,
two on the Southern Pacific Line to Sonora, and even the
Vera Cruz line had been put in jeopardy at Esperanza where
it crosses the highest and wildest part of the mountains in
the State of Puebla. We tarried thirty-six hours in the unbear-
able heat of Vera Cruz and then boarded a banana ship bound
for New Orleans. She was licensed to carry thirty-six passengers but besides ourselves there were on board only sixteen
holiday-makers from St. Louis, Missouri. They were charming companions and I do not think any of them had previously
met a European. It was a delicious calm voyage and I made
friends with Julie, the stenographer-secretary of a wholesale
leather merchant at St. Louis. We spent a hot star-spangled
night discussing the merits and behaviour of two of her young
men, and she promised and failed to write and tell me when
and how she decided between them. If this should ever meet
her eyes, let it remind her that she is well remembered and
that it is not too late for that promise to be fulfilled.

Except for Taxco everything that I had seen in Mexico
seemed to have flowed round and over me without making
any more impression than a documentary film would have
done. None of it got into me and became part of me as
China and many other countries have done before and since.
This may have been because we lived in Mexico City which
lies in a hollow in the hills with no exit to the sea at a height of

about eight thousand feet. Such an elevation is known to have peculiar effects on the human body and mind not noticeable in Davos, for instance, which stands only six thousand feet above the sea. Or it may have been because the *mestizos* or half-castes which form the bulk of the population are racially immature, the mixture of Spanish and Indian blood being only three centuries old. I think perhaps a race or a culture may have to be matured like wine if it is not to disappoint us in the way that Americans and Australians and other " new " peoples are liable to disappoint us, if we see much of them. Or, finally, it may have been because Mexico seemed to me, of all the places I have ever been in, to be one of the most godless and spiritually corrupt. The history of the country before the coming of the Spaniards must have something to do with this. There is, it is true, a rather pathetic charm in the accounts we read of Montezuma but this is only part of the story : another part of it records countless human sacrifices ; and it is not unreasonable to suppose that the sufferings of hecatombs of prisoners whose hearts were torn out upon the temples now casually visited by tourists still infect Mexico City, and that the visitor, without knowing the reason, is still affected by the rank sickly smell of blood and entrails just as cattle suffer when they smell the slaughter-house. It was unfortunate for the country that the Aztecs with their predilection for the smell and sight of blood should have mated with the Spaniards whose contempt for suffering and death is well known. It was an added misfortune that for the many years before I was appointed to Mexico the practice of religion should have been an object of hatred and persecution only paralleled in modern times, so far as I know, under thoroughgoing Communist régimes ; and it was perhaps one consequence of all this that in Mexico City a dozen or a score, and in the whole United States of Mexico several hundreds of murders were committed every night. I never got into close contact with such things, but I never got completely out of contact with them either, and may be that is why I was not sorry to leave the place.

After twenty-four hours in New Orleans and three days at

the Embassy in Washington we joined the *Aquitania*, most graceful and comfortable of liners. She had been re-engined and broke her own record with an average of 25.9 knots. On June 5th I landed at Southampton and before many days had elapsed I was under instructions to take charge of the British Embassy to Spain, then located at Hendaye just over the French border from Spain. A few weeks' leave were, however, due to me and it was during this holiday with my wife in Ireland that we decided to buy Rockfleet.

CHAPTER 18

SPAIN

SO far as professional advancement went, the point at which
I had arrived on return from Mexico was crucial. Foreign
affairs in 1938 absorbed everyone in London to the ex-
clusion of most other departments of public life ; consequently
the Foreign Service was, so to speak, the marching wing of
public administration and so continued till September 3rd,
1939, when it yielded this position to the Armed Forces. I
was at this time fifty-one years of age, and if the Foreign
Office thought that in me they had a useful servant, now was
the time for them to use me. My record, however, did not
stand high in their esteem. During the years which I had
spent in the Foreign Office before going to Mexico, while
there had been no bad feeling between me and the higher
departmental authorities, I had frequently offered them uncongenial advice ; I had thought that they allowed the public
to hope too much from that will-o'-the-wisp, Disarmament ;
that however justly they distrusted German intentions, their
subtly offensive attitude to the German Government only made
things worse ; that they were unnecessarily and unwisely
indulgent to the French and too credulous of the pretensions
of the Little Entente. Above all, I thought it unnecessary
and almost fatal to allow Mussolini to drive a coach and
horses through the League of Nations. I may have been
wrong or I may, perhaps, have been partly right, but either
way I was swimming against the tide, and to swim against
the tide is not the way to get on in the Foreign Office unless
one can swim underwater ; and although my subsequent
activities in Mexico had throughout been explicitly endorsed
and approved, this was not enough to dissipate the smell of
obstinate inconvenience which I emanated. However, the
Foreign Office were, according to their own view, acting

considerately in sending me to take charge of the Embassy to Spain which was admittedly a sinecure, because this was a way of avoiding the reduction in my emoluments which " unemployment " would have entailed. I, to my surprise, found that the position to which I had been nominated was, from the personal point of view, extraordinarily rewarding.

In September of 1938 I drove alone to Hendaye, following for the first time the road through Bourges, over a corner of the Auvergne and down to Pau and conversing *en route* with many people, including the chemist in Aire-sur-l'Adour who was taking his leeches out in jam-pots to the *place* in order to give them the benefit of the sun. Most of them had the same thing to say, namely, that poor France could not do much, but that Mr. Neville Chamberlain was wonderful ; that England, so strong and adroit, was going to save them, and—by implication—save France from the unpleasant necessity of pulling herself together and paying taxes and preparing to fight the Germans again. I reached the outskirts of Pau about seven o'clock in the evening, and stopped by the green side of a poplar-bordered road before entering the town. The Snipe had proved a good car, and here at last were the Pyrenees on the horizon. A drive from Paris to Pau was a small thing but a first sight of famous mountains is never at all a small thing ; and so, sitting under the poplars, the outline of the Pic du Midi d'Ossou set me ruminating as I had often done before about mountains and journeys. It was nice to think that I had seen so much of these wrinkles in the earth's surface between the 35th and 45th north latitudes ; Swiss, Austrian, Julian and Carnic alps, Karavanken, Serbian and Bulgarian mountains, Caucasus, Ararat and Elburz ; but I regretted very much that I had not, as I had planned, been able to return from China by the Great Road through Lanchow and Hami to Kashgar and then over the Karakorum to Leh and Srinagar and Sarhad, emerging through Afghanistan and Meshed at the place under Demavend in north Persia where Percy Loraine had taken me in his yellow Vauxhall in 1925. That would indeed have been worth attempting even though with my bad back and stomach I might have come to the last of all journeys as did Pereira with his game leg in Szechwan and Reginald Farrer with his humped back and cleft palate far up the valley of the Irrawaddy. It was, of course, too late for that now, so I should have to put up with being one of the people who had never done anything heroic.

My ditch under the poplar trees and in sight of the Pyrenees was a nice place and it had been a good drive ; but my back now ached and I wanted a bath, so cutting short my regrets I pushed on to look for an hotel and see what this famous place Pau was like. Ever after I spent that first night at Pau I was very fond of the " Hotel de France ". I liked the top rooms, I think mine was No. 414—and I liked very much the politeness of the old *valet de chambre* and the chambermaid in starched gingham and the noise of the weir at night and the view which I got in the very early morning, drinking a cup of tea at the window in my pyjamas. The air of Pau is bland and life-giving, and there is always the knowledge that a few short miles will carry us into the heart of those lovely mountains. But the mountains were to come later ; on this September morning I had much to do, and so I drove on to Hendaye through Orthez and Bayonne and St. Jean-de-Luz and in the afternoon entered the grocer's shop just this side of the International Bridge where the Embassy had settled when the tide of Spanish civil war had rolled as far as the French frontier. One might say that the Embassy had been cast up rather than settled at Hendaye, that I and my staff were castaways ; and having taken one look at the location and the amenities of the place I decided to remove the Chancery to St. Jean-de-Luz, and did so during the ensuing week. St. Jean-de-Luz having been described by my wife in " Frontier Passage " I shall not here write anything about it. My main interests lay over the river in Spain.

Of the stories which we invent and tell to children some have to be retold many times, and in the re-telling not only must nothing be omitted, but much in the process of time must be added. " No, Daddy," the children say, " you've got it wrong ; as Alice went upstairs she saw them sneaking to and fro in the moonlight under the trees. Please don't leave that bit out ! " or " Daddy, you've never told us where the Vampire lived. Did he live up in the roof? And what did the inside of the roof look like ? " Of such stories some come to have a special significance ; they are not stories to be trifled with ; they are for birthdays or Christmas Eve ; there must be a special harmony between teller and listeners ; and when the teller has gone to change for dinner and the listeners are tucked up in bed, all must feel that they have taken part in some exciting and satisfying ritual. Similarly for me Spain is a place and a story which I prefer to discuss only when all is harmony. I do not care to argue about it. I particularly dislike argument about Red Spain and White Spain. To those who have seen in Spain what I saw I am pleased to relate my experiences, but not to critical listeners who would think I had been bemused by the Castilian sun or bewitched by the gypsies on the road.

I entered Spain with no preconceptions as to what I should find there. Someone with more industry might well have run through the standard works on the country which he was about to have the opportunity of visiting ; but ever since on getting into the Foreign Office I destroyed my notebooks and sold my textbooks I have had an aversion from serious reading, and so it was that I came to Spain with a mind prepared only by its emptiness to receive whatever impressions contact with this new country and people should make. The first local comment on Spaniards which I heard was from the inn-keeper at Laruns. I had driven through St. Jean Pied-de-Port and Oloron up the Laruns valley intending to have a long walk by myself in the mountains ; and I did have a very long walk up through the forest and onto the high alps where a farmer told me how he had shot seventeen bears in his time, but that the eighteenth had clawed one of his cows, and that was why she had those queer marks on her quarters. Before starting on this walk I had asked the innkeeper where the frontier was and whether I could safely go where I pleased. " Oh, yes," he said, " but you need to be prudent if you meet any Spaniards. They are not like the rest of us, French or Germans or English. They are queer people in a way, for if you disagree with them you can't do anything with them, you can't do anything about it. We have an expression hereabouts : ' *têtu comme un Aragonais* '." This seemed to me afterwards as sound a judgment on Spanish character in relation to politics as could be put into four words ; but a distaste for compromise was, of course, only one aspect and a negative aspect at that of the Spanish character—*muy noble pero muy bruto*—of which I tried during the ensuing months, with growing amazement and humility, to learn a little more.

I went to Burgos at the earliest opportunity to see the British Agent there, Sir Robert Hodgson, and the Minister for Foreign Affairs. My relations with these were anomalous, for Sir Robert's mission conducted all important business with General Franco's administration on instructions received directly from the Foreign Office and not through me ; while General Franco, for his part, was naturally unwilling to recognize the official status of an Embassy and a Chargé d'Affaires not located on Spanish soil. I was in fact only a kind of symbol of the unity of Spain now split into two halves, and an observer on behalf of the Foreign Office of what passed in both. The General's ministers, however, received me in a personal capacity very kindly and politely and made me wish I was to have more to do with them than was likely to be the case. My daughter Kate accompanied me to Burgos and we had a notable drive from St. Jean-de-Luz.

The road, after passing through San Sebastian and Tolosa, mounts steeply to a pass from the top of which over the right shoulder the outlying summits of the Cantabrian mountains can be seen. It was at this point that we crossed the watershed which divides Basques from Spaniards ; and to us, seated now for lunch on a flowery upland slope, these steely ridges seemed to give preliminary notice of the character of the people with whom we were about to mix. Somewhat exalted by this sight Kate and I next passed through an open forest of oak and dropped gradually to Alsásua, here leaving the Basque province of Guipuzcoa and entering the old kingdom of Navarre. Between Alsásua and Burgos through Vitoria and Miranda the main road traverses for the most part flat open country bounded on either side by a horizon which with every mile becomes less serrated and assumes instead the shapes of immense flat-topped downs. Some of this land is grazed but most is cultivated, and the extent and configuration of the plough-land is thrown into relief by infrequent villages from which the peasants must often have a long walk every morning and evening to and from their work. The houses of cream-coloured stone, which gathers up and reflects the hard sunlight, are substantially built and have suffered little at the hand of improvers. Kate and I stopped in more than one of these villages and cursorily explored the narrow streets and the square and the churches ; but we took equal pleasure in sitting by the side of the road and directing our looks towards those scattered at a distance among the brown autumnal fields. At one point we counted no less than fourteen of such villages spilled at intervals of some miles upon the umber plain which extended in all directions for a great distance. Growing thus out of the labour of the farm and existing for no purpose but to shelter the labourers and the produce of their labour, comprising with themselves whole worlds of family histories and personal relationships, these distant townships stimulated our imagination very agreeably. Perhaps if the day had been less kind we should have had a less happy impression but the day was very kind ; it was a perfect autumn day, and the benevolent sunshine made the furrowed fields look as rich and soft as an otter skin and set every roadside tree alight with cream, chrome, lemon and butter-yellow leaves. Cut out of blue sky and backed by red-brown tillage, these poplars and willows attended us all the way to Burgos. This arresting sight, the insistence of these flaming trees which accompanied our passage, dominated the mood in which we drove into Spain and taught us, I think, that a proper understanding of the people depends on a certain disposition in the observer and is withheld from cold and unsympathetic visitors. In Spain, it seemed, trees were not just trees nor villages and mountains just villages and mountains but reflections of some shining or heroic quality in life of which Spaniards are the exponents and custodians. Perhaps it is for this reason that in Spain we cannot for long turn our eyes away from the country through which we pass ; that however sombre and monotonous the view, however long and straight the road— and some Castilian roads are very long and very straight—a significant and dramatic quality in the landscape soon recaptures our attention.

It was not to be expected that this transfiguration of the countryside, this startling apprehension of recondite force, would wholly survive contact with the disorderly congestion of Burgos, a provincial city now converted into the political capital of a people at war and thronged with distracted officials and soldiery fresh from the field ; but another revealing experience for me was provided a few weeks later by a drive from Burgos to Seville. This second journey was intended to be continued through Valencia and Barcelona in order to give me an insight into republican as well as nationalist Spain ; but although for reasons which I shall explain in due course it was interrupted at Gibraltar, what I saw on the way there through Leon, Estremadura and Andalusia was enough to revive and confirm impressions of Spain as a whole formed on the road from Tolosa through Navarre and Old Castile.

In December 1938 there was no reasonably convenient means of transport between town and town unless a traveller could get the use of a motor-car. I could not take Kate on a journey which was to be extended through Valencia, Madrid and Barcelona but preferring not to drive alone, I had let it be known in the Ministry of Propaganda in Burgos that in case they wanted a seat for anyone in a car going south, I should be happy to take a passenger. No applicant for these facilities came forward in Burgos, but on reaching Salamanca late in the evening of my first day on the road I was asked on the telephone from Madrid whether I could accommodate a Swedish girl engaged on Red Cross work, and told that if so, she would join me at my hotel in twenty-four hours' time. I was glad to do this and spent the intervening day seeing the sights of the city with the Rector of the *Collegio de los Nobles Irlandeses*, then appropriated to the use of the German Ministry of Information. My Swedish companion, the Baroness Beata

Bonde, aged about twenty-one years, turned up late at night and I told her firmly that we must start at six o'clock on the following morning. Women do not like being turned out of bed at this hour or look their best if they are, but at six o'clock the next day I found Beata in the hall of the Grand Hotel of Salamanca, very tidy and composed, as if it was the most natural thing in the world to be up and about at that time of night in an empty and somewhat war-worn hotel. I discovered my car to have seven Chryslers and Chevrolets in front of it in a dark garage deserted by all but a huge negro who was fast asleep on the floor, and by the time he and I had man-handled those infernally heavy cars out of the way, I was in a muck-sweat. By seven o'clock we were on the road with the rain streaming down the windows and the wind howling against the car.

About a dozen times in my life when thrown into the com-pany of a total stranger it has been immediately, intuitively and reciprocally recognized that I and my companion were not strangers at all but dear and trusted friends. Before this conjunction and after it the intricate pathways of our separate lives may have wriggled all over the globe, perpetually separ-ated by space and time ; but when the conjunction was made we seemed to have been fitted into place, like the two last pieces of a jigsaw puzzle, with predestinate perfection. This is one of the nicest things in the world that can happen to anybody because it mixes the pleasures of surprise and dis-covery with the delights of assurance and the appearance of immutability ; and it happened to me—and I hope to Beata—as we settled into the front seats of the Snipe and drove through the atrocious Castilian night.

By the time we reached Plasencia the weather had cleared up. This town is partly built on the side of a declivity above the road whence the cathedral is approached by several flights of steep steps. Driving slowly past these I had the idea of stopping and looking into the building, for who knew when I should be in Plasencia again ? And perhaps there was here something singular or memorable well worth a few minutes' delay. But I said, No, we would go on : many miles still

185

lay ahead of us, and besides that there was at one point a kind of " Tom Tiddler's ground " between the two armies which had to be passed before dusk or not at all. Beata said " But yes ; of course we must stop. If you feel you must do a thing it is very important to do it. This is not simple. It is a principle that you must always let things happen to you if they want to happen and if there's no good reason why they shouldn't be allowed to happen. Otherwise you will be full of regrets. We regret things we don't do more than things we do do." I said, " No, but all this may make us late." Beata answered " But I say yes, and will not argue any more. We will now get out and go up these steps to the cathedral." And so we went up into what Beata afterwards called " our cathedral ". I have never found out who built it or when or why, nor anything about it, nor about the men and women who had worshipped there and had at last lain in their coffins beyond the sanctuary, nor of the vigils that had been spent there, nor of the gratitudes or tears or fears or desperate resolutions laid as an oblation before the dusky blood-flecked image of Christ. But all these things had, it seemed, been gathered up and safely stored in the shadows and scented silences of this building where mass had just been sung ; and I was after all very glad that we had come up the steps and been into it, for I was again violently confronted as I had been in the Cantabrian hills and on the road to Burgos by the Spanish awareness, expressed here in the idiom of architecture, of the ephemeral nature of men's individual experiences and of the continuity and tragic dignity of man. In this or some- where near it must lie, I thought, the quality which differen- tiated Spain from other countries, and it was an apparently fortuitous series of occurrences which was discovering it to me.

By the time evening approached and we had traversed at high speed the no-man's-land between the two armies and we were saying to each other that if indeed we made Seville that night we would have the best dinner the town could provide. Having passed in fifteen hours from the bitter fury of the central plateau to the African warmth of the Guadalquivir valley we reached the city at about nine o'clock in the evening and sat down to two plump partridges in the rather macabre emptiness of the Hotel Alphonso XIII. That was the last I saw of Beata for a year or two. When I said goodbye to her I thought to myself—as many times before and since—what a lot there is to be said for " pick-ups " and chance acquaintances ; that they often turn out to be made of pure gold, not susceptible to the corrosion of time and mutual responsibility.

I spent the ensuing week at the Rio Tinto Company's mines and in Seville cathedral. German architects took a hundred years to build this, the largest Gothic church in the world ; so large that the tourist would be unlikely to notice, unless it were pointed out to him, that it contains eighty-three altars or that the choir is furnished with about two hundred choir books each three foot high and two foot broad. It is interesting to see how Spain has breathed into an exotic design her own peculiar atmosphere of awareness and sombre glory, not competing with the aspiring light-filled loveliness of north European cathedrals, but with shadows and secrets completing the story of our spiritual experience. I first entered the cathedral at about five o'clock in the evening of the octave of the Feast of the Immaculate Conception, when the interior was already dark but not too dark to notice that every facet of each of the immense groups of pillars on which the roof of the nave is borne was clothed in strips of crimson velvet some two foot broad hanging from capital to plinth. The velvet dated, I was told, from the sixteenth century and there must have been more than a mile of it. I remembered once buying a couple of square feet of the same sort of thing in Duke Street for thirty-five shillings. When I got as far as the *capilla mayor* I was astonished to see six or eight boys dressed in pale blue or cream-coloured velvet uniforms of the period of Philip II dancing a kind of minuet on the steps of the high altar before the Cardinal Archbishop and to the accompaniment of four or five instruments. I have since informed myself about the origins of this well-known ceremony, but at the time I was much surprised and at a loss to fit it into the picture of Spain which was building itself up in my mind. At the conclusion of the performance the Cardinal, preceded by his secretaries and canons in purple and scarlet and black, and followed by six train-bearers, walked in procession to the sacristy brushing past me in the obscurity heavy with incense. One of the canons, well over six foot tall, carried his right hand with extended fingers over his heart; and his head was thrown back, and his eyes lifted towards the vaulting now lost in darkness many feet over our heads. The repose of his dusky and aquiline features recalled the impassivity which in Moors often veils the turbulence of an African temperament; and it might, I thought, well have been like this that St. Augustine of Hippo looked, walking from the baptistry to the basilica in Milan on Easter Sunday of the year 387, when the excitements and fatigues of his conversion and instruction had at last been concluded. Thagaste, where Augustine was born, was only just over the water in Algiers, and whether or not they had the same rich African blood in common, at least this canon and St. Augustine had shared the sun and the faith and the general confusion of the world in which each had grown up. My canon may for all I know have been thinking only of his supper or of nothing at all but, as I walked back to the hotel afterwards, the imagined resemblance between the two men seemed to me to throw a little more light on something dramatic and heroic in the Spanish character; and as for the dancing before the high altar, was not this a symbol of the Spaniards' aptitude for integrating his experiences; the Real Presence on the one hand, fun and games on the other; the natural and the supernatural joining hands in a man's life. *Benedicite omnia opera.* If the Lord be praised with trumpets and shawms, why not with dances and castanets also? Spaniards, I thought, must be very much aware of this thing which I cannot define but which has been partially disclosed to me on the Burgos road and in the church at Plasencia and now in the cathedral of Seville; perhaps it is this which Spanish traditionalism and obstinacy is designed to preserve, this which they are now desperately fighting about, this which is in jeopardy.

I spent the evening reading a book about Spain which had been lent to me in St. Jean-de-Luz and in conversation with a local resident who pretended to a knowledge of Islam ; and according to what these told me, the Moorish University of Cordoba had in the year 1000 or thereabouts been the highest centre of light and learning in Europe. Here was an astonishing fact which illuminated my own ignorance of history just as a visit to Hué, recorded earlier, had shown up my ignorance of geography. But Cordoba had been much more important than Hué, and I was surprised to think that during the fifteen years covered by my education, my tutors had told me no more about this African culture than they had about our own Irish church which had at the same time been keeping alight the lamps of civilization in the opposite corner of Europe, displaying severally in the Ardagh chalice and the Bettys-town brooch on the one hand and the Alhambra on the other a sophistication hardly paralleled anywhere in between. It was an odd thing to find myself stumbling like this amidst the obscurity of my own mind against these pillars in the antechambers of mediaeval history.

The next morning I revisited Seville cathedral in company with a Gibraltarian guide who pointed out to me that the main doors of the building—made of brass and some thirty foot high—were those which had formerly hung in the mosque which had stood on the same spot in Mohammedan days. They were covered all over with a repetitive sentence in Arabic characters which, he said, meant " There is but one God, and Mahomet is his prophet." It was a striking circumstance that this message should still be announced from the gates of a Christian edifice and I compared it in my mind with the mosque called Kahriyeh-Jami' in Constantinople at the extreme opposite end of Europe, which had been a Christian basilica before the Turks crossed the Bosphorus in 1453. After the Turkish occupation of the city, this church—like St. Sophia —had been converted into a mosque, but the mosaics had not been covered up or destroyed, with a consequence that Moslems worshipping there had for five centuries passed through a narthex on whose walls the Christian story was still brilliantly pictured. The world was indeed a delightful place which could send my thoughts in the course of a few hours dashing about from Cordoba to Ardagh and to Hué, and from Seville to Constantinople ; but it would have been much more delightful if the tolerance had been more general which was exemplified by the doors of Seville cathedral and the narthex of the Kahriyeh-Jami'.

Perhaps it is because those aspects of Spanish life to which this chapter has been devoted eludes precise definition that Spaniards, anxious to explain themselves, so often have recourse to stories, ending the telling of them with the words " that is very Spanish, that is ". During the civil war many stories of recent incidents were passing from mouth to mouth of which no collection, so far as I know, has yet been made. There was, for example, the story of *á mi la legion* and the story of the nurse with the crushed fingers. I shall tell only two which are short and commonplace but came within my own experience.

A car belonging to the British Agency on the way to San Sebastian had the misfortune to run over a boy in the streets of Vitoria, and all efforts were in vain to save the life of the child who was the only son of a couple living in the poorest part of the city. The British Agent himself proceeded to Vitoria on the following day to condole with the mother, the father being away at work, and to enquire whether it was within his power to alleviate her distress. She thanked him for his attention, expressed the view that the Agency chauffeur was in no way to blame, repudiated any idea of indemnity or assistance, and begged him not to allow recollection of the accident to prey upon his mind. A week or so later a labouring man obviously in very humble circumstances presented himself at the front door of the Agency in Burgos and asked to be received by Sir R. Hodgson. The doorkeeper, unable to elicit the nature of his business, was told to bring him upstairs, and the travel-stained visitor was accordingly shown into Sir Robert's study. It was the dead boy's father who, just as a matter of courtesy, had come the seventy-odd miles from Vitoria to return His Excellency's call. The second story relates to a poor widow who with five sons cultivated her late husband's small property on the outskirts of Burgos. One son had been left by the military authorities to do all the work of the farm but four had been taken for service with the army. On hearing that the fourth and last of these had been killed the widow reflected that she had now no man fighting for Spain. This seemed a shameful situation and astonished that her only remaining boy had not at once seen things in the same light, she ceased to cook for him, saying in reply to his remonstrances " I do not cook for cowards." The young man, mortified, left at once for the front and within a week he too was dead.

I think I must, after all, tell a third story of Colonel Moscardo of the Alcazar, for there are many in England and America who do not know it. It has several versions, and mine may not be accurate. I should be happy if Moscardo, which is unlikely, would correct me if I am wrong ; but, anyhow, I am sure he will not mind it if I repeat the tale as it reached me, for he and his son and the story are now part of the history of his country.

Colonel Moscardo, at the time when General Franco was precariously transferring his troops from Morocco to Spain, found himself in command of the Alcazar at Toledo with a garrison of some eight hundred men in a fortress beleagured by superior forces of the Left. To those unfamiliar with Spain it may be a surprise to hear that telephone communication between the Alcazar and the investing troops had not been interrupted, but such was the fact. In the early days of the siege Moscardo was called up from enemy headquarters and told that his son, aged about fourteen years and a prisoner in their hands, would be shot unless the fortress were surrendered. On the colonel replying that surrender was out of the question, his son was brought to the telephone and the following conversation ensued :

" Father, they say they will shoot me unless you surrender."

" My son, you know that I cannot surrender."

" What then am I to do, father ? "

" Pray for us, my son, and remember that you die for Spain and Christ the King."

" That is easy, father. I will do both." Upon which

Colonel Moscardo heard the shot which at once killed his boy and wrote the names of both in imperishable letters into the annals of Spain. *Eso es muy castizo.*

From Seville I pursued my way alone to Jerez, where I learned how sherry is manufactured, and towards Gibraltar, leaving behind me somewhere near Fascinas the avenues of eucalyptus which characterize this part of the road, and winding instead through and over scrubby downland. Suddenly I found the sea below and the African coast in front of me. To have arrived alone on a lonely road within sight of a new continent furnished one of those moments which so well reward the traveller. Between Algeciras and La Linea in the gathering dusk, I saw something pink on the road ahead of me, which presently proved to be the Royal Calpe Hunt returning to Gibraltar. It threw much light on both Spaniards and Englishmen, that at a time of acute international tension when all frontiers were shut, a British pack could still hunt Spanish foxes on Spanish soil.

I spent five days at the Convent—as Government House is called—with Sir Edmund and Lady Ironside. I went to bed with influenza and they were very sympathetic and attentive to me, though Ironside, who weighs about 18 stone and has a forearm like a leg of mutton, said he had never been ill himself. " What do you mean—never been ill ? " I asked. " What I say," he said, " that I've never been ill. I was in bed once but that was because my aeroplane crashed and I broke both my legs. I well remember, when I was pulling the pilot out, how odd my feet looked because they were pointing backwards instead of forwards. What's more," he said, " I've never been tired."

" Nonsense," I said, " that can't be true."

" Well," said he, " perhaps it's not quite true. At the beginning of the 1914 war I was on duty once for fourteen days and nights on end, and I did feel a bit queer at the end of it." I asked him how he accounted for all this, and he explained that one of his ancestors had got into a bit of trouble with King Harold of the Saxons and had been exiled to a district later called Ironside somewhere near Peterhead. He said the climate of that part of Aberdeenshire was such that only people like him and his forebears could survive.

As soon as I was out of bed I was ordered from London to return with all speed to St. Jean-de-Luz to investigate the circumstances in which a British diplomatic bag had been opened by the Spanish frontier authorities at Irun. Accordingly with my car I boarded a P. & O. steamer for Marseilles and started thence to drive the four hundred miles to St. Jean in the worst snow and frost which had been known in those parts for a generation. There were thirty-seven cars snowed up outside Narbonne where I was forced to spend the night. I skidded into a tree at St. Gaudens and abandoned the Snipe, reaching the Embassy very late and very tired on December 24th to find that Patrick and Jane had joined us there for Christmas. From Marseilles onwards it had been a trying drive, but oh ! how much better than wearing out my trousers on an Office of Works chair in London ! I will now briefly describe the facts of what became known at the time as the " bag incident ", and explain the relevance of these to the " Francs Case " referred to in an earlier chapter.

At the time in question the British Vice-Consul in San Sebastian resided at St. Jean and motored to and from his office daily, and on these journeys he was accustomed to carry in his car any correspondence which required to be exchanged between the Embassy in France and its dependent Consulate over the border in Spain. One evening in December he was approached by the Spanish frontier authorities who said they had reason to believe that among his papers was a communication from a " Red " spy in San Sebastian to a " Red " agent in St. Jean and that they therefore wished that a full examination of the contents of his car should be made by them and the Vice-Consul jointly and before witnesses on the spot. This request was put forward firmly, but, of course, with the proverbial Spanish politeness. The Vice-Consul replied that if there were any grounds for such suspicions, he would be as glad as the Spanish authorities to ascertain the truth in respect to what would constitute a manifest impropriety ; and the papers in the Vice-Consul's custody were accordingly examined. Among them was discovered a parcel addressed by a party in San Sebastian to a party in St. Jean containing a shirt into which certain military maps had been sewn ; *prima facie* evidence of a crime had been detected ; the " exhibit " was impounded by the police ; the Vice-Consul was exonerated of any personal responsibility and allowed to proceed on his way.

While these events had been in progress all members of the staff of the British Vice-Consulate at San Sebastian had been arrested ; and in due course judicial proceedings were set in motion against them by the Spanish Government. The British Government were naturally concerned at this incident which at the time attracted a great deal of notice in the Press. While no technical breach of diplomatic etiquette had apparently been committed by the Spanish Government, it seemed possible that there had been carelessness or misbehaviour or both on the part of British employees, and it was therefore decided that a British inquisition should be held at once in order to ascertain the real facts. I had been appointed to preside over this Board of Enquiry. I went immediately to London to find a person of judicial experience to sit on the Board along with myself and Mr. Jerram from the Agency at Burgos. Sir Wasey Sterry was the man, and the three of us began in St. Jean-de-Luz the examination of witnesses. I did my best to make the proceedings impressive by buying a long trestle table and an enormous piece of green baize to cover it. Before describing the proceedings of this Board, that is to say before dealing with that aspect of the story which has relevance to the " Francs Case ", I will relate the conclusion of the matter so far as concerns Spanish judicial proceedings, the results of which have long ago been made public. Of the persons under detention a Spanish employee of the British Vice-Consulate at San Sebastian was observed some days after his arrest by persons in the street falling from a second floor window on to the pavement. He died without recovering consciousness and the Board of Enquiry was thus deprived of what should have been their most important witness. The others were kept in prison for some time, then put under domiciliary arrest, tried by due processes of law and acquitted on all counts. The acquittal covered also the dead man, and the judgment of the High Court in Burgos, published in the ordinary way, declared that the military maps discovered in the Vice-Consul's car had been introduced into it by agents who supposed themselves to be acting in the interests of the Burgos Government and that no more blame attached to any British official than it did to the accused. I will now return to the proceedings of my Board.

In the course of preliminary investigations it transpired that the bag between Burgos and St. Jean-de-Luz had from time to time been used by subordinate persons attached to the Agent's staff for the transmission of Spanish currency which could be sold at an enhanced price on the French side of the frontier. These transactions, as it turned out later, were not of an important kind, not entered into for improper motives, and due solely to the abnormal currency situation then obtaining in Spain, but I did not know this at the time when the Board began its enquiries, and I accordingly found myself in the position of Chairman of a Board appointed to enquire among other things into " transactions in foreign currency " by civil servants and the question whether these had been " engaged in transactions of which the propriety was open to doubt ". The words in quotation marks are quoted from the proceedings in the " Francs Case ". The wheel had indeed gone full cycle. The ironies of official life could go no further, for here was I on the Bench where formerly I had been in the dock.

The first thing which the Board had to do was to settle its procedure. Once bitten twice shy. Though these were only quasi-judicial proceedings my own earlier experience had convinced me that " when we consider a system of law from the citizen's point of view rather than the lawyer's, as a material element in the political stability of the commonwealth, we may almost say that certainty in procedure is more important than certainty in the substance of law ". [1] In settling our procedure, to what precedents could we look for guidance?

[1] " A First Book of Jurisprudence ", Sir F. Pollock, Bart.

There were apparently only two that were closely applicable, and of these the " Francs Case " enquiry was one. Chapter 15 will have made clear my view that in some respects the procedure followed by the Board of Enquiry into the " Francs Case " was defective. These defects I was determined in the " bag incident " enquiry to remedy. Accordingly as each witness came before us for the first time I read and offered to him a copy of a statement explaining the subjects of enquiry, the position of witnesses and the status of the Board. This statement contained among other things the assurance that if the Board found that the witness had been to blame in any respect, then that he should be furnished in writing with a statement of what it was which we held against him, and given the opportunity to reply to this orally or in writing or both.

The Board was never able to conclude the investigation, since it could not compel the attendance of material witnesses, of whom one was dead and others under arrest in Spain ; but had it done so it would, of course, have submitted its report to His Majesty's Government who might well have seen fit to lay this report before Parliament. In this report I should on even the narrowest construction of my duties have been obliged to describe the procedure which it followed and the reasons for it. Even the most scrupulous avoidance of any attempt—or the appearance of it—to exploit the circumstances for my own satisfaction, could not have prevented this report from implying a criticism of the procedure followed by my own judges in the " Francs Case ". Perhaps, therefore, it is as well that circumstances brought my investigation to an unfruitful end before this point was reached. There is nothing in the world a Government Department likes less than being scored off.

The Spanish Civil War came to an end early in 1939, and I went across to Perpignan to see the *débâcle*. The Republican army pitched its guns and armour off the road into a deep *barranca* or glen, building up what I suppose to have been the biggest scrap-heap in the history of the world. The soldiers marched into France or dispersed on the mountains.

French Communists were all over the place buying revolvers from them at twopence a piece. Four hundred thousand civilian refugees marched up the road cut in the side of a hill to the frontier chains at Cerbère. I could see this queue of misery extending for miles, blasted by torrential rain and a howling wind. The French were apparently unmoved by all this suffering, sending Senegalese troops to control the situation. A day or two afterwards I went to Argelès and found ninety thousand Spanish Republican soldiers penned on the shore without any shelter in a tearing wind. They had burrowed into the sand for shelter like rabbits. Apart from sending in some dead horses and truck-loads of bread the French had ignored their sufferings. I went to Paris and told the Ambassador, Sir Eric Phipps about it, but there was nothing else I could do about the greatest aggregation of human misfortune I had ever seen, so I went to Amélie-les-Bains to see that the British agent and his staff, also in retreat from Barcelona, got accommodation and hot-water bottles in their beds. Meanwhile, I heard that I was appointed to the Legation at Budapest, for which I had applied some months earlier, expecting to find here another set of people very imperfectly comprehended in London or by me. And so I said goodbye for the moment to Spaniards, having learned in a short time a good deal, as it seemed, of the unique personality of Spain : of the tenacity of Spaniards, of their lofty humility and sombre pride, of their courtesy, of their contempt for danger and suffering and of their preoccupation with the tragedy and majesty of death.

More nonsense had been talked by more people about the Civil War in Spain than about any other comparable disturbance, but nobody in London wanted to know what I thought about it, so I could devote all my time to preparations for departure to Hungary. My opinion, for what it is worth, was and is that the stability of General Franco's regime was fortunate for Spain. This view is not based on an appraisement of the relative merits of " White " or " Red " policy in Spain but on the facts that the Franco regime is, for the time being, by far and away the best available guarantee against a recurrence of civil war, and that of all human calamities a civil war is the most dreadful. The Caudillo, like the rest of us, must die ; but the best service foreign lovers of Spain can render to her is not to interfere with their clumsy fingers in the crucial question of what is to happen then. I think most instructed and impartial people in English political life would agree with what precedes, but most of them have so far been afraid to say so.

CHAPTER 19

HUNGARY

ON giving up Bridgend we had taken a flat at No. 1
More's Garden, Cheyne Walk. I left this with a newly-
joined member of my staff on May 4th, 1939, and drove
to Hungary, sleeping at Arras, Strasbourg and Ischl on the
way ; and, having dropped my companion at Bratislava,
continued by myself to Budapest. Although nothing less
adventurous than motoring along the main roads of Hungary
can be imagined, even here, in a humble way I picked up some
of the crumbs which fall from the explorer's table ; for this
was after all the road to the East, and all of it in front of me
was new. Accordingly, the brave way the silver snipe on
the bonnet of my Humber car flashed on into the great plain
of central Europe suited my mood very well. The character
of the wayside villages altered as I went forward : the houses
here were built sideways not frontways to the road ; the pots
and jugs hung out to dry had patterns on them that were
new to me ; the names of the towns were strange indeed :
Györ, Szöny, and Pilisvörösvar. Stimulated by all this and
rattling over the tramlines of Ujpest and along the south
embankment of the Danube on the evening of May 8th, I
felt quite ready to meet all the novelty of taking charge of a
Legation right in the middle of what was clearly going before
long to be a political whirlpool.

There is no doubt that to be a British Ambassador or
Minister can be highly enjoyable. In the first place it is good
to travel the world in comfort at Her Majesty's expense ;
nice to have the best places in trains and ships and at the
opera, big houses to live in, lots of good servants (in every
country in the world being a servant in the British Embassy
is a much sought-after job) and a staff which attends to all

the boring time-wasting details of travel, house-keeping and social obligation : above all nice to be the cock on top of one's own little dunghill, master of one's time and movements and able to give instructions which will be punctually and thoroughly carried out. In the second place nearly every foreign Government and society do their utmost to make the British Representative happy and comfortable. All doors are open. The best of entertainment is offered, and anything anywhere he wishes to do or see will be arranged with all the goodwill in the world. Foreign Governments treat all foreign Representatives thus but I always had the impression that they were especially kind and indulgent to Representatives of the British Government, this being perhaps the unearned increment of the preponderant position of England in the nineteenth century and of the fact that British Ambassadors and Ministers were formerly recruited from the upper classes of society. In the third place the Ambassador or Minister (the distinction has now ceased to have any meaning) will be served by a nice, considerate, intelligent, loyal staff. Naturally there are a few exceptions but in the great majority of cases everything possible is done by Counsellors, First, Second and Third Secretaries, Service Attachés, and the rest of them to surround their chief with a cosy atmosphere, provided of course that they feel that he, for his part, is going to give them a fair deal. If he is wise he will not only give them a fair deal, but draw them into his family circle ; make each member of his administrative staff feel that there is always a place for him at the Ambassador's table and that the Ambassador is not an unsuitable person with whom to discuss difficulties with his wife or mistress. Very agreeable relations will also be the rule with other foreign Representatives. Inevitably some of them are bores, but most Ambassadors or Ministers of the more highly civilized Powers will be intelligent people with whom it will be possible to discuss with profit and entertainment everything under the sun. Finally, I must say that so far as my experience goes the Prime Ministers and Foreign Ministers and Permanent Under-Secretaries of State of foreign Governments were as a rule more highly gifted intellectually than we who represented the British Government, and consequently people with whom it was not only a pleasure but an education to deal.

If there is a fly in the diplomat's ointment, it will probably be the Foreign Office. In his dealings with his parent department a difference will be found between what might be called " hot " and " cold " diplomacy. What I call " hot " diplomacy covers anything like a crisis, the negotiation of an international agreement, or affairs which attract public or parliamentary attention. In such cases telegrams fly to and fro, contact with the Foreign Office is close and continuous and the Ambassador, though he may disagree with Cabinet Ministers at home, will have the satisfaction of being able to carry out their wishes with precision and full understanding on both sides. What I call " cold " diplomacy has to do with the background of all this ; the building-up in the Foreign Office of comprehension of the instincts, habits and passions of a foreign nation and of the personal characteristics of the men who govern it ; the building-up in the minds of the foreigners of understanding, if not of approval, of the policy of the British Government. The well-meaning Embassy will spend much devoted labour on this and will in many cases get the impression that so far as the Foreign Office is concerned it has been largely in vain. The impression is often a correct one ; for higher officials in the Foreign Office are mostly much too busy to bother about anything but " hot " diplomacy and they have not got enough time—and Cabinet Ministers have no time—carefully to read or maturely to reflect upon descriptive and argumentative despatches. Consequently, there are cases where an Ambassador or Minister has been at his post for two years without receiving a single political instruction from the Foreign Office ; and of all the " background " despatches I ever wrote from abroad to the Foreign Office, I do not suppose that more than a dozen were read by anyone above the rank of an Assistant Under-Secretary. Diplomatic officers should not be unduly disturbed by this but continue in patient well-doing. They will find that the appearance of being forgotten by the Foreign Office has its compensations ; they will be able for long periods to forget the Foreign Office themselves.

What I have just written is applicable to my life in Budapest from the middle of May 1939 till April 1941, when Hungary entered the war. When towards the end of it relations became very " hot " I felt that I was working in satisfactorily close contact with my masters at home. Otherwise and so far as " cold " diplomacy were concerned, I personally felt that the Foreign Office and Ministers in London knew nothing to speak of about Hungary or Hungarians and did not want to learn—anyhow not to learn from me. This was never more clear to me than when all Central and South European Representatives were summoned to London for consultation in the spring of 1940. Mr. Neville Chamberlain entertained us, and he began a conversation with me about Hungary, but it soon became obvious that this worthy Birmingham industrialist knew nothing about Hungarians and that his mind was not open to such facts or impressions as I could offer him. There was, I think, in the Foreign Office and in most Ministers' minds a hard core of feeling and opinion about central Europe built up by what may roughly be called the pro-French school of thought and by the patient labour of Czechs—of the charming and persuasive Jan Masaryk and the astute and deceptive Edward Benes. This was of a nature to make Hungarians, and me also, feel that no burning Hungarian question, such as the merits of the Treaty of Trianon, would be considered fairly in London.

However, in every other way than this I had a most enjoyable time in Hungary which, as all must agree, is a lovely country. The middle of it is flat and consists of very deep rich soil, heavily tilled. Some people might find it dull to race along the main roads through the *Alföld* as it is called, in winter when a frozen sun glares under a great arch of steel-blue steel-grey sky at the silent bitter fields or even in summer when the flat straight roads are carpeted with the fallen blossoms of honey-sweet acacia ; but my farmer's heart was always nourished and satisfied by the prospect. If one wanted a change from the *Alföld*, one could easily reach the surrounding foothills where the country breaks up into stream and meadow and coppice or find deep forests where in the autumn the red deer cough and bark, the roe deer bolt like rabbits from the thickets and wild pigs come down at sunset to drink and wallow in the mudpools. If this was not enough, one could, within the compass of a weekend, visit Vienna and the charms of the Ostmark ; the mountains of High Tartary ; the waving grainlands of Slovakia, ridge after ridge of rye and barley, bronzed and kilted girls bending and singing like Ceres in the corn ; Ruthenia with its peasantry polite and poor but rich in their embroidery ; the white stony ridges of Giulia and Fruili ; or the pretty small roads which lead the traveller to Maribor and Vorozdin and many Slovenian villages, which, though Slovenia was in 1940 a word unknown to most English people, nourished a life as intricate, as dignified, as old and as seemly as anything to be found in the Cotswolds or the valley of the Thame.

In the second place I had an enjoyable time in Hungary because those Hungarians with whom most of my time was inevitably spent, were very much like the gentry of England. The hall-mark of the English gentry is what the French call *désinvolture*, translated in Cassell's Dictionary as " easy graceful bearing, unconstraint, ease, gracefulness ". This was precisely what was encountered among Hungarians, either of the aristocracy or bourgeoisie. To walk right into a French family (whether aristocratic or bourgeois) is a formidable adventure, but among Hungarians it was like being at home. There was always a house within a potter of the Legation where I could go in between five and eight o'clock for a drink and conversation. One or two other friends would look in and perhaps also a journalist and a priest and the children back from school ; and we would all stand and sit about on the floor if it pleased us, or on a creepy-stool in front of the fire and talk scandal or nonsense—Hungarians enjoy just the same sort of scandal and nonsense as English people—or engage in vigorous and indeterminate discussions about religion or sex or politics until it was time to change for dinner. The Hungarians talked English, French, German, Italian and

Hungarian with equal ease though as between Hungarians the language was always Magyar—that melodious and vigorous speech which was, as it were, the banner of their uniqueness among all their European neighbours.

Weekends in Hungarian country houses also followed a familiar English pattern ; breakfast in the dining-room with kidney and bacon ; then a walk through the village to Mass, the countrymen standing about rather taciturn and very bony and tough-looking in top boots and skin-tight white breeches braided with arabesques ; then a visit to the stables to see the mares in their paddocks, the yearlings on range and plough oxen by the score chumping maize-stalks ; then a dip in the swimming-pool, lunch, siesta, walks, drinks and dinner ; everybody doing precisely as pleased them all the time with an informality which was as much an art as the most stylized behaviour. The principal difference between England and Hungary was that in Hungary I never went to a weekend shoot where we had less than three hundred beaters or shot less than two thousand cock pheasants.

The outbreak of war confronted Hungary on every side with problems of nightmarish complexity about which I shall say very little. The man with whom more than any other it was my business to discuss these was the Prime Minister, Count Teleki. He was of the Transylvanian nobility. There was nothing remarkable about his physical appearance, except that his face suggested a connection with the horsemen who riding into the West from the uplands of Asia many centuries earlier had founded the family from which he sprang. His manner was calm and gentle, but his movements quick, his habit of life modest to the point of austerity. He was intellectually eminent, a distinguished naturalist and a geographer of European repute. (When, incidentally, the British Army landed in Norway he at once explained to me in great detail and with maps the difficulties they would encounter and the absolute necessity there had been of taking Trondhjem.) He respected and liked the English, though he did not think much of Mr. Neville Chamberlain or Lord Halifax or Mr. Eden. He was very much a family man, inspiring his intimates and subordinates with unbounded devotion. Under this unassuming but not unimpressive exterior feelings of passionate intensity throbbed and burned ; ended by burning him up altogether. The passion I had to keep my eye on was his devotion to his country ; all other motives had to take station behind that except his religion. He lived a dedicated life, untortured by conflicts originating in his own character and beliefs. All the conflicts came from outside ; from the ineluctable pressure of political circumstances on his judgment and conscience.

In many respects and especially in his pre-eminence over other contemporary politicians he resembled de Valera and Salazar ; for all three displayed or display, as the case may be, a most engaging combination of characteristics ; being all men of the world, Christians, shrewd, intellectually powerful, patient, supple, inflexible in respect to certain matters of principle and utterly incorruptible.

The British Legation was a commodious house of the eighteenth century built round a courtyard and standing on the great rock of Buda with a big view from the back windows over low-lying Pesth and the Danube. Soon after my arrival Jane joined me. When the balloon went up there was nothing exceptional for me to do except send home as many British subjects as possible and start an intensive propaganda or information service. The Chancery on September 4th and 5th was, as I suppose, like the inside of the control tower at an aerodrome. We enlisted the help of some British air-line pilots who happened to be in Budapest and together with these and my Service Attachés we spent the night in the Chancery drinking cocoa and telephoning to aerodromes all over Europe about weather conditions and availability of aircraft. In the end I chartered two K.L.M. machines at Amsterdam at £400 a flight from Budapest to Holland. I took a chance on getting Treasury cover for the expense, and the K.L.M. took a chance on flying by night over German military areas. It was a relief when we had got the last of the mothers and babies into the air. On September 4th also we started the issue of a news bulletin, based on B.B.C.

broadcasts, of which I made Jane the editor. It had to be roneo-ed and called for personally by our clients, anything else being illegal. The Hungarian Government looked the other way—being almost to a man pro-British—and we soon had a circulation of thousands.

My wife and Kate joined me in March 1940. The fighting in France started, it will be remembered, in the second week of May, and it was a very anxious and unhappy family—now reunited but for Patrick—which listened to the broadcasts on those warm June days while Patrick sat amidst the desolation of the Dunkirk beaches. It is no good pretending that any national disaster can be as painful as a private anxiety. It was a pity, of course, that civilization and Christianity and things like that were in jeopardy, but this had happened before and they had survived or regenerated themselves. The O'Malleys' trouble was that Patrick had got caught up in this present emergency and that while his survival had for a good many days and nights been a matter of doubt he had, should he be killed, no faculty for regeneration. It seemed a long time before at last we heard that he had got out, and had, during the moments of our most acute anxiety been resting somewhere on the borders of Wales signing orders—being then a Second Lieutenant—as " O.C. Troops 48th Division ".

September came when, as it seemed to us, the Germans should go into England for the kill. Owing to lack of space elsewhere the official wireless machine was housed in one of the bathrooms in the guests' chambers at the back of the house ; and it was here, sitting on the edge of the bath and on the seat of the w.c. that with our little contraption we caught the princely and immortal words out of the startled ether :

" We shall fight in France ; we shall fight on the seas and on the oceans ; we shall fight with growing strength and confidence in the air ; we shall defend our island whatever the cost may be ; we shall fight on the beaches ; we shall fight on the landing-grounds ; we shall fight in the fields and streets ; we shall fight in the hills, we shall never surrender . . ."

Well, that was all right so far as it went, but it looked as

LIEUTENANT PATRICK O'MALLEY (1940)
Ox. and Bucks, L.I.

KATE O'MALLEY DRESSED IN LOCAL BRIDAL
COSTUME BY HUNGARIAN PEASANT WOMEN

if these encounters on the beaches and in the streets and
fields and hills were going to be a bloody and mortal business.
Anyhow for better or worse we knew now where we were.
Alone. Up against it. No allies now to bother or wonder
about ; only the astonishing benevolence of America to up-
hold us ; and our past ; and the Invisible Army of all brave
men who from time to time in the history of many nations
had turned to face desperate odds with bared teeth and
resolute hearts.

Immediate anxiety about Patrick having been removed we
turned our thoughts with increased composure and zest to
the Polish soldiers of whom there were now some forty thousand
in Hungary. As unobtrusively as possible, and with the hearty
connivance of the Hungarian authorities and particularly of
the Regent, we did what we could to help them escape into
Yugoslavia and re-form in France or Great Britain. As all
the world knows, a very large number succeeded.

Our next pre-occupation was British prisoners of war in
German camps situated in Poland. A postcard reached me
from Jack Poole (Rifle Brigade, I think) from Oflag VII C.
I answered it, and experience soon proved that communication
with prisoners of war in German hands was easy and regular.
That postcard of Jack Poole's turned out to be a regular
snowball ; and before many weeks had elapsed the Legation,
scouring the Balkans for stores of every description, had
become a depository and transmitting station for tons of food
and clothing. For months all available British subjects
worked at this like navvies. It had, strictly speaking, nothing
to do with the Foreign Office, but it naturally gave all of us
immense satisfaction. The Germans behaved very well ; even
the guitar and five hundred mouth-organs for camp bands
were safely delivered.

The only real live British prisoners of war who came my
way were two " other ranks " who had been captured at
Calais and had escaped from a camp in Poland. After being
looked after from October 1940 till February 1941 by the
Polish Underground Movement, they had reached Budapest.
I was having a nap after luncheon when Kate stepped into

my bedroom and handed me a bit of paper, with the names written on it.

" I've got two prisoners for you," she said.

I said : " Oh ? where ? "

She said : " Down in Pesth . . . is looking after them."

This was exciting. I did not want to embarrass the Hungarian police, so I sent a guide down for them and let them into the Legation after dark myself by the garden door and put them in an empty wing under lock and key so as to keep my servants guessing. Clothes and razors were bought and we settled down to think how to get out of Hungary two young men who could not have succeeded in following any of the Polish escape routes. I decided to take them with me to Belgrade disguised as members of my staff, some passports with visas were produced for them, and off I went with a retinue by the night train to visit Sir R. Campbell in Yugoslavia, which I anyhow wanted to do. At this time the Germans had pretty thoroughly infiltrated the Hungarian frontier police, and when we reached the Hungarian–Yugoslav frontier I was woken up by one of my staff and told that the authorities did not like the look of the Hungarian exit visas on my prisoners' passports. Smuggling p.o.w. out of the country was no part of a Minister's duties and I began to sweat, particularly in the palms of my hands. However, all went well. I sent for the head policeman, lay in bed with my hair rumpled, got very very angry, and said I would take my whole party off the train and telephone there and then to the Regent if he did not let all my staff through with me instantly. Luckily he did not call my bluff, and so we slid on out of the station into Yugoslavia.

The arrival of these two p.o.w. put ideas into my head and I began to concoct plans with Christina for a regular escape route for British p.o.w. from Polish camps. This was Christina Gizycka, G.M., O.B.E., Croix de Guerre, later called Christina Granville, who was murdered in London in 1952. She was from a Polish noble family, the Skarbeks, young, beautiful and gifted, famous afterwards in the French *maquis*. The Germans had put her photograph up in every station in

Poland and £1,000 on her head, dead or alive ; but she went back for us from Hungary into Poland several times. She was the bravest person I ever knew, the only woman who had a positive *nostalgie* for danger. She could do anything with dynamite except eat it. I loved her dearly—God rest her soul. Her husband, George, was doing some underground work for the British military authorities in Abyssinia. I got him to Budapest, made him into a British subject and appointed him to be my Military Attaché's clerk. With these two to maintain liaison with one of the numerous Polish underground associations we had strong hopes of getting a steady stream of p.o.w. down to Athens and so home to England. I had to reveal these plans to the War Office in London because they were going to cost a lot of money. For the first and last time in my life when applying for money for government purposes, I at once got a telegram saying that the sky was the limit. All these thrilling schemes were on the point of maturing when relations between the United Kingdom and Hungary were broken off.

Some months before this I had realized that the German police net, working through disloyal members of the Hungarian police or the Hungarian General Staff, was closing round Christina. I begged and implored her to leave the country while there was still time but she was obdurate. Finally, at the eleventh hour, she agreed. It was a Saturday afternoon. Now the Gestapo had many curious habits, and among them was a great attachment to a weekend without engagements. We therefore felt confident that we had till the early hours of the Monday to put a planned escape into operation ; and accordingly, I told a junior member of my staff to drive to Belgrade on the Sunday with a Legation car and Christina rolled up in the boot. On Sunday after breakfast I noticed signs of perturbation in the courtyard, and found that inadequate preparations had been made and that in none of the cars available for the trip was the boot big enough to hold Christina. However, I had a very large Chrysler of my own and from the back of this we ripped spare tyres and other impedimenta. Time permitted of no concealment.

The policeman at the entrance to the Legation stared sombrely at the proceedings, but they were nice men and accustomed to get hot cocoa on snowy nights in the porter's lodge. So Christina went off sitting demurely beside the driver, rolled up in the boot when the frontier was approached, and managed to avoid sneezing or coughing at critical moments. I went down to Belgrade shortly afterwards and we had a fine party at the Serbski Kral and went to see the stomach-dancers in some low haunt afterwards. I did not embarrass the Foreign Office by reporting to them Christina's escape which, like my transactions with the two p.o.w., were not part of a Minister's duties.

During the early months of 1941 the Germans closed in on Hungary. In April their army marched through Budapest almost under my windows " From Morn till Noon . . . from Noon till dewy Eve " ; splendid men, splendidly equipped, buckles shining like a dragon's scales in the clear Hungarian air. A German army on the march, armed and accoutred for battle, is an awful and majestic thing ; particularly awful when it is a hostile army marching against our friends and the friends of our friends. And yet, in my strange and rather lonely situation, anger and consternation gave place to compassion. What fine young men they were ! What a pity to die so young and so strong ! But of course they should have thought of that before and not egged Hitler on or let him get so much above himself. It was too late now. If they were going to die, they were going to die ; and what was worse, a lot of other people would die in the process of killing them. Meanwhile I had my business to do with the Regent.

By this time—the first days of April—the pillars of the State had begun to crack and its walls to bulge. We heard the rustle and crepitation of stanchions and girders as the undermined edifice began to settle which had so long sheltered these Hungarians to whom I was now much attached. The Regent was an honest decent man and a friend of mine. I thought I had persuaded him to send Bethlen and Eckhardt and Baranyai and other respectable Hungarians out of the country to form an Emigrant Government, himself retreating when the emergency arrived with what loyal troops he could collect to the frontier of Yugoslavia. But when the moment of decision came he thought with invincible and utterly misplaced optimism that he was going somehow or another to weather the storm in his palace in Buda, and Bethlen thought so too. Teleki knew better and shot himself when all hope was gone of reconciling divergent loyalties. Horthy's optimism was ridiculous. When I went to say goodbye to him he said : " It's absurd your dragging Kate all round the world with you. You had much better leave her with me, and I and Ili (his daughter-in-law) will look after her." I said : " You've got this all wrong. Things are a damn sight worse than you suppose. If you are going to stay here, your best line is to get yourself shot by the Germans," for I knew well that he would not have hesitated to get himself shot if it would have done Hungary any good. He listened to me kindly as always, but it was clear that my words left him unmoved. Although I did not know it, the Hungarian General Staff was already deeply committed to a different course. There was nothing for me to do now but hurry on with preparations for instant departure.

CHAPTER 20

THROUGH RUSSIA AGAIN

FROM April 8th to the 11th, 1941, the drawing-room and halls of the British Legation in Budapest resounded with the affectionate goodbyes of all our friends ; and there were many tears shed, for most of them, much less optimistic than the Regent, felt that the departure of the British sounded a sort of tocsin heralding the end of the old order in Hungary. My butler cried as he kissed my hands, repeating many times : " *Sie sind immer so gut mit mir gewesen.*" In the midst of all this we got about eighty-five suitcases packed for the journey. My silver had all gone home a year earlier. Everything portable now had to be packed so far as possible in articles which could be easily handled, for we were not at all sure what sort of a journey lay before us. Books, pictures and all household equipment had to be left behind, and all was later completely destroyed in the long and bitter battle between Germans and Russians which eventually laid waste the beautiful streets of Buda.

Italy being enemy territory only three possible routes from Hungary to England were worth considering : through Germany or Austria to Switzerland and Boulogne or Lisbon ; through Moscow and Tokio or through Moscow and Erzerum to Constantinople. I was advised that except for a small party of males the third route was impracticable. I have no doubt that if I had asked them for it, the German authorities would have provided a sealed train to Lisbon complete with heel-clicking waiters and champagne, but it would have been distasteful to have accepted favours from them. Accordingly, I decided with the approval of all to go round the world. I was accompanied by the Belgians and the Dutch and together we made up a party of about fifty souls.

Providentially for us a little railway across Ruthenia connecting Hungary with the Ukraine had been put into use some three weeks before the date of our departure. By this we proceeded to Ungvar and Csap to the Russian frontier ; the Soviet Government having been asked by the British Government to make suitable arrangements for the further journey. We got to the Russian frontier at 10 p.m. on a very cold night and here began to experience the perversity and discourtesy of the Russian administration. The train which we were to enter, for instance, was drawn up about one hundred and fifty yards beyond the platform and we were expected to remain in a comfortless station for the best part of the night before being allowed to enter it. The enforcement of this arrangement was in the hands of a scruffy little man who proved to be a Lieutenant-Colonel and soon discovered that nothing short of physical force could prevent the personnel of the British, Belgian and Dutch Legations from shouldering their own bags down the line and through the snow and settling themselves without further delay into the unlighted and dilapidated four-berth carriages which were to carry us through Lwow (Lemberg) and Kieff to Moscow. Although when we arrived at the Embassy in Moscow it was explained to us that the Soviet Government possessed no modern, clean or comfortable sleeping berths which could have been put at our disposal, we had observed that half a dozen highly placed Communists had been accommodated at Kieff with a brand-new coach of *wagon-lits* which included an observation car.

Three days were spent in this train watching from the windows companies of politically unreliable citizens being driven to work in the flat featureless fields of the Ukraine and in inspecting the sights of Kieff. In Moscow Sir Stafford and Lady Cripps received us with abundant hospitality and here we stayed until April 24th. Sir Stafford, than whom no man radiated more kindness and charm, would not talk politics. He spoke about Russia with the kind of reticence to be expected from a politician still in doubt about the line he would take when he got back to the House of Commons ; but I got the impression that disillusionment was already well

at work. I for my part forbore to tell him that before I had
spent many hours in the " Workers' Paradise " the sensation
was again strong upon me which I described in an earlier
chapter, of being in a spiritual gas-chamber. In Moscow we
were never out of sight of bent railings, broken hinges, leaking
gutters and untidy courtyards. Up and down the streets,
ten to sixteen abreast, still trudged the uniformly glum dirty
dun-coloured population, just as they had trudged in 1925.
There was hardly a bright colour to be seen apart from the
white woollen berets of the girls for which communally-owned
Soviet rabbits had, we supposed, been laid under contribution.
This was all very unlike the poorest parts of Stepney High
Street or Limehouse, for even in the very poor parts of London
there is always laughter and high spirits—the young men
swaggering along and the girls swinging their hips on the way
to a gin-palace or a cinema. When Kate burst into a hearty
laugh one day coming out of a shop into the street a member
of the Embassy who was with her said : " Hush ; one doesn't
laugh here like that in the streets, it is liable to attract attention
and unpleasantness." What a country where a child must
not laugh !

Having dropped some of our party to reinforce the Embassy
establishment, I left Moscow on the Siberian train on the
morning of April 24th in company with my family, five members
of the Budapest staff and the Dutch Chargé d'Affaires from
Budapest and his family who were under my wing—they not
enjoying full diplomatic status. The resources of the Soviet
Government did not extend to providing separate compart-
ments for each of us, so I and Kate doubled up together.
Jane was not with us, having gone back to England from Budapest just before Italy entered the war. We were put into a
pre-1914 coach of the conventional second-class *wagon-lit* type.
The dining-car was old, dirty, ill-lit and villainously served.
Butter was plentiful and excellent, bread tolerable and the
rest of the food more or less uneatable. There were no fleas
nor bugs. After the first day no milk or eggs were obtainable ;
not because they could not be bought, but because the dining-
car contractor saw his way to make a larger profit out of

inferior food. The crew of our coach were prepared to tolerate us so long as we accommodated ourselves to their ideas of how passengers should behave, but they were certainly not ready to study our convenience, much less our whims. For instance, one of the horrors of a Russian train is the wireless machine which never stops. This is so arranged as to fill the whole coach with the Moscow transmission in Russian. It was useless to turn it off or to explain to the sleeping-car attendant that we were all foreigners urgently wishing quietly to rest or read or converse together. If the sleeping-car attendant wanted to listen to the broadcast or thought it proper that we should do so, he insisted on turning it on and plainly showed his resentment at any objections or interference from ourselves. Breaches of the train rules were punished with summary fines. I myself was fined 25 roubles within a quarter of an hour of leaving Moscow for trying to let down a bed. I was later again fined 25 roubles for lighting a spirit stove. The imposition of these fines upon a travelling diplomatist clearly gave the management much satisfaction. Many rather embittered arguments took place through the intermediary of the *Intourist* [1] interpreter on the subject of ventilation. Siberia still being partially under snow, all windows were hermetically sealed. Consequently the atmosphere soon became foul and we asked that at least the doors at either end of the coach might be periodically opened to admit fresh air. The only response to this by the attendants was to turn off the heating. We explained that what was making some members of the party feel ill was not too high a temperature but lack of oxygen. "I quite understand," said *Intourist*, "the chemical and physiological facts; but you must realize that you are in Soviet Russia and not in England, and that Soviet laws and customs which are different to your laws and customs must here prevail. Our regulations say that passengers may have either fresh air or heating but not both ; and although you are all foreigners in this coach, we cannot disregard the rules in order to suit your convenience. Anyhow," she added, "you would get a great deal less

---

[1] *Intourist* means an official guide in charge of foreigners.

fresh air in the air-raid shelters in London where you are going."

Towards the end of the winter the country between Moscow and Manchuria is uniformly dreary. For the most part it is uncultivated and covered with scrub. Two or three times a day the train stopped in dreary filthy poverty-stricken towns. Between whiles it passed at infrequent intervals an aggregation of the timber-built huts, or rather styes, around which the inmates were beginning to stir from their winter's hibernation. Climatic conditions, while more severe in Siberia, do not differ very widely from those which prevail in winter in the great plain of Hungary ; but there is a world of difference in the appearance which the two present to the eye, and we were naturally led to dwell on this contrast by the fact of having so recently exchanged the *Alföld* for the steppe. An idea is often met with in London that the agricultural population of Hungary consisted in 1941 of down-trodden peasants labouring in servitude and dejection to keep a feudal aristocracy in ease and luxury. I can only say that I had driven over nearly all the main roads and innumerable by-roads in Hungary without finding any foundation to speak of for this conception. An agricultural proletariat indeed existed and required energetic attention from the Hungarian authorities, but the general impression that I got from having passed through or stopped in a large number of country townships and villages in Hungary was that of sound, neat and sufficiently commodious houses inhabited by tough upstanding self-respecting well-mannered agreeable countrymen. We had, of course, no opportunity of getting anything but the most superficial glance at the Russians of Siberia and at the manner of their existence ; but, for all its superficiality, our impression was strong that, whatever may have been the case in towns, the inhabitants of the purely rural districts of Siberia enjoyed an extremely low standard of life. Judged so far as one could judge them by their faces, demeanour, clothes, houses, domestic animals and equipment, the life of these people seemed to be without any comfort or beauty, without any hope or purpose except the preservation of life itself. It was apparently all undifferentiated proletariat. The appearance of the country-side and of the population showed considerable improvement beyond Irkutsk ; and *Intourist* told us that this was because the most easterly parts of Siberia are those to which the Soviet Government had, during the last fifteen years, transferred from European Russia a considerable population ; and that money had been more generously appropriated to the new than to the old settlements. This, said *Intourist*, was the reason why numerous freshly-completed factories and communal houses were observable in Chita and to the east of it. Maybe this, too, was the reason why it was in the neighbourhood of Chita that we saw a cross country metalled road for the first time after leaving the vicinity of Moscow three thousand miles to the west.

By the afternoon of our seventh day in the train we were looking forward eagerly to crossing the frontier into Manchuria and our disappointment was correspondingly acute when we were informed by the local authority at Atpor or Otpor—the Russian frontier station—that, since we had no Manchurian entrance visas, we could not be allowed to proceed without special authority from Moscow ; that if this authorization had not arrived in a few hours when the train was due to proceed, we were to wait where we were till further orders. Atpor is an insignificant village with no accommodation for travellers. On the night of April 30th it was under snow and subject to the full force of a bitter Siberian wind. The following conversation took place between me and a laconic and sinister-looking member of the police ; *Intourist*, with obvious satis-faction, acting as interpreter :

" Do you know that we were assured by the Foreign Office in Moscow that no difficulty of this kind would arise ? "

" No."

" Do you not realize that there is no official in Russia who could have granted a Manchurian visa but that we all have Japanese visas ? "

" No."

" Do you know that the British Consul in Harbin and the Japanese Embassy in Moscow have both assured me that there is no obstacle to our entering Manchuria ? "

" No."

" The chief of Police at Chita told me all was in order : will you kindly telephone to him ? "

" What I do or don't do is nothing to do with you. You must wait here till I get instructions."

" May I telephone to Harbin or Manchuli ? "

" Both are impossible."

" May I get a car or cart and go on with a policeman to the actual frontier and speak to the Manchurian authorities there ? "

" No."

" May I telegraph to the British Consul at Harbin ? "

" No."

" Can we telephone to Chita or Moscow ? "

" No."

" May I telegraph to Moscow ? "

" Yes, in Russian."

" Is there an hotel in Atpor ? "

" No."

" Can we get any food here ? "

" None is provided."

" Will the heating be kept up in the train ? "

" No."

" Does the fact that I have two invalids with me affect the matter ? "

" No."

" May we go on to Vladivostock, or back to Chita ? "

" No. Your passports have not the necessary visas."

" Where, then, are we to go, or what are we to do if we are all turned out on the platform in the middle of the night in this weather with no immediate prospect of getting forward or back ? "

No answer.

At this point the policeman, tired of the discussion, turned his back and left the train. With *Intourist's* help a telegram in Russian to Sir Stafford Cripps describing our plight was despatched, but we learned subsequently that it was never delivered to the Embassy. Having assisted me thus far,

Intourist and the crew also got off the train leaving only two sentries in the surrounding snow in charge of it and us. In view of the malevolence of the police and the uncertainty of our future, I decided to burn the despatches which I was taking to Tokio ; and, having done so, I gave Kate a sleeping pill and rolled myself up in a fur coat on the floor, all bedding having been removed from the train. My own discomforts and distresses during the preceding twenty days had been increased by anxiety on account of Kate who had left Budapest after an attack of influenza, with acute inflammation of the ear and infected antra. For this reason I had been counting each kilometre and hour which separated us from Tokio. The prospect of indefinite detention at Atpor of my whole party, deprived as they would have been of every comfort and subject to the ill will and caprice of the Soviet police, brought shamefully to light my own lack of fortitude ; and I must have looked a very poor figure lying on the floor, feeling as if my stomach was jumping up and down inside me and, at intervals, being sick. My wife, however, is tougher than I am and she made tea for me and others when she was not busy stoking the " chauffage " at the end of the coach. It was a very unpleasant night. At about seven o'clock the next morning our passports were returned and we were told we could proceed over the frontier to Manchuria. I do not know how to account for the unkindness and insolence of Communist officials to an inoffensive party of diplomatists to whom every conceivable facility had been promised by the Kremlin. Was it all due to muddle ? or to a sort of official and Party sadism ? or was it all a calculated insult ? Later, from Tokio, I reported the affair to the Foreign Office in London, but, so far as I know it did not interest them. I never heard any more about it.

Having in what precedes written in unfriendly terms of the Communist gang who govern Russia and her satellites, I wish to add that my words are in no way directed against the unfortunate peoples under Communist rule. My distaste is for the parent fungus in Moscow from which infective spores have been so widely disseminated ; and I shall always try to bear in mind the words in which Sir Thomas Browne [1] marked the distinction between peoples and their Governments :

" There is another offence unto Charity, which no Author hath ever written of, and few take notice of ; and that's the reproach, not of whole professions, mysteries and conditions, but of whole Nations ; wherein by opprobrius Epithets we miscal each other, and by an uncharitable Logick, from a disposition in a few, conclude a habit in all.

> Le mutin Anglois, & le bravache Escossois ;
> Le bougre Italian, & le fol François ;
> Le poultron Romain, le larron de Gascongne,
> L'Epagnol superbe, & l'Aleman yvrongne.

St. Paul, that calls the Cretians lyars, doth it but indirectly, and upon quotation of their own Poet. It is as bloody a thought in one way, as Nero's was in another. For by a word we wound a thousand, and at one blow assassine the honour of a Nation."

Manchouli is remotely situated on the borders of Manchuria and Mongolia, but it possesses a decent hotel where we got excellent coffee and milk and bread and eggs and apples. The waiters and porters were northern Chinese and to me and my wife it was inexpressibly delightful to be surrounded again by these men from Shantung and Chihli, heaving, shouting, laughing, quick to understand and do what was wanted ; cheerful, dignified and, to our eyes, beautiful. Here I was again, as at Poti in 1925, crossing at a stride into what seemed like Paradise out of the dirty crazy barbarism of Soviet Russia.

All along the line we now followed to Tokio through Harbin, Dairen, Kobe and Yokohama, Consuls and other British subjects were loud in their complaints of the inefficiency and suspicions and disobliging behaviour of the Japanese, but we were in a mood to take the latter quite simply as we found them ; and we found them clean, courteous and obliging. The Japanese South Manchurian Railway Company's train was, I suppose, one of the cleanest trains in the world. One could have eaten off the floor of the w.c. The food and beds were excellent and boys passed up and down the train offering

[1] Works of Sir Thomas Browne. Ed. Charles Sayle, 1904, Vol. I, p. 90.

the passengers towels freshly wrung out in boiling water with which to wipe their faces and hands or the window-frames. Sitting at the windows, it was delightful now to see again the blue linen-clothed figures of Chinese peasants working in the fields. The weather and the landscape of this afternoon of May 1st were in harmony with our mood. The snow had been left behind at Irkutsk. For many miles on both sides of the railway stretched the flat grassland ringed with hills which in the intensely clear and dry air and a brilliant sun glowed like topaz and sapphire. Here and there we could see the felted tent of a Mongol, and near it the mounted herdsman pasturing his stock on the dry grass from which this spring's green had not yet driven last year's gold. Exchanging these sights later for the well-ordered rice fields and gardens, bright clothes and cheerful faces of Japan, some of my party, having expected only to exchange one form for another of the uncomfortable, the bizarre and the alien, were surprised at the transition from Russia where all was raw, inchoate and barbarous to the Far East where we returned to order, beauty, continuity and politeness ; but I had been both to Russia and the Far East before and enjoyed being able to say " I told you so ! "

The Ambassador, Sir Robert Craigie, and Lady Craigie entertained us most generously in Tokio for a week, and we proceeded to San Francisco via Honolulu in the Japanese *Tatsuta Maru* ; the ship and personnel being, as was to be expected impeccably clean and polite. On arrival in the United States my wife stayed for some weeks in Los Angeles, trying unsuccessfully to sell a story to the Film Companies. Kate and I wandered on to Washington, inspecting on the way Santa Fé and the Grand Canyon which we found dull. My wife stayed on in America for a year. I delayed along with Kate for three months until I had succeeded in getting Tibor Eckhardt (see Chapter 19) from Cairo where he had got stuck to Washington where I hoped he might be useful among Hungarian immigrants in the U.S.A. The less said about these three months the better, for they were filled with boredom and frustration. In every other country in the world the British Embassy is, for a member of the Foreign Service, a home from home. Not so in Washington in 1941. The place pullulated with British officials. The British were tremendously busy with their war, and Americans with their neutrality. Naturally no one welcomed the arrival of flotsam from the wreck of central Europe.

And oh what am I to say about these poor dear Americans who mean so well and try so hard? I think I had better not say much for many of them seem to mind what the British think of them, whereas of course the British do not ever mind in the least anything Americans say or think of us who sit back feeling safe and superior. Why is it that Americans look funny to me when they are playing baseball in those extraordinary caps with huge peaks, whereas there is nothing funny at all about the equally foreign spectacle of a Basque playing pelota? Why is it that a photograph of a group of American Generals or even the sight of two ordinary G.I.s walking down Piccadilly is slightly funny, whereas there is nothing funny at all about a Norwegian or Pole or Turk in uniform? Why is it that in spite of the power and the glory we not seldom get a whiff—aye, even in Boston—of preparatory school or servants' hall? The answers to these very indelicate questions are certainly not to be found in any superiority of the British over the Americans in cleverness, goodness, courage, industry or humour ; for Americans are surely in those respects quite as good as or better than any other people. It may be that the answer lies in the highly developed self-satisfaction and Narcissism for which the British are universally notorious. But perhaps it is possible to see a little further into the matter by comparing the British with the French ; for the wine-drinking French have I think rather the same sort of feeling about the beer-swilling English that the English have about Americans, namely that they are in some way—not susceptible of exact definition—superior. And for my part I think this French sentiment is well founded. If an average French household is minutely examined, it will, I think, be found to be more thoroughly penetrated by that complex of thought and feeling and habit and custom which, in a rough and ready way, we call " civilization " ; and the reason for this is perhaps simply that the process of penetration has been going on rather longer in France than in England. So, coming back to the Americans, I think the answer to all my questions is that they are a very young people and that the English are in comparison a very old people ; and that the moral to be drawn from this answer is that we should not take this feeling of superiority to Americans at all seriously. It is not more respectworthy than the feeling of superiority which a man of ancient lineage often entertains for the parvenu. Time will remove it.

But the three months I spent in the United States was not enough time to enable me to get used to Americans or turn to advantage the modest opportunities I was afforded of making friends with them. I was ill at ease with them because we thought and felt and spoke in a different idiom ; and their idiom was very much more foreign to me than anything I was used to in any country in Europe. And so the very hot damp days in Washington and the equally hot but dry days in New York dragged themselves out, relieved only by short visits to Ipswich and Martha's Vineyard ; dragged themselves out amidst vast and comfortless hotels, shops which combined the business of snack-bar and apothecary and crowds where everyone seemed to be rushing to and fro and round and round without achieving anything but the propagation and growth of a human jungle where few flowers bloomed and few birds sang. I blamed myself at the time, as I do now, for my narrow and unsympathetic outlook, but self-blame did not prevent me from longing for the vulgarity of Leicester Square or the ugliness of World's End. I knew that in the interstices of such squalor familiar and comforting social habits could still germinate ; and of course, besides all that, Kate and I wanted to get on to the places where bombs were falling and exploding among our friends.

Kate and I were to go home by air, but in 1941 there were only three aircraft available for civilian passenger traffic from America to Europe : three flying-boats called Bristol—and two other names beginning with B—of which one made the round journey every three weeks or so. We had to wait a month for our passage. At last the appointed day arrived ; and at Baltimore in the early hours of the morning Kate and I went on board. The flight to Botwood in Newfoundland was without incident. Here, however, the captain, Kelly Rodgers, decided that we must wait until some small broken part of the machine had been replaced ; and so Kate and I were enabled to spend two whole days and nights in this novel environment. Botwood was reminiscent of the sea-inlets of Argyllshire ; a remote, pale pinegirt inlet of the sea. It was a logging station without any amenities beyond what the garrison—the Prince Edward Island Highlanders—could offer. This hospitable regiment made us honorary members of their mess ; and Kate and I slept in the Colonel's bedroom. I was allowed to drive a Bren-gun carrier over hedges and ditches. It was all as pleasant as could be. It was nice to be with a people at war.

On the evening of the second day the sea-plane was declared ready for flight, and at sundown we took our places. The eastern horizon was coloured like a wood-pigeon's breast ; the western sky was pale lemon green like the waters of Loch Carra. Nearly the whole arch of heaven was empty : only in the west did cumulus mount up in tower above tower, and it was towards this imposing cloud-structure that Bristol taxied into the head of the bay, then turned and thundered back, lifted her nose from the bow-wave and bore us serenely into the empyrean. We mounted up with wings as eagles and the darkness of the clouds enfolded us. It was a proper moment for serious reflections : nothing between us and the next world but the snoring engines. In a few hours we were to be two miles up in the air and a thousand miles from land ; a lonely place for Kate and me ; a solemn thought for earthbound man and girl. Kate said " Go out into the darkness and put your hand into the hand of God. That shall be to you better than light and safer than a known way." [1]

To us unaccustomed—as indeed was everybody in 1941—to the idea of flying across the Atlantic, a safe landfall seemed

[1] Miss M. L. Haskins.

improbable ; " but," said I, " if we really do get there, if
tomorrow morning we really do get onto the earth again, it
will indeed be *un beau moment*, one of the very best things
that's ever happened, or ever will happen to us in life ". And
so it proved. At about half-past five o'clock in the morning,
after sound sleep, we first saw the wrinkled sea through holes
in the cloud floor. In a little time the mountains of County
Clare—Slieve Elva and Slieve Callan—were visible upon the
horizon, and we swung twenty degrees to starboard. Presently
we were overflying white cottages and fields green with the
aftermath and pock-marked with yellow circles where tramp-
cocks had stood. And then at last we touched down upon
the broad Shannon like a swan upon her downy breast, and
got out and walked again along the Irish lanes. It had
indeed been a very nice homecoming.

CHAPTER 21

POLAND

No. 1 MORE'S GARDEN was naturally looking the worse for wear by September 1941, when we got back. Most of the windows were gone and the bomb that knocked down Chelsea Old Church had messed up the drawing-room and blown into a thousand pieces the Dresden candlesticks that had come from Belclare. However, Jane who had been in residence and fire-wardening had made the place habitable and here I settled down to wait for orders from the Foreign Office. The Foreign Office could not think of any way in which I could help to win the war till February 15th, 1943, when His Majesty King George VI, moved thereto by Mr. Eden, decided that I was a " Person of approved Wisdom, Loyalty, Diligence and Circumspection " and that he " reposed especial trust and confidence in the discretion and faithfulness of His Trusty and Well-beloved Owen St. Clair O'Malley " who was " hereby nominated constituted and appointed " Ambassador to the Polish Republic. Mr. Eden added that I should stir my stumps and make as much of the job as I could. The Polish Government were at this time located in London. Apart from trying to keep out of the way of bombs, and fussing about my wife's illnesses, I cannot remember a single thing I did during the seventeen months I was unemployed except that I was appointed chairman of a committee of three persons to screen Hungarians detained as enemy aliens in the Isle of Man. That did not last long, for I disapproved so strongly of the way one of my two colleagues cross-questioned the men who came before us, refusing to accept my guidance in this matter, that I resigned and the committee's activities lapsed.

On appointment as Ambassador to the Poles, I went to the Palace in the usual way to " kiss hands " as it is called. The appointee to high office does not actually kiss His Majesty's hands. All that happens is that he is received alone and converses with the King for twenty minutes or half-an-hour. I do not know whether members of the Foreign Office nowadays are instructed by their elders in the matter of their personal relations with the Sovereign. In case they are not, I record what I was told by Sir Eyre Crowe when I was young, hoping that this may be useful to them. Crowe said that the proper relation between the Sovereign and someone holding the King's Commission was unique. When in course of time it became my privilege to converse with the King it would be my duty to tell His Majesty—if His Majesty encouraged me to do so—precisely and without reserve what I thought on any topic which came up. Crowe reminded me that no one in the Foreign Service should criticize the Secretary of State for Foreign Affairs to persons outside the Foreign Service ; but, said he, though the case is not likely to arise, to the Sovereign you can if you wish, and you should if you think it just and useful, say anything you like in criticism of any Ministers or their policies. He gave me an instance drawn from his contacts with King George V than whom no occupant of the throne had a nicer sense of such things. On one occasion King George V had quoted something which a Minister of the first rank had said to him. " If . . . told you that, Sir," said Crowe, " he told you a lie." " Yes," answered His Majesty, " and it wasn't the first and it won't be the last." Crowe warned me of course that it was not the business of the Sovereign to open his mind to the subject, nor, ordinarily His Majesty's custom. This, however, was neither here nor there : it was the Sovereign's business to listen to anything material the subject had to say, and it was the subject's duty to tell the truth to his King. This is a delicate and moving relationship but inherent in a true conception of kingship, for the King is father of all and of the least of his subjects, and the subjects' allegiance, particularly a commissioned officer's allegiance, is, so to speak, the fruit of a sacrament. It follows that a newly-appointed Ambassador or Minister when he is received by the King should be respectful but not servile, diffident but not hesitant, communicative but not garrulous and frank but not pert.

I continued as Ambassador to Poland till August 1945 when I went to Portugal. Of what I thought and said during that time I can, for the reasons I give in my Foreword, say very little ; but a retired official is perfectly free, with due regard to law and propriety, to say what he likes about current politics —to offer himself for election to Parliament if he chooses— and I shall avail myself of this liberty to say what I choose about our grievous situation *vis-à-vis* Russia between 1947 when I retired and 1953 when Stalin died. The reader may judge for himself whether the heart of the matter was the same during the years 1943 and 1945 as it has been between 1947 and 1953.

During this latter period we, on this side of the Iron Curtain, wanted an agreement with Russia to live and let live : for the sake of a quiet life we were ready to acquiesce in the inclusion of a large part of the globe under a regime which we detested and feared. But the negotiation of an agreement to live and let live postulated something in the nature of common ground, however small, between two negotiating parties ; and the Communists on their side did not in my view want to live and let live : on the contrary they wanted the destruction of every-body and everything which they found unassimilable. For propaganda purposes, in order that politicians might attract the votes of the doubtful voters and on the chance that things might be less black than they seemed it was indispensable to be ready, and to show readiness, to negotiate an accommoda-tion with Stalin, but in my view it was of no more substantial use to argue and negotiate with Stalin and his associates than to argue and negotiate with a lot of gorillas [1] and rattlesnakes. There was in the sombre depths of their hearts and minds no desire for a genuine accommodation, nor any moral principle or sentiment to which we could successfully appeal. Conse-quently there was for us no hopeful possibility of protecting all

[1] In his Mansion House Speech of February 19th, 1919, Mr. Churchill said that we were then " engaged in fighting against the foul baboonery of Bolshevism ". With respect, I prefer the comparison to gorillas ; but I am afraid both expressions are, so to speak, libellous on the animal kingdom.

that we held dear except in a preponderance on our side of physical force and, what is more, a known readiness to use it if necessary.

The reader may, as I have said, judge for himself how far things between 1943 and 1945 were as I believe them to have been between 1947 and 1953. What is perfectly certain is that a majority of Poles in those earlier years thought them to be exactly as I have described them above ; and, though behaving with commendable restraint, they were puzzled by the ostensible belief of the American and British Governments that by making political concessions or sacrifices (at the expense in the first instance of other nations) they could put Stalin in a good temper and induce him to do what they wanted. A classic example of such a concession or sacrifice which touched the Poles closely concerned the question of their eastern frontier. A committee of the Paris Peace Conference of 1919 had recommended the allocation to Russia of a belt of country lying between Poland and Russia which was inhabited partly by Russians and partly by Poles. For various reasons the recommendation was never carried into effect in the final peace settlements ; the debatable territory, east of what was called the " Curzon Line ", remained with Poland ; and argument and hot feeling had raged on all hands about this issue ever since. The British Government's attitude was made clear by the following statement by Mr. Churchill in the House of Commons on December 15th, 1944.

" If the Polish Government had agreed [to yield the contested territory to Russia] there would never have been any Lublin Committee [viz. the puppet Government of Poland]. If Mr. Mikolajczyk [Polish Prime Minister in London] could have returned to Moscow early in November . . . with power to conclude an agreement on the frontier line, Poland might now have taken full place in the ranks of the nations contending against Germany, and would have had the full support and friendship of Marshal Stalin and the Soviet Government."

The merits of the suggested new frontier line need not be discussed. The point is that Mr. Churchill thought, or anyhow said that he thought that Russian friendship to Poland was a purchasable commodity and, if purchased, would be durable. Everybody ought to know by now that Mr. Churchill was wrong on both points, but most Poles had known it all along. Many other concessions to Russia were promised or made in central and eastern Europe, and the English explained their policy by saying that these were necessary to induce Russia to go on fighting the Germans as hard as possible and—later—to join the fight against the Japanese. The majority of Poles thought this nonsense ; thought that Germans and Russians hated each other so much that neither party could disengage ; and that, being a fight to the death, both would have to go on fighting as hard as they could. That part of England's explanation which had to do with the Pacific rested they said, on a misapprehension of Stalin's character. If it suited Stalin to go to war with Japan, he would go to war with Japan. If it did not, he would not. It was not within the power of England and America by promises and inducements to deflect from his own chosen course a man for whom no contractual and honourable obligations had the slightest validity. This difference of view between the Poles and their allies was natural, for Poland is situated next door to the jungle where the gorillas and rattlesnakes live, and the Poles thought they knew much more about the nature and behaviour of these animals than Mr. Churchill and Mr. Roosevelt. In respect to the handling of Stalin by these two pre-eminent men, most Poles felt—like Isaiah—the " the suckling child shall play on the hole of the asp, and the weaned child shall put his hand into the cockatrice's den ". Who now can say that the Poles were wrong?

And to them it seemed also that the mischief went deeper than what looked like the delusions of great men. They were not indeed surprised at the *naïveté* of American public opinion and they knew that the mind of the illustrious President was near the end of its tether. Also they could understand that British public opinion needed tactful handling, having been misled for many years into wishfully thinking that Stalin & Co., though a bit rough in their methods, were not bad fellows at bottom and would yield to and eventually reciprocate patience, tolerance and amity. But they could hardly believe that the British Government—usually sceptical of the professions of foreigners—were equally ingenuous ; and they were mystified and disconcerted by seeing British Ministers not only expensively courting Stalin at Tehran and Yalta but propagating through every channel those very illusions about Russian policy which in turn constrained the British Cabinet to pretend that the dangers of yielding to Russian pretensions were negligible. Confidence in Russian intentions being unwarranted by any known facts why was it, the Poles asked themselves, that it was stimulated by all Government departments, nearly all newspapers, the B.B.C., the Army Bureau of Current Affairs, the Army Education Department, the Political Warfare Executive, and every other organ of publicity susceptible to official influence ? Why indeed ? Why was it that in all these establishments were to be found individuals with curious foreign names or persons who had changed their names, or were of mixed blood or of multiple allegiance, self-appointed saviours of society, bitter little Messiahs, do-gooders, cranky professors, recognizable fellow-travellers and numberless camp-followers from among the frustrated and ambitious intellectual proletariat—all burrowing like wood-beetles, corrupting and softening with their saliva and excrement the oaken heart of England ? The generation of Poles with whom I had to deal had grown up in the bracing atmosphere of new-won independence and their perceptions and instincts had been kept simple and bright by knowing very well that they were surrounded by gorillas and rattlesnakes in the East and exceedingly warlike Germans in the West. They had not realized how far the political demoralization of England had gone in the 1920's and 1930's. What they did know very well was how sad for Europe and how perilous for England would be the fruits of conjunction between the highest in the land and this monstrous brood of beetles.

While the beetles grubbed and burrowed, the Poles had much to put up with ; and their position was particularly trying because out of deference to the British who were at once their hosts, their allies, their fellow-soldiers and the repository of all their hopes, they were obliged to suffer the following grievous things without making much fuss in public about them. When Russia invaded their native country, she declared that Poland had ceased for ever to exist as a political entity. This was followed by persecution of Poles in many barbarous forms which persisted after as before the date on which Russia became the ally of their allies the British. When the German retreat from Warsaw commenced the Russians watched with satisfaction from the east bank of the Vistula the Polish population which was fighting with teeth and nails against the last spasm of German atrocity to prepare a path for the victorious Soviet army. When the Russians passed the river they set up, with British and American acquiescence, a species of puppet government composed of renegade Poles. When the Prime Minister of Poland went from London to Warsaw to try to negotiate an accommodation with the Russians he only got out again—unsuccessful of course—by the skin of his teeth. When in May 1945 a galaxy of Allies were at San Francisco arranging for the abolition of war and the reign of law and good faith between the United Nations, sixteen leading Poles who had been persuaded to go to Moscow under Russian safe conduct to negotiate with Stalin were all clapped into gaol where all but one, if still alive, have been ever since. All but the Russians were startled, but, after appropriate gestures of disapproval by other delegations, every-thing went on as before. All this was very trying for the Poles, and it was very trying for me too, for we both knew that these were the formative years when the shadows of coming events were discernible which proved disastrous for our first and staunchest ally and for many other people as well.

It was by no means only the Poles who suffered. Between 1943 and the autumn of 1945 when I went to Portugal, much more than the sacrifice of Poland was esteemed necessary to keep Stalin in a good temper ; and to appease him an indiffer-ent eye was turned upon his destruction and dismemberment of a number of smaller nations. One after another they were seized ; Esthonia, Latvia, Lithuania, parts of Finland, a quarter of Poland, all Poland, Czechoslovakia, Ruthenia,

Yugoslavia, Hungary, Bulgaria, Rumania, Albania, a quarter of Austria and a third of Germany. Oh, it was grievous to see so many pleasant and diverse communities being herded into a spiritual and cultural gas-chamber ! What a falling off was here from the bright morning of the Atlantic Charter and the sun-capped waves and good timber of the U.S.S. *Augusta's* quarterdeck ! All this also was trying for the Poles. It was trying for me too, for I had numerous friends in the countries named. The lucky ones—if they were women—were just raped. Of the unlucky ones, one had water poured into his lungs through a rubber tube ; another had all his fingertips sawn through with a hacksaw half way up the nails. The last I have heard about the widow of Stephen Bethlen, Hungary's celebrated Prime Minister, was being used as a scarecrow on a Hungarian farm with branches tied to her arms and feathers stuck in her hair. After I had retired from the Foreign Service things changed for the better. The mighty American Republic woke up, scratched its ears, rubbed its eyes and bellowed a challenge at the gorillas and rattlesnakes. England too rolled over and yapped in chorus with the United States ; but listening closely, anybody can hear the beetles still at work in the timbers of the house.

While the events I have referred to were in progress or preparation I was little more than a spectator with a very good seat in the front row which I was glad to vacate when the time came. In September 1944, the Secretary of State told me that he and the Prime Minister had decided that I was to go as Ambassador to Madrid. He was kind enough to say that I had fulfilled satisfactorily and without losing my head duties in respect of Poland which he knew had been difficult and often uncongenial ; but it was impossible to remove me from the Embassy to Poland for the moment without the appearance of putting a slight upon the Poles, and I was therefore to stay where I was until a more propitious moment. In March 1945, Mr. Eden said that it was still impossible to move me but imperative to appoint a new Ambassador to Spain ; I was therefore to go on staying where I was for the moment and presently go as Ambassador to Portugal. I said that I would of course do my best wherever he sent me, but that what had now been decided was to send me to a second-class instead of a first-class Embassy with a consequent diminution of the pension which I should enjoy when, after the lapse of a couple of years, I should, in the ordinary course, retire. Mr. Eden was good enough to say that he had not realized this but that the matter could and should be adjusted in my favour. At the beginning of June Mr. Eden got a duodenal ulcer and at the end of the month Mr. Churchill's administration went out of office. My departure for Lisbon in August approached, and I asked the Foreign Office to go into the question of emoluments which I had raised with Mr. Eden. This they could not see their way to do. Since my work with the Poles had been largely conducted personally with Mr. Churchill and Mr. Eden and not through departmental channels, I suggested to the authorities that they should at least ask the outgoing Secretary of State for a " character ". If, as I had every reason to hope, Mr. Eden said that I had been " honest, industrious, obliging and clean in work and person " this might, I thought, do me some good. I was disappointed that the Foreign Office could not see their way to speak to Mr. Eden about the matter. What was much worse was that at this point a general re-organization of the Foreign Service took place the effect of which was to make Portugal a " Grade III " post. Poland had been a " Grade II " post, so that instead of getting a step up I was now due for a step down. The Foreign Office said this was appropriate to the circumstances ; and so there was nothing for me to do but prepare for my transfer. I'd better hurry out to Lisbon, thought I to myself, or perhaps I shall find myself a Consul.

Lisbon is a most enjoyable place but in the estimation of the Foreign Office only of third-class importance—not a very distinguished appointment with which to terminate a career. Before leaving England, I asked two very prominent members of the Foreign Service what was the reason for my relative unsuccess in that Service, bearing in mind that nothing I had done had ever met with explicit criticism or disapproval. The first said that I had been too often too right too soon. That was nicely put, and of course I recognized that such a record would not endear me to my superiors. The second said that my trouble was that I was arrogant, intolerant and obstinate. This, I think, was a just remark, but I consoled myself with the reflection that it is in the long run in the interests of the Foreign Service not only that a majority should be more elastic and less uncompromising than myself, but also that there should be a minority—a smallish minority—of heretics. But of course those who live by the sword must not complain if they perish by the sword, and a heretic must not complain if he is burned. Thus he fulfils his function. So I went off to my last job— as a third-rate Ambassador—in good spirits.

CHAPTER 22

PORTUGAL

I WAS anxious to be once more a guest in a man-of-war before the opportunity for this sort of thing came to an end with my retirement. Fortunately I had friends in the Admiralty who said they could arrange a passage for me to Lisbon ; but the Foreign Office said that the Portuguese Government would be embarrassed by a request to allow one of the King's ships to enter the Tagus ; and accordingly it was arranged that I should disembark at Gibraltar. My wife had to stop behind in London to clear up at More's Gardens, for we now gave up for good the idea of having any residence in London.

I went on board H.M.S. *Enterprise* at Portsmouth. She was trooping to the Far East and this was to be her last voyage before being broken up. *Enterprise* was sister to *Emerald*, Captain England, in which I had been entertained in Nanking in 1927, but in the earlier stages of her career she had been cut in half and lengthened by the addition of a middle section. She was the shape of a pencil and had in her time been the fastest light cruiser in the Navy. It was a great pleasure as well as a great surprise to be welcomed on the quarterdeck by Captain Church who had commanded *Wishart* in the Yangtse in 1927 in the circumstances described in Chapter 12. It was a very nice voyage and, as usual, I enjoyed being allowed —like the ship's cat—to wander about all over the ship.

In Gibraltar the Governor, General Sir T. R. Eastwood, put me up for a night or two in the Convent where I had stayed with Ironside in 1937. When the final dissolution of the British Empire has been completed ; when the English have handed over Gibraltar to Spain and Cyprus to Greece and Hong Kong to China and the West Indies to the U.S.A. and the Falkland Islands to the Argentine Republic and Malta to the Maltese and Aden to King somebody or other and Penang and Singapore to the Republics of this or that, British officials will no more enjoy the experiences of their Victorian, Edwardian and Georgian predecessors whose good fortune it was to perch as birds of passage on these little bits of England ; but I experienced and delighted in them, and to all the Governors who ever entertained me I give my heartfelt thanks. The unique quality of this enjoyment comes, I suppose, from a combination of hospitality, comfort, order, dignity, familiarity and traditionalism together with the cloak of majesty which covers the men and the environment, recalling the wonderful story of the expansion of England and of all the seamen and merchants and soldiers and adventurers and administrators who in the course of four centuries had erupted from England into most parts of two hemispheres. These beams of memory and consciousness seemed to be focused onto the keys of the Fortress which customarily lie on the dinner-table in front of the Governor and Commander-in-Chief of Gibraltar.

The drive from Gibraltar to Lisbon was the hottest drive I ever had. The air that flowed through the car beat upon us with a searing and tireless malignancy, incomparably more uncomfortable than anything I had ever felt in Persia or Annam or the Red Sea. My Press Attaché, Geoffrey Stowe, had come to meet me and his conversation with the chauffeur was the first I heard of the Portuguese language. He kept saying "Oh, George, drive slower" or "Oh, George, don't take corners so fast" and I asked why all these "ohs"? He explained that Portuguese still used the vocative form, which made me think perhaps it was true, as I had been told, that of all living languages Portuguese most nearly resembles in pronunciation classical Latin. This was a shocking idea calculated to upset one's feelings about Horace and Virgil, because of all living languages Portuguese is the most cacaphonous. In due course we reached the *posada* on the Spanish-Portuguese frontier at Elvas ; and in this small town, as had so often happened to me in my earlier travels, I encountered something wholly unexpected—a town made, as it appeared, of alabaster, blazing like a jewel in the sun, set in a flowery plain, uncontaminated by any ugliness or vulgarity. The sight of such architectural chastity was to be repeated many times in Portugal. My Counsellor, Ashley Clarke, and his wife had come to meet us. We dined and slept well and by the following evening were being ferried over the Tagus to Lisbon and entering the Embassy house which was to be my home for the next two years. I am afraid after my long hot drive I looked very untidy and dishevelled to all the members of my staff paraded in their Sunday best to receive me ; but if they thought so, they did not show it.

The reader who has followed my peregrinations thus far must by now be sick to death of being told how full the world is of beautiful and interesting places and things. If I have not persuaded him already of this, I shall not be likely to do so by dwelling on the multiform riches of Portugal in races and classes and plains and mountains and towns and birds and flowers. Besides, my wife has done this much better than I could do it in a book called " The Selective Traveller in Portugal " by Ann Bridge and Susan Belloc Lowndes which anyone can buy for a guinea. Portugal was my last appointment ; perhaps, therefore, I may suitably bring my narrative to a close by supplementing with some fragmentary observations what I have already written in previous chapters about the way the Diplomatic machine works.

What is an Embassy ? I will answer this question by making a list of the people who worked in the Lisbon establishment in 1945. There were about four hundred of them, excluding private domestic servants. As taxpayers need to know if they are getting value for money my list will indicate how these four hundred persons were employed. Starting at the bottom, there were cleaners and charwomen ; a gardener ; a stoker and two chauffeurs. Official cars with official chauffeurs are sometimes spoken of as needless luxuries : in fact, they were indispensable for messengers taking " bags " to and from the airport, to and from outlying departments of the Embassy or fetching government stores from the docks, and for clerks with no cars of their own sent on government duty to the business quarter of Lisbon or to station, airport, docks or banks. In

the second place there were porters and messengers, as necessary to the life of the Embassy as are the porters and messengers
in government offices in Whitehall. Thirdly there were
guards : experience shows that no mechanical or physical
safeguards are as good as a man awake, sober and armed.
Fourthly telephonists, both in the main Chancery building and
in the affiliated offices in other parts of the town : I am grateful
to all those who have worked for me, but to none more than
these indefatigable, obliging, bilingual, trilingual or quadra-
lingual girls.   Fifthly the Representative of the Office of Works
who was responsible for buildings, furniture, lighting, heating,
water and comparable services.   Sixthly the cypher staff, all
trained experts on day and night duty.   Repeated instructions
used to come from London not to send telegrams when anything
else would do ; nevertheless the increased pace at which all life
seems to go on nowadays made a large amount of telegraphic
correspondence unavoidable.   Seventhly the Archivist and
his clerks.   The Archivists are responsible for accounts ; Parliament and the Comptroller and Auditor-General are rightly
inquisitive and pernickety about the outlay of public funds ;
the Treasury and the Finance Department of the Foreign
Office consequently watched our operations with sleepless
vigilance ; every penny spent had to be accounted for and
justified.   The Archivists were responsible not only for the
custody and manipulation of a huge number of files relating
to subjects with roots spreading downwards into the labours of
previous years but they were also, in practice, responsible for
a hundred and one things which could not be classed as anybody else's job.   The Head Archivist is the lynch-pin in the
hub of an Embassy wheel.   No reward is too great for a good
Archivist.   He is assisted by a team of stenographers, and
copyists, generally good-looking, well-dressed, overworked,
underpaid young women.

Now we come to the outliers.   First, the Consulate (I mean
the Consulate in Lisbon, not the Consular posts in the provinces) which since the amalgamation of the Consular with
the Diplomatic Service is a direct responsibility of the Ambassador.   The Consul is answerable for the care of all British

subjects in his district including everything in the case of Lisbon from very numerous and important merchants to drunken seamen. Secondly Passport-Control Officers who work in close touch with the local police. Thirdly there is the British Council. This is not a direct Embassy responsibility but it is a government agency on which the Embassy must give advice to the Foreign Office and with which the Embassy must in consequence keep in the closest touch. Finally and on the top of all this there is the Diplomatic staff proper : Counsellor, First, Second and Third Secretaries ; honorary Attachés ; Military, Naval, Air and Press Attachés and—very important—Commercial and Financial Secretaries, all the last six with their necessary clerks and typists. All the people and duties listed above were indispensably necessary to conduct the foreign relations of Her Majesty's Government with the Portuguese Republic and its important colonies. These related to almost every conceivable human activity. At one end of the scale was discussed with the Portuguese Government the use of the Azores for American and British aircraft in time of war ; at the other we studied the habits and distribution of the Colorado beetle. Somewhere in between I should place the necessity under which I once found myself of arranging for the burning on a pyre of the body of a Maharajah in a country where cremation is illegal. The British Electorate can take it or leave it. If they take it, they must pay for it ; if they do not want to pay for it, they must not expect the Government to do so much for them. Anyhow, I can assure them none of their money was wasted in Lisbon in 1945. I spent about a third of my working time in pure administration, largely looking for opportunities for economy and simultaneously trying to get better pay for the lower-paid members of the staff.

I sat on the top of this imposing human pyramid and often viewed my situation with surprise, remembering how frequently I had had my bottom kicked at school, how inconspicuous I had been at Magdalen, how—in spite of an auspicious start—the Foreign Office had come to take but a modest view of my capacity, how inglorious I often appeared to my wife and children and how many hours of my life I had spent mucking out pigstyes and henhouses at Bridgend or washing-up and blacking my boots at More's Garden. However, it was very nice, and I did my best.

Apart from the time he spends having fun on his own account, an Ambassador's life seemed to be divided into three intercommunicating departments. Part of my time was spent in giving and going to parties, opening bazaars and making speeches. Most of this was rather boring ; and as it is a side of life fully described in many of the books written by retired members of the Foreign Service, I shall say nothing about it except that I enjoyed reading the lessons in the English church in Lisbon wearing, on rare occasions, a uniform plastered with gold lace back and front. Part of my time was spent on business interviews and hard straightforward work at a desk with plenty of electric bells and telephones. The job might be to compose a review in a hundred pages of the whole social and economic life of Portugal or, on the other hand, a frenzied application to the Foreign Office for a compassionate allowance for a set of false teeth for a typist, the expense of which she could by no conceivable means have defrayed unassisted. This sort of thing was always interesting and exhausting. A third part of my energy was spent in *making the whole machine work* : by which I mean getting the best work out of every member of the staff and keeping them happy. An Embassy is just like any other co-operative and hierarchical organization. It begins to lose power whenever one man gets discouraged or another too cocky or a third jealous or suspicious. When wives quarrel it is hell. Trying to prevent all these things happening will not earn for the Head of a Mission any thanks from the Foreign Office any more than will whatever trouble he takes to teach new entrants how to do their work ; but it is very absorbing and brings its own rewards.

Each Ambassador has got to find out in what way he can best do his work. An Ambassador may work very much like an Under-Secretary in the Foreign Office, spending laborious days at office desk transferring papers from " IN " to " OUT " tray, and glad to get away from it all to his residence in the

evening. That did not suit me. I never went near the building which housed the Chancery (not chancellery, as many
journalists called it). I sat in my house, which was about five
minutes' walk away from the Embassy offices and when I was
not paying or receiving official calls, struggled with the telegrams and despatches which I could not foist off onto someone
else. I was " At Home " to the heads of the various departments of the Embassy at any time in case of urgency, but
normally between tea and dinner. It was then that I liked
them to come in, bring their papers and say exactly what it
was that we had to decide ; say, not write, and say in the
smallest number of words exactly what it was they wanted to
get settled. I would then say, not write, what I thought or
wished or decided, and I expected my interlocutor to go away
and work out for himself the result of our consultation. If
two or three were concerned ; they came together. These
discussions took place in the garden in the summer or before
my study fire in the winter. The average consumption of
whiskey was about two bottles a day. At the end of my two
years of office several members of my staff had learned the
superiority of Irish to Scotch whiskey.

The evening might end in a variety of ways ; sometimes at
my dining-room table ; sometimes we had to separate for
dinner engagements, but sometimes—and these were the best
evenings—we would decide to go and sup at the Guincho.
The Guincho was a solitary shack about twenty miles from
Lisbon perched between the pine woods and sandy cliffs and
coves where a continuation of the road to Estoril meets the
Atlantic. Here a good sole or lobster was always to be had
and afterwards, when many stories had been told and much
nonsense talked, we would pair off and walk or sit among the
rocks, contemplating the starry firmament, watching the great
Atlantic rollers, conversing about the things which related to
our private lives and our human destiny and all our happinesses
and miseries. And then in our swift cars we would flash back
to Lisbon past the clumps of cistus and the fields of deep blue
dwarf iris and the fishing nets hung up to dry and the blinking
lights in the Tagus and the blatant hotels of Estoril—back to

our quiet beds there to be refreshed till another day should be announced by the crowing of cocks and the cries of the Phoenician fish-wives parading our streets with sardines and red mullet and octopus and the other fruits of their husbands' industry on their heads.

I now turn from the inside of an Embassy to an Ambassador's relations with the Government to which he is accredited. I should like to write a whole book about this ; indeed I did do so once, but lost the manuscript along with most of my other possessions when the Germans got to Budapest. I am here going only to make some fragmentary observations.

On pages 116 *et seq.* of his book " The Ruling Few ", Sir David Kelly, lately H.M. Ambassador in Moscow, says much that is just and useful on the subject but includes these words : " I have often felt there is a close analogy between the diplomatist and the barrister ; for example, just as a barrister should defend his Client without *personally* committing himself or identifying himself with his Client, so an Ambassador must state the views of his Government, and argue the case for them, to the Foreign Government, even though he may privately consider the policy is ill-advised or even morally wrong. If he feels too strongly about it he should resign . . . so long as [an ambassador] takes the money . . . he must keep his private opinions for his intimates."

Without disagreeing with all that Sir David says I should like to add something in qualification of his propositions. I think an Ambassador sometimes finds himself in a position where the general interest is best served by acting not wholly as an advocate but in part as an arbitrator. However conciliatory the British Government may conceive itself to be ; however categorical the instructions which they have given to him, circumstances from time to time arise where in a residual corner of his mind, the Ambassador is clear that the general interest—which in the long run is nearly always identical with the British interest—requires that the scales of argument should be slightly tipped against the clients whose brief he holds and in favour of Counsel for the opposite side. So to tip the scales involves the nicest possible questions of judgment and duty, but no Ambassador should be unaware that in certain circumstances it is his duty, like Nelson, to put his telescope to his blind eye. What an Ambassador will nearly always need to do is to explain with the utmost precision what his Government thinks and wants ; but I have myself on occasions to a Foreign Minister said " Well, that's what the British Government think. I don't altogether agree with them. I think that point you made just now is good, and that the agreement we should aim to reach is such and such . . ." and have been perfectly sure afterwards that I was justified by the result.

I must say also that I see difficulty in the application of Sir David's principle that if the British Government is set upon some course which is morally wrong and if the Ambassador feels strongly about it he *should* resign. This principle does not, presumably, apply only to Ambassadors ; it must surely extend to the Secretaries who carry out the Ambassador's orders and the typists who type them and the cypherers who encypher them, in the same manner as the duty to refuse to carry out a wrongful order was declared in the deplorable Nuremberg Trials to extend all the way down from Hitler's Chiefs of Staff to the humblest member of the German Armed Forces. No one has yet succeeded and no one is ever likely to succeed in reducing to unambiguous language consistent with common sense the moral rules of conduct to which Sir David Kelly adverts, but I know that I personally have seen the British Government do dishonourable and reprehensible things in respect of which I was, among others, one of their agents ; and that I have no sense of guilt because I did not resign. In Sir David's context I should not go further than to say that a public servant should not be afraid to say so to Ministers if he thinks the course they contemplate is dishonourable or morally wrong. Such action would go far beyond what is now the general practice.

A great deal of time can be wasted in advocacy such as Sir David recommends, but I did not have to waste much of it in Portugal. The man I had mostly to deal with was Dr. Mathias, the official Head of the Portuguese Foreign Office.

He was much cleverer than I, and could in many cases have argued the British case as well as I could myself. So clear also was his power of exposition that I, for my part, was never long or much in doubt about the Portuguese case. This being so it would only have soured us both to go on and on arguing ; and as a rule we could agree, after a few words on both sides, that he knew precisely what the British Government thought and that I knew precisely what the Portuguese Government thought ; and we could then advance to the stage of " Well, and what are we going to do about it now ? "—to the stage where combined ingenuity and warm co-operation often produces a solution in the general interest to which both sides can agree. To such ends an Ambassador must make the foreigners he has to deal with like him ; and if they are to like him, he must really and truly like and respect them. If an Ambassador is liked by the foreigners he can speak to them very forcefully and frankly without giving offence. But he must not only be liked but trusted. One of the many illusions about diplomacy is that it consists in diddling the other fellow. Nothing could be further from the truth. It consists more than anything else in precision, honesty and persuasion, which three things should hang together. An Ambassador should never deceive a friendly foreign Government and never try to persuade them to do something contrary to their own best interests. Behaving thus an Ambassador may occasionally be able slightly to incline the policy of the Government to which he is accredited in the direction favoured by his own Government ; but he cannot hope to do this often or much, for foreign Governments are in general little affected in their actions by the personality or reasoning of the British Representative. I was guided by these principles, among others, in my dealings with the Portuguese Government. I cannot presume to say how far I was successful, but, since it is nothing to boast about, I think I can with propriety say that an Ambassador with an outlandish name and *provenance* like myself enjoys a certain advantage over purely English officials ; for the fact is that foreigners incline to think that an Irishman can look with something more like their own detachment at the foibles of the English which those who like me have had an English upbringing should be competent to explain and interpret sympathetically.

I was lucky in Lisbon in having such completely friendly and trustworthy people to deal with as Dr. Salazar, the Prime Minister, and Dr. Mathias. One advantage of this was that it enabled me to avoid a very common ambassadorial fault which consists in the inaccurate reporting to the Foreign Office in London of conversations with foreigners. After an important interview with a foreign Minister, an Ambassador sits down at leisure in his own study to write a despatch about it—a " recorder " as we call it—to his own Foreign Secretary. Inevitably there come into his mind, and all too often flow from his pen, not the words he actually employed but something much more pungent, witty and creditable to himself than what he actually said in the cut and thrust of conversation or disputation. On several important occasions I avoided this by writing recorders of my interviews in advance of them. When I got to the Portuguese Foreign Office I gave the draft to Dr. Mathias and said : " Here you are. This is the account I am going to send home of the conversation we are about to have. If you don't agree with the words I have put into your mouth, please take the draft up to Dr. Salazar this evening and let him correct it." The following morning I would get the draft back with the Prime Minister's corrections or additions. It saved a lot of time, the result was dead accurate and incidentally my " recorder ", without departure from the truth, contained all the nicely turned phrases which, as I hoped, gave to it elegance and force.

Much nonsense is written and talked in England about the political system in Portugal as also about the political system in Spain with both of which I am acquainted. The fount and origin of this nonsense is the supposition that English Parliamentary democracy, as it is called, could prudently be substituted for these systems. This nonsense is sedulously propagated by the wood-beetles referred to earlier, and, alas, is believed by many well-meaning ill-informed people. It was heartily subscribed to by Mr. Ernest Bevin who, when not engaged in trying to overthrow the British Constitution by a

AUTHOR AND DR. SALAZAR

General Strike, had a lot of sense. This book—this somewhat
trivial account of the sort of life I have lived—is not the place
to go into the matter ; nor, considering how offensive parts of
it are to Leftish opinion, should I expect to do any good if I
did so. But I cannot close this chapter on Portugal without
saying that under Dr. Salazar's government the country has
made and is making great progress away from revolution,
bankruptcy, intolerance and sectional oppression and rapacity ;
and towards stability, comfort and preservation of the decencies
and traditional nicenesses of social life. There is a catch in
this. I used to say to Dr. Salazar : " You are not immortal.
What do you suppose is going to happen when you die ? "
He answered : " Well, I really don't know. But one does
what one can while one is alive ; and I am trying to educate
a governmental *corps d'élite* who can take over when I go.
I do not see that I could do anything different." Nor do I.
Portugal will need several generations of clean and businesslike
administration before experimenting with the popular English
system of vote-catching. In this matter, France, from whom
Portugal draws much intellectual and cultural nourishment,
provides an urgent warning and by no means an example.

In the second week of January 1947 I received a letter
marked " Private " from the Permanent Under-Secretary of
State saying that " the Secretary of State " (Mr. Bevin) " had
decided that he would wish to replace me in Lisbon when I
reached the normal retiring age of sixty ". This I was due to
do on May 4th, 1947. That was all the " notice " I ever got.
As the letter was in what typists call " single spacing " on
duodecimo paper and did not seem to need any answer, I sent
none. Later, after getting home to Ireland I got a letter
beginning

" Sir, I am commanded by the King to convey to Your
Excellency an expression of his regret at the termination of
your long and distinguished career etc. etc. . . ."

going on to recite the dates and places of my various appointments, and ending up " Yours sincerely, Ernest Bevin ". This
was on quarto paper and though odd as to form was kindly

meant, so I sent a civil reply. In October I got a letter from the Paymaster-General's Office saying that I had earned a pension of £1,093 15s. per annum gross and a lump sum of £3,281 5s.

That was the last I had to do with Whitehall.

CHAPTER 23

EPILOGUE

I LEFT Lisbon in a 14-h.p. Vauxhall car on April 28th, 1947. This was the last of the transcontinental drives I used to like so much. With an agreeable companion I drove for the last time across the eastern plain of Portugal now literally carpeted with every description of wild flower, leaving the country, as I had entered it, by Elvas. A kinsman of mine in the 13th Foot had fought at Albuera in 1811, and I wished therefore to inspect this field of slaughter, and did so. We also went through Badajoz and made a thorough examination of the walls and bastions. This was by way of tribute jointly to my son Patrick and to the past ; for Patrick had been in the Oxfordshire and Buckinghamshire Light Infantry and it will be remembered that it was the 43rd and 52nd Regiments of Foot which had led the great assault on the breaches (still observable) in 1812, on which Napier tersely commented [1] : " Many died, and there was much glory." In this way here and now were made manifest some of those tenuous tortuous threads which link one generation of men with another. From Badajoz we turned north through Merida to look again on the rose-pink stones of Salamanca ; and so through Avila to Madrid and Toledo.

From Madrid we took the Burgos road, running into deep snow—though it was the month of May—on the Guadarama mountains ; but the gallant little Vauxhall beat all the other cars on the road which got snowed up. On the descent, the silencer dropped off and I spent an hour under the car in a barn, encouraged as was to be expected by the truly Spanish kindness and courtesy of the farmer. From Burgos we retraced the road through Alsasua and Tolosa to Irun, and from St. Jean-de-Luz we climbed as high as the season permitted

[1] " Peninsular War ", ed. 1834, vol. iv, p. 421.

towards the Col d'Aubisque, where *Primula farinosa* and *Gentiana acaulis* were to be seen in flowery cushions by the square yard. We slept at Louvy-Juzon and dined off trout and goats' cheese ; paused in Pau where the well-liked Hotel de France had been defiled by the Gestapo, rushed on through the dull Landes to Touraine, inspected the famous and now lifeless chateaux and came to rest in Chartres where all was peace and dignity and beauty. Two days later we were driving up the Old Kent Road. I was not an Ambassador any longer, but such were some of the pleasures incidental to having been one.

I dropped my companion in London and went on alone in the Vauxhall to Rockfleet.

The house at Rockfleet crouches like a little fortress among some storm-lashed sycamores and alders fifty yards from high-water-mark on an inlet of the sea opening out of Clew Bay, and within a hundred yards of the old castle. There is nothing dramatic about the low green hills and islands which enclose our bay ; nevertheless we stand here close under the mountains of Mayo which, for all they are no more than 2,600 feet high, have the same authority to provoke high thoughts as more imposing ranges in other lands ; and on the other side of us is the ocean, and the knowledge that the first rays of the morning sun must traverse two thousand miles of restless water before striking the coast of Labrador and summoning the Eskimos to their watery toil. When I first bought the place, it had been nothing but a ruinous small house and a starveling farm. I had started work on it before the war, and it was now my business to finish turning it into a place of beauty and fruitfulness. This was going to call for much skill and energy, not to speak of money ; and as I drove alone to Liverpool and then across the midland plain of Ireland I felt anxiety as well as excitement at the prospect.

It might, I thought, have been more sensible to do what many of my seniors had done on retirement : seek directorships ; apply for work on Government Commissions of Enquiry into this, that or the other, and in general, try to make the transition from official to private life as little violent as possible. It might have been more sensible in the emotional disarray

ROCKFLEET.   HOUSE AND CASTLE

ROCKFLEET.   FRONT DOOR

which retirement generally entails, to cling for safety to the
" IN " tray and the " OUT " tray and to dockets and com-
mittees and memoranda : to snuffle under the table of official-
dom for titbits of Service news and crumbs of Service reminis-
cence dropped by the younger man who now exercised power
and enjoyed the prestige of high office ; perhaps even falling
back prematurely on cross-word puzzles before luncheon and
Bridge in the afternoon. But it was too late to think about
that now : I was already committed to something quite
different.

When we were children at Denton we used sometimes to go
for a picnic to the site of a large house which had been long
ago totally destroyed by fire. The park wall still stood and a
postern door in it led through a jungle of copsewood, bright
in spring with celandines and anemones, to the foundations of
the house now covered with close-cropped grass and making
a pleasant place to spread out the bread and butter and
lettuces and boil the kettle under tense observation by startled
rabbits and jays. The moment of leaving the busy road and
closing the park door behind us was full of pleasurable anticipation, for here in the deserted tranquillity magic lay about
us, thick as dust in long-unlived-in rooms. Similarly, arriving
at last on a June evening at the mouth of a lane, tunnelled
through hedges and leading to the house and castle of Rockfleet, I felt the same sort of surprise and delight ; for here was
the same sort of magic in our secluded beaches and meadows
now brilliant with the promise of the flowering seaweed. And
as the days passed, and as I settled down to the manifold
labours and anxieties of farming and building I was able to
accept with humility and love the wonder and discipline which
the place was going to impose upon us, reflecting that all life
is a matter for wonder and discipline and that I was lucky to be
where these are so regularly and benevolently exercised.

Here I sit now among a lot of old things which, like me,
have travelled far. There is the china pot which was the only
thing left unbroken in one of our houses outside Castlebar
when the French occupied it in the invasion of 1798. There
are the two stuffed grouse and the eagle owl which had stood

in the hall at Belclare. There is a little picture of Teig, my great-great-great-great-great-great-great grandfather who fought with Sarsfield at the Siege of Limerick in 1691 ; and there are a lot of other pictures and old books and letters and papers. Most of these things have wandered about from Mayo to Lowndes Street, to Eastbourne and to Denton before coming back here to Mayo. I sit here among these things looking at our swan-haunted curlew-haunted shore or walk through the meadows and pasture where I have to produce milk for eighteen souls off some of the worse acres in Connacht ; and I think to myself what a long road it was from Denton and Belclare by Radley and Magdalen and Skipness and Bridgend and China and Mexico and Chelsea and Spain and Hungary and Portugal to Rockfleet, but—taking the good with the bad—what fun it all was.

INDEX

INDEX

255

INDEX

INDEX